Communicating in Professions and Organizations

Series editor
Jonathan Crichton
University of South Australia
Adelaide, SA, Australia

This ground-breaking series is edited by Jonathan Crichton, Senior Lecturer in Applied Linguistics at the University of South Australia. It provides a venue for research on issues of language and communication that matter to professionals, their clients and stakeholders. Books in the series explore the relevance and real world impact of communication research in professional practice and forge reciprocal links between researchers in applied linguistics/discourse analysis and practitioners from numerous professions, including healthcare, education, business and trade, law, media, science and technology.

Central to this agenda, the series responds to contemporary challenges to professional practice that are bringing issues of language and communication to the fore. These include:

- The growing importance of communication as a form of professional expertise that needs to be made visible and developed as a resource for the professionals
- Political, economic, technological and social changes that are transforming communicative practices in professions and organisations
- Increasing mobility and diversity (geographical, technological, cultural, linguistic) of organisations, professionals and clients

Books in the series combine up to date overviews of issues of language and communication relevant to the particular professional domain with original research that addresses these issues at relevant sites. The authors also explore the practical implications of this research for the professions/organisations in question.

We are actively commissioning projects for this series and welcome proposals from authors whose experience combines linguistic and professional expertise, from those who have long-standing knowledge of the professional and organisational settings in which their books are located and joint editing/authorship by language researchers and professional practitioners.

The series is designed for both academic and professional readers, for scholars and students in Applied Linguistics, Communication Studies and related fields, and for members of the professions and organisations whose practice is the focus of the series.

More information about this series at
http://www.springer.com/series/14904

Darryl Hocking

Communicating Creativity

The Discursive Facilitation of Creative Activity in Arts

palgrave
macmillan

Darryl Hocking
AUT University
Auckland, New Zealand

Communicating in Professions and Organizations
ISBN 978-1-137-55803-9 ISBN 978-1-137-55804-6 (eBook)
https://doi.org/10.1057/978-1-137-55804-6

Library of Congress Control Number: 2017949877

Cover illustration: Paper Boat Creative / Getty Images

Printed on acid-free paper

This Palgrave Macmillan imprint is published by Springer Nature
The registered company is Macmillan Publishers Ltd.
The registered company address is: The Campus, 4 Crinan Street, London, N1 9XW, United Kingdom

To Rose, Lucia, and Isaac

To the dedicated and outstanding art and design educators and professionals who provided me with access to their practices

In memory of Chris Candlin

Contents

List of Figures

List of Tables

1

Creativity and Communication

Introduction

The last decade has seen an increasing focus on creativity and creative practice across a broad range of professional and educational settings. The contemporary business environment, for example, consistently highlights creativity as crucial for success, while the fields of architecture, art, design, film, music, and software design, among others, are now collectively referred to as the creative industries; a consequence of policy initiatives within advanced free market-oriented governments as they position these disciplines as pivotal to economic progress. Aligned with such developments, the field of creative writing is now currently one of the largest growth areas in tertiary education, and not far behind is creative technologies, an emergent field situated at the interdisciplinary nexus of science, mathematics, and new digital media, and motivated by the emergence of web-based technologies with their emphasis on social networking and creative production. Perhaps influenced by these different developments, attention to student creativity has also recently reappeared in the context of art and design education. This return follows a relative hiatus in the mid to late twentieth century, when the view of student creativity as an individual ability to be harnessed and developed was

D. Hocking, *Communicating Creativity*, Communicating in Professions and Organizations, https://doi.org/10.1057/978-1-137-55804-6_1

replaced by a conceptualisation of artistic production as something that could be taught according to standardised outcomes and formalised curricula.

This post-industrial resurgence of creativity presents a new challenge for both educators and researchers as they attempt to comprehend the increasingly complex and diverse senses of creativity and creative action as it occurs across these multiple sites and practices. Compounding this difficulty is the influence of social and cognitive psychological traditions in creativity studies, which to date, have largely viewed creativity as an essentialist and objectively measurable reality. These studies have largely focused on investigating the thought processes and personal attributes that underlie creative behaviour, mostly through the use of controlled experiments, computer models, or the evaluation of eminent artists' and scientists' lives, personalities, and processes. What typically informs this research is a taken-for-granted definition of creativity as the production of ideas or products that are both *novel* and *useful* (Mayer 1999; Kaufman and Sternberg 2010; Hennessey and Amabile 2010); a definition which is used whether creativity is viewed as a personal cognitive ability, of either gifted or normal individuals, or whether it is viewed as a socio-cultural phenomenon, where the idea or product's creative worth is validated, often posthumously, by the larger community or gatekeepers of the domain in which it takes place (Csikszentmihalyi 1999). Nevertheless, regardless of the relative consensus regarding the definition of creativity and despite claims to scientific rigour, social and cognitive psychological creativity studies can produce quite divergent findings, even when they investigate similar types of creative practice and phenomena (Sternberg 2005).

The creative process of the highly influential twentieth-century modernist, Pablo Picasso, has been the subject of a number of such studies and these provide an example of how creativity research has traditionally treated the visual arts. One of Picasso's most critically acclaimed works, *Guernica*, completed in June 1937, has been of particular interest to creativity researchers, primarily because he left a numbered and dated collection of preliminary sketches for the painting which purportedly enable a close examination of his creative processes. Using his preliminary sketches as evidence, these cognitive psychological studies have resulted in two contrasting descriptions of Picasso's creative process.

The first argues that when examined in the order produced, Picasso's preliminary sketches are said to show little systematic development towards the final composition of *Guernica*. Simonton (2007), an advocate of this position, points out that many of the figures found in the final work, such as the weeping woman, appeared only in the early preliminary sketches, while other figures in the sketches, such as Pegasus, failed to appear in the final version of *Guernica* at all. Hence, in the process of creating *Guernica*, Picasso generated various diverse and often unconnected sketches, without knowing at the time which of these he would eventually select for development into the final product, and it is only with the benefit of hindsight that any degree of continuity can be identified. Accordingly, this view of Picasso's creative process for *Guernica* supports the conceptualisation of creativity as a messy and chaotic process, involving 'false starts and wild experiments' (Simonton 1999, p. 197), where an often gifted creator is unable to see where they are going until they eventually reach their destination.

In contrast, the second description of Picasso's creative process, argues that the development of *Guernica*, involved a more ordered and structured process of exploration, whereby a coherent sequence of sketches was generated, each systematically building upon the preceding one, until an end result was obtained. The series of preliminary sketches are seen as arising from, and extending, a kernel idea, one which can even be seen as emerging well before *Guernica*. According to Weisberg (2006), for example, the figures found in the preliminary sketches, such as the bull and the horse, can be seen as having continuity with earlier compositions by Picasso, as well as with earlier works of other artists. This view of Picasso's creative process for *Guernica* supports the conceptualisation that creativity is a systematic and straightforward step-by-step process, similar to ordinary everyday approaches for problem solving, rather than a series of unpredictable and chaotic leaps.

Not all psychological studies on Picasso's creativity have focused solely on *Guernica*. Stokes (2006), for example, examines the collaborative development of cubism by Picasso and his close associate George Braque. In her attempt to understand the creative processes used by the artists to develop the ground-breaking new geometric new style of cubism, she suggests that the two artists consciously set specific constraints on their practice, most of which were a rejection of the prevailing representational style of the late nineteenth century. A first constraint precluded the painting of an object from a single point of view and instead promoted depicting the object from multiple viewpoints. A second constraint precluded reproducing the colours of the objects being depicted and instead promoted the use of a monochromatic palette, and a third precluded representing the illusion of depth and instead promoted the depiction of a flat and patterned picture surface. For Stokes, this supports a conceptualisation of creativity as involving the ability to move from a prior initial state to a novel goal state, which as seen here, necessarily involves a series of paired constraints: one of the pair preventing a conventional response to a problem, with the other promoting a novel outcome. These sets of paired constraints ultimately lead towards the creative goal state.

Although quite understated in her study, Stokes' inference that the creative development of cubism was a collaborative process involving both Picasso and Braque raises a point that is central to this book. As with many other creativity studies, what is absent from these largely decontextualised investigations of creativity and the creative process is attention to the interactions that artists have with other artists or their acquaintances and other individuals that were directly or indirectly involved in their creative practice, and furthermore, how these interactions might have shaped the ongoing development of the artists' creative products and processes. This absence is particularly evident, for example, in Locher's (2010) comprehensive overview of empirically based creativity research in the visual arts where there is no mention at all of verbal interaction or language use—even where studies involving creative practice within team environments are discussed. As regularly indicated in the literature (e.g. FitzGerald 1995), Picasso did not work in an isolated vacuum, and like most other creative individuals, was in constant dialogue with a network of fellow artists, friends, and dealers about his work, its progress, and its successes. It is well documented, for example, that Pablo Picasso and George Braque would meet daily to exchange ideas about their work in what have been characterised as 'intense conversations' (Ganteführer-Trier 2004, p. 12), and it is of note that both artists have personally commented on the significance of these interactions for their creative outcomes. In a letter to Françoise Gilot, Picasso, stated that:

> Almost every evening, either I went to Braque's studio or Braque came to mine. Each of us *had* to see what the other had done during the day. We criticized each other's work. A canvas wasn't finished unless both of us felt it was. (Picasso, cited in Gilot and Lake 1964, p. 76, original italics)

Similarly, Braque, in dialogue with art critic Dora Vallier recalled:

> [W]e used to meet every day, we used to talk … In those years Picasso and I said things to each other that nobody will ever say again, things that nobody could say any more … It was rather like a pair of climbers roped together. (Braque, cited in Friedenthal 1963, p. 264)

In his often-quoted text on cubism, Daniel-Henry Kahnweiler (1949), Picasso's dealer for a large part of his life, makes the point that these daily conversations formed the basis for many of the creative advances that took place in Picasso and Braque's work. He also suggests that the term *cubism*, one whose emergence would collectively frame the creative practice of Picasso, Braque, and a succession of other early modern painters, materialised as a result of a conversation between the art critic Louis Vauxcelles and the artist Henri Matisse after the latter had described Braque's paintings as being composed 'avec les petites cubes' (Kahnweiler 1949, p. 5). According to Kahnweiler, Vauxcelles subsequently developed the term *cubism* and used it to refer to two works of Braque in a review he wrote on the 1909 Salon des Indépendants. As a result, what was initially constructed as a derogatory term eventually came into common usage. It has also been noted that when Picasso and Braque were on their summer vacations, they continued to correspond in writing, often lamenting their inability to interact on a daily basis (Gantefúhrer-Trier 2004). Picasso wrote to Braque in 1912, bemoaning that 'I miss you. What has become of our walks and feelings? I cannot conduct our discussion about art in writing' (p. 12).

This book, then, takes as its starting point the idea that communication plays a crucial constitutive role in both the production and reception of contemporary creative practice. As with Picasso and Braque, artists are consistently in dialogue with their peers, gallery dealers, collectors, critics, technical experts, viewing public, and acquaintances, among others, on the subject of their creative activities, and these ongoing interactions impact on, and continually shape, the artist's creative practice. Commercial gallery dealers, for example, work hard to build an ongoing dialogue with the artists they represent, so that they might have a degree of input into the quality and direction of the work they receive. Likewise, the information gathered by the dealer during these interactions enables them to more successfully represent the artists' work to interested collectors and curators, a process that also involves lengthy conversations. The relationships that emerge from these interactions facilitate a sense of trust between the dealer and the collector, and are often viewed as a necessary precursor to the sale of works. For collectors, these ongoing dialogues also provide a source of knowledge about emerging art practice and help identify potential future acquisitions (Winkleman 2015).

Communication that facilitates the production or reception of creative practice is not always spoken. The visual works in public galleries, for example, are almost always accompanied by written information, which typically provides the viewer with an interpretation of the artworks exhibited, describes the creative intentions of the respective artists, and details their backgrounds. Traditionally, this information is found in small brochures, or texts placed at the entrance of each room or section of an exhibition, commonly referred to as wall panels. Public galleries also usually place what are called either labels or didactic panels besides individual works. As well as providing details identifying the work, known as the tombstone, these written texts also contain interpretative or educational information. Such information, which is usually produced by the curatorial team, inevitably brings a particular way of understanding the work into being for the viewing public, and as indicated by Duncum (2001), viewers of art tend to depend on these interpretative statements for their understanding of the works on display.

> I enjoy Parsons (1994) account of a newspaper photograph that shows about a dozen people, all of whom are looking, not at the Malevich painting hanging on the wall, but at the accompanying text. (Duncum 2001, p. 18)

In an increasing number of galleries, wall panels and labels are being replaced by the oral texts of hand-held audio devices, or more recently the multimodal texts of portable digital technologies, for example, dedicated iPads, which provide access to a varied range of content, including artist interviews. Following the conventions of many social media platforms, these digital devices also enable the viewer to 'like' or 'dislike' particular works, thus providing a way for viewers to interact with the curatorial process.

Another important communicative form that discursively frames the way a work is conceptualised is the artist statement. The artist statement, usually written by the artists themselves, provides a description of their creative practice and focuses, in particular, on the themes that inform the work. It is usually produced in the form of a single page handout, or as a text on a gallery website, to accompany an exhibition. An artist statement, however, is also included in applications for grants, or with the portfolio of work sent to a gallery when canvassing for an exhibition. Contemporary artists' statements are frequently informed by the post-structural theories of French literary theory, and as a result they are often written in a similar scholarly register. French literary theory was introduced into Western art education in the late 1970s, and the kinds of post-structural tropes central to the works of Foucault, Bourdieu, Baudrillard, or Deleuze and Guattari, among others, have increasingly provided visual artists with a textual catalyst for their creative practice. As pointed out, somewhat disparagingly, by Kester (2011):

> Post-structuralism, for many in the art world, is less a tradition that is actively engaged *with* than a system of thought that one subscribes *to*. The result is often a liturgical relationship to theory, and a related tendency to simply invoke theoretical precepts as axioms and then apply them to practice in an illustrative manner. (Kester 2011, p. 58, original italics)

The interdependency between communication and creativity can also be seen in the world of design. The design process often commences with a series of discussions about the client's specific needs, between the client and the designer, or between the client and another representative of the creative or design team (such as the account manager in advertising). Subsequently, the results of these verbal interactions are almost always translated into written form, in what is normally referred to as a brief.

Producing and using briefs is a multi-layered process, and as a result there are various kinds of briefs, each whose specific language impacts on its target audience in different ways. In advertising, for example, the initial client brief is often developed by the account manager and involves business and marketing jargon. Its primary aim is to facilitate dialogue between the client and the agency to ensure they understand each other's requirements. A communications brief is designed to emotionally convey the client's brand and consumer relationship through metaphorically colourful language, while the creative brief provides the stimulus for the creative team and is more strategically oriented (Hackley 2005). Overall, however, the crucial communicative function of the brief is one of alignment between the individuals involved, a process which necessarily involves ongoing interaction and the building of relationships (Thorson and Duffy 2011). Indeed, a number of studies have shown that in the initial stages of brief interpretation, concepts for the design are brought into being verbally, rather than visually (Tomes et al. 1998; McDonnell 2012), and it is generally not until designers have verbally formulated a core design concept that they begin to translate their concepts into visual forms. These visual outcomes are nevertheless again translated into verbal forms during meetings with the clients where the designs are negotiated.

It could also be argued that communication in creative practice can also work to orient individuals or groups towards particular identities, and the activities related to those identities, within the particular context of that practice. For example, Cuff's (1991) description of the communication that takes place in a design briefing for a ski resort development shows how participants orient towards their different roles and respective positions of power, largely through the employment of a range of conversational strategies:

> Here, the client wants all those who work with him to share his vision of the ski lodge as a luxury resort. He wants to assert who's boss, and he does so by laying out the topic for conversation ("back of house"), by assuming personal responsibility for positions (I don't like frozen foods; I don't want employees mixing with guests), by ignoring the conversation when he chooses (making phone call, cutting meeting short), and be telling the architect and the consultant to take notes on important issues. The archi-

> tect also establishes his primary role in the threesome by speaking more frequently than the kitchen consultant, by speaking for the client, and by steering conversation ("Let's get back to ..."). (Cuff 1991, p. 190)

Processes of categorisation, as evidenced here, are instrumental in the construction of an individual's or a group's identity As Antaki and Widdicombe (1998) have pointed out, 'for a person to have an identity—whether he or she is the person speaking, being spoken to, or being spoken about—is to be cast into a *category with associated characteristics or features*' (p. 3, original italics). It is in this sense that Oak (2009) has also shown how individuals perform the roles of architect and client through the verbal interaction of a design meeting.

What is of interest about these different examples of communication found in creative settings is that most could be described as belonging to a broad interdependent set of communicative genres. Communicative genres are generally understood as written or spoken texts that commonly occur in certain contexts, and serve distinctive communicative and social purposes relative to that context. As a result of their specific purposes and their particular socio-historical origins, genres tend to evolve distinctive norms of content, style, and structure. While there is evidence that generic conventions are sometimes manipulated by the 'private intentions' (Bhatia 2004, p. 4) of individuals or organisations, generic conventions, more often than not, shape or delimit the types of interaction that occurs in any particular context. The generic nature of communication in creative settings will contribute to the way such interactions are understood and analysed throughout this book, and how they contribute to the facilitation of creative activity.

Communication in the University Art and Design Studio

In order to open a window into the role played by communication in the facilitation of creative practice, and ultimately into the nature of creativity itself, this book will focus on a specific situated context involving creative activity—that of a university art and design studio. Like the professional context, communication in the university art and design studio is typically structured around an interdependent set of spoken and written communicative genres. As will be seen throughout this book, these genres not only play a central role in facilitating and guiding the students' creative practice, but also in constituting the way in which the tutoring staff conceptualise and structure the future creative options of the students. They also contribute to the development of the students' identities as artists, designers, sculptors, or graphic artists, and furthermore to their habitus (Bourdieu 1993) as cultural producers.

The set of communicative genres in the studio context around which this book is focused, is more or less representative of most contemporary university art and design programmes worldwide. A two- or three-page written document, commonly referred to as the *brief*, is the most significant genre of these contexts, and one around which the other communicative genres in the studio are structured. The brief typically includes a provocation, often in the form of a set of quotations from artists, or an extract from a philosophical text, which acts as a stimulus for the students' creative projects. It also includes a statement outlining the specific requirements for the presentation and the assessment of the creative works. A new brief is usually presented to the students in a *brief launch*. This involves a reading of the brief and an elucidation of its important points to the students, and a subsequent question and answer session. Students may be provided with different versions of the brief depending on the particular art and design area they are interested in, for example, visual art, graphic design, or 3D. In the specific studio context that this book focuses on, there is usually a five-week period between the brief launch and the final presentation of the work produced for that brief. This five-week period is referred to as an assessment event.

Well before the commencement of each new assessment event, the students' tutors typically spend a substantial amount of time drafting, debating, and redrafting the contents of the different versions of the new studio brief in *brief writing meetings*. Furthermore, throughout the period following the launch of the completed brief, there are usually regular *studio tutorials* between an individual tutor and a student, as well as a number of *group critiques* attended by one or two tutors and a larger group of students. While students are developing their creative work in the studio, they also routinely discuss their creative activities in what I have referred to as *casual studio interaction*. They also usually make notes in *student workbooks*, which are included with their final presentation of works. The final major generic activity of the brief cycle is the *assessment*, where one or more tutors collaboratively assess each student's presentation and complete written *feedback*, although this was often followed by *moderation meetings*, and other assessment-related administrative activities. These genres largely comprise the primary data collected for this study of communication and the facilitation of creative practice.

This emphasis on the educational context does not reduce the significance of this book's key points for those interested in professional communication. In contrast, a central proposition of this book is that unlike the professional and institutional worlds, whose practices are often viewed as constituting those carried out at the educational level (Candlin et al. 2002), the practices of the creative professional, including the visual artist and design practitioner, are, in effect, powerfully shaped by the practices that take place in the educational context. Chapter 9 will address this view in more detail, by examining the primary themes that emerge from this study within the context of two professional sites of practice, that of a successful practising visual artist, and that of a professional design practitioner.

Conceptualisations of Creativity

As creativity is a central focus of this book, it is important to provide an overview of the concept and the different ways in which it has been conceptualised. According to Pope (2005), while cognates such as 'creation', 'creator', and 'create' have been in existence for some time, the first recorded mention of the abstract noun 'creativity' was not until 1875, and the term only came into common usage in the 1940s. Table 1.1, which shows the occurrences of creativity and its cognate terms in the 400 million word Corpus of Historical American English (Davies 2010), supports Pope's point that the term *creativity* was not widely current until the mid-twentieth century. Interestingly, an examination of the sources of these results around this time shows that the disciplines predominantly associated with the emergence of the term are education (all nine results in 1930 and four of the nine results in 1940) and philosophy (four of the nine results in 1940 and approximately 70 per cent of the 109 results in 1950). What is also of interest in Table 1.1 is the relative decrease in the use of the word 'creator' from about 1880 when it was commonly capitalised to refer to the Christian deity. However, as its frequency appears to revive toward the end of the twentieth century, the word 'creator' is increasingly used to refer to the producer of some object or artifact, especially literary or artistic works.

The cognitive and social psychology focus of much Western creativity scholarship in the past 70 years is frequently attributed to a presidential address titled 'Creativity' given by J. P. Guilford to the American Psychological Association in 1950, where he identified creativity as a subject of immense social importance which was seriously neglected by psychologists. Guilford's address focused in particular on the creative personality and the nature of creative behaviour, and hence it is not surprising that the subsequent groundswell of psychological research that resulted from the address was primarily concerned with establishing a definition of creativity and identifying the attributes that underlie creative behaviour. The emphasis on providing a definition of creativity is still seen as central to psychological studies of creativity. Kaufman and Sternberg's (2010), for example, suggest that prior to the pursuit of understanding creativity, one first needs to define it, and Plucker, Beghetto, and Dow (2004) lamented that of the 90 peer-reviewed creativity-based articles they reviewed, 62 per cent failed to provide an explicit definition of the term.

Table 1.1 Frequency of the abstract noun 'creativity' and its cognates in the nineteenth and twentieth centuries

	1810	**1820**	**1830**	**1840**	**1850**	**1860**	**1870**	**1880**	**1890**	**1900**
creativity	0	0	0	0	0	0	0	0	2	0
creation	67	225	581	815	744	628	739	634	665	565
creator	18	156	235	344	339	295	264	214	169	162
create	23	151	282	382	404	349	397	472	390	426
	1910	**1920**	**1930**	**1940**	**1950**	**1960**	**1970**	**1980**	**1990**	**2000**
creativity	0	1	9	9	109	93	139	148	267	262
creation	574	648	623	549	638	600	734	645	912	778
creator	138	167	155	94	130	120	173	170	204	286
create	574	711	728	766	928	1044	1070	1492	2301	2604

As mentioned earlier, the conceptualisation of creativity as something that is both *novel* and *useful* (Hennessey and Amabile 2010; Kaufman and Sternberg 2010; Mayer 1999) is commonplace in social and cognitive psychology; however, this definition is also used by creativity researchers across many other disciplines. Novelty generally refers to something viewed as innovative or unexpected because it diverges from existing practices in unforeseen ways. However, because too much divergence is perceived as potentially leading to something that is socially irrelevant (Kozbelt et al. 2010), the creative outcome must also be valued as useful, appropriate, significant, relevant, or meaningful within the domain for which it is intended; an attribute normally understood as being determined by the larger community or gatekeepers of that domain (Csikszentmihalyi 1999). Literary theorist, Pope (2005), in a thoughtful deviation from novel and appropriate, offers the definition *original* and *fitting*. He states that the first term, *original*, represents the idea of newness as well as the notion of origin. This, he suggests, evokes a conception of creativity as 'historically informed and theoretically aware' and thus 'sensitive to ancient precedent as well as modern preference' (p. 58). With this in mind, Pope's second term *fitting* evokes a dynamic conception of creativity as the ability to accommodate existing patterns, but also the ability to develop, though a process of 'active exploration' (pp. 59–60), new patterns that anticipate the continually changing state of affairs. Such a view of creativity as exploration will be further developed in Chap. 6.

There are a number of qualifications to the definition of creativity as something novel and useful; the most common, which not unlike the second description of Picasso's creative practice above, views creativity as an everyday, ordinary, and regularly occurring personal phenomenon. Computer psychologist Boden (2004), for example, suggests that creativity can simply exist as a personal experience or breakthrough, and as a result, she makes a distinction between 'psychological' or P-creativity, which she defines as an idea that is both novel and valuable only to the person who considered it, and 'historical' or H-creativity, which she defines as an idea viewed as both novel and valuable within the broader context of human history. This is not dissimilar to the often cited distinction between 'Big C' and 'little c' creativity (Amabile 2014; Craft 2002). 'Big C' creativity is described as path-breaking innovation that advances a domain and is therefore only ever achieved, often posthumously, by a few eminent and talented individuals, while 'little c' creativity is seen as the commonplace resourcefulness of ordinary people as they engage with everyday challenges, for example, developing an inventive meal from an assortment of leftovers. In an interesting addendum to this distinction, Kaufman and Beghetto (2009), believing that these categories are too broad, have added two further descriptions of creativity to the Big C/little c distinction. The first is 'mini-c creativity', which they describe as involving the transformative personal insights and development of individual knowledge that occurs in the learning process. The second is 'pro-c creativity', which refers to the high-level creativity of experts in their fields who will normally never achieve the status of eminent. According to Kaufman and Beghetto, pro-c creativity is exhibited by professionals in their field and is often the manifestation of decades of experience. Finally, Richards (2007) also identifies a difference between the eminent creativity of celebrated artists, authors, or scientists, which dominates early social and cognitive psychological studies of creativity, and everyday creativity, which she argues requires further scholarly attention. However, while she reinforces the psychological conceptualisation of everyday creativity as novel and meaningful, unlike the previous definitions, she foregrounds the nature of everyday creativity as 'a fundamental survival capability' (p. 27). As such, it is not a trivial activity, but one that often involves risk and deep commitment, potentially resulting in personal as well as social transformation and growth, and ultimately key for a healthy and purposeful lifestyle.

A limited number of studies have challenged the conceptualisation of creativity as novel and useful. In the field of Applied Linguistics, for example, Carter's (2004) investigation of creativity in everyday spoken language use also comes to the conclusion that rather than solely being the preserve of the gifted, creative language play is endemic to everyday spoken language and therefore the common property of human beings. However, and in contrast to the psychologists' emphasis on novelty, Carter demonstrates how one of the most common types of language creativity emerging from his corpus-based study is the use of echoing and repetition. He makes reference to Tannen's (1989) studies of casual conversational which support his findings:

> Repetition is a resource by which conversationalists together create a discourse, a relationship, and a world. It is the central linguistic meaning-making strategy, *a limitless resource for individual creativity* and interpersonal involvement. (Tannen 1989, p. 97, italics added)

Another applied linguist, Pennycook (2007), also argues that creativity is manifested through repetition, rather than divergence. Drawing upon the theories of post-structuralist scholar Deleuze (2004), Pennycook suggests that the habitual reoccurrence of socio-cultural practice will always result in a degree of transformation, and thus it can be argued that divergence and novelty is the norm, rather than the exception. As a result, Pennycook (2007) suggests that:

> Repetition, even of the 'same thing', always produces something new, so that when we repeat an idea, a word, a phrase, or an event, it is always renewed. From this point of view, sameness (language structure, identity, cultural norms) needs to be explained rather than assumed, and when we produce something new, this must always be a case of repetition. (Pennycook 2007, p. 585)

Pennycook supports his argument using examples of contemporary hip-hop culture where creativity emerges from recontextualisation, appropriation, and recycling. Similarly, Slutskaya (2006), using the context of contemporary improvised dance as exemplification, is critical of the received view of repetition as restricting creativity. She argues that in order to provide a meaningful sense of structure to any new contemporary dance performance, the dancers necessarily repeat habitual movements that, over time, constitute and provide a sense of unity to what is essentially the arbitrary social construct of contemporary dance.

Such values align with many non-Western conceptualisations of creativity, which have been described by Lubart (1999) as less focused on originality and directed instead towards the development of personal or spiritual fulfilment. According to Lubart, for many artists, this process often takes place through the reactivation or reinterpretation of tradition. Art theorist Danto (1994) provides an insightful exemplification of this non-Western emphasis on reinterpretation in his critical essay on a major exhibition of traditional Chinese painting. In his essay, he examined how the significance of each work in the exhibition resulted from its skilful ability to reinterpret, rather than transcend, prior works of the genre; a characteristic of creativity still largely attributed to the performance of Western classical musical works. In his essay, Danto concludes that:

> [T]he Chinese painter would be judged as we judge performers of known pieces or of known roles—as an interpreter rather than composer or author, whose interpretation may be compared in terms of virtuosity with respect to the way the spirit of the motif is transmitted. There would be room for dazzling skill and for eccentricity, *but not for a kind of originality or innovation.* (Danto 1994, p. 34, italics added)

There is a similar disagreement in creativity research regarding the tension between freedom and constraint and its role in the creative process. For many researchers, constraint is essential for creativity. Candy (2007), for example, writing in the area of digital design, holds the view that 'creativity may be seen as a process of exercising free choice in the context of a range of existing constraints' (p. 366); computational psychologist, Johnson-Laird (1988), argues that 'to be creative is to be free to choose among alternatives' (p. 202), adding however that 'which is not constrained is not creative' (p. 202), and psychologist Stokes (2006), states that constraints possess a crucial role for structuring creativity by acting as a series of 'barriers that lead to breakthroughs' (p. 7). Moeran (2006, 2009), in his study of the creative industries, even goes so far as suggesting that the concept of creativity is meaningless 'unless considered in tandem with the constraints under which it operates' (2009, p. 4). He has highlighted the constraining role played by the creative brief in facilitating creativity in advertising:

> Both copywriters and art directors often yearn for freedom from the constraints of [the] brief, but it is the constraints found therein that provide the 'stimulus for invention'. (Moeran 2006, p. 88)

For Moeran (2006), the constraints found in the design brief are necessary because they provide some sort of direction for creative action;

however, the relationship between freedom of choice and constraint is often discussed as one that is delicately balanced:

> Too little constraint and nothing happens (because there is no pressure for change)—or it just occurs haphazardly. Too much constraint and again nothing happens (this time because the system is seized)—or it all happens in a rush, willy nilly. (Pope 2005, p. 122)

In contrast, Hennessey and Amabile (1988), reviewing research that looks at the effects of surveillance, time pressure, rewards, and expected evaluation on creative behaviour, suggest that there is convincing evidence that such constraints undermine a person's creativity:

> There is no doubt that salient factors of extrinsic constraint in the social environment can have a consistently negative impact on the intrinsic motivation and creativity of most people most of the time. (Hennessey and Amabile 1988, p. 34)

Hennessey and Amabile do concede that for some individuals—for example, highly trained professionals at the top of their field—rewards will support creativity; however, they conclude that this is extremely unusual and that, for the most part, such constraints can be damaging to both intrinsic motivation and creativity. In the organisational context, West, Sacramento, and Fay (2006) also argue that external demands—for example, uncertainty, time constraints, and competition—inhibit creativity, which they define as 'the development of ideas' (p. 137); however, they add that the application of creative ideas into products, services, or working processes is actually facilitated by such demands.

The belief that creativity results from some kind of tension was also raised by Thomas Kuhn (1959, 1977) who was writing, in particular, about creativity in scientific research. Kuhn was critical of the received view that creativity was the result of divergent thinking (i.e. the ability to generate numerous and diverse ideas to solve a problem). Kuhn suggested that convergent thinking (i.e. the generation of a single solution using existing knowledge and rules) was also required for scientific creativity.

For Kuhn the dynamic interplay between divergent and convergent thinking, which he referred to as 'essential tension', was fundamentally a tension between the scientific tradition and the breaking of this tradition. According to Kuhn 'the productive scientist must be a traditionalist who enjoys playing intricate games by preestablished rules in order to be a successful innovator who discovers new rules and new pieces with which to play them' (Kuhn 1977, p. 237).

What is clear in this brief discussion is that creativity is conceptualised and defined in multiple different ways. It is also apparent that perceptions of creativity are often shaped by the specific contexts in which they are located. The next section examines the concept and role of creativity in the context of art and design education.

Creativity in Art and Design Education

Like definitions of creativity, the role and significance of creativity in art and design education is also multifarious. According to Fleming (2010), and reinforcing the information in Table 1.1 above, the use of the term *creativity* within the context of art education is noticeably absent in early twentieth century educational reports, and even the more common term 'creative' was rarely used to refer to the art practice of students. However, following World War I, and influenced by the pedagogical views of Viennese artist educator Franz Cižek, the rise of the Expressionist art movement, and the increasing interest in Freudian psychology (Efland 1990), new expressive ideologies in art education facilitated an emerging focus on student creativity, which was eventually manifested through the development of a pedagogical approach referred to as *creative self-expression*.

Cižek, who also influenced the Bauhaus master Johannes Itten (see Chap. 6), observed that children's art had an important intrinsic value when produced without any influence from adults. While there is some debate regarding the exact nature of Cižek's unpublished teaching methods, and whether he actually adhered to his non-interventionist philosophy, they are usually described as working to facilitate the true creative vision of children through an emphasis on free choice and the avoidance of any focus on technique or formal study (Efland 1990; Smith 1996). Following Cižek, Rugg and Shumaker's (1928) widely read and highly influential *The Child-Centered School* played an important role in further promoting creative self-expression in education. Although a critical evaluation of the new progressive schools of the 1920s, the book saw the new schools as ushering in an educational revolution, which had a significant impact on the role and teaching of art in the curriculum:

> This success is due not so much to the changed viewpoint concerning the place of art in education as to the whole new theory of self-expression, the emphasis on the place of creative originality in life. Art in the new school is permitted; in the old it is imposed. The new school assumes that every child is endowed with the capacity to express himself, and that this innate capacity is worth cultivating. (Rugg and Shumaker 1928, p. 63)

While there were opposing voices, the centrality of creative-free expression as a pedagogical approach continued to grow in strength after the end of World War II, reaching a peak in the 1960s and 1970s. This is largely seen as a consequence of Victor Lowenfeld's widely influential text *Creative and mental growth*, first published in 1947 and later co-authored by W. Lambert Brittain. Lowenfeld, a student of Cižek and one of America's most influential mid-century art educators, convincingly argued that not only was creativity and creative intelligence inherently connected with the artistic ability of students, but it also contributed to their abilities in other areas of study, as well as their own overall social development. In the 1964 edition, for example, Lowenfeld and Brittain stressed that 'the teacher should consider the development of creativity as one of the most vital areas of the art program' (p. 250), which they argued should focus on independent and spontaneous thinking, curiosity, and the various stages of self-expression.

By the 1980s the place of creativity in arts education once more began to disappear across the Western world. This was partly a reaction to the previous decade's overemphasis on creative self-expression, but mostly due to the increasing realisation that the role of culture was absent from the art curriculum (Burton 2009). In the United States, this curriculum change was driven by the discipline-based art education (DBAE) movement and the work of art education theorist Dwaine Greer. For Greer (1984), art was an academic discipline, which like others, involved content, concepts, procedures, and modes of enquiry that could be systematically studied and assessed in a structured curriculum. The result was a curriculum focus on four parent discipline areas, aesthetics, art criticism, art history, and art production, which, together, Greer identified as defining the discipline of art within an educational setting. It is of note that the term *creativity* or *creative* is never mentioned in Greer's defining article and that the ideological shift away from the emphasis on creativity that underpins discipline-based art education is clearly evident in the title and contents of the subsequent report *Beyond creating: The place for art in America's schools* (Getty Centre for Education in the Arts 1985), which provided the rationale for the DBAE programme along with case studies of its implementation in a number of school districts. Interestingly, however, in a 1987 article, where Clark, Day, and Greer clearly situate DBAE as a reaction to the creative self-expression approach, they do identify the way creativity is differently conceptualised in each of the two approaches:

> *Creative-self expression*
> Innate in child; develops naturally with encouragement and opportunity; lack of development is usually result of adult intervention.
> *Discipline-based art education*
> Creativity as unconventional behaviour that can occur as conventional art understandings are attained; untutored childhood expression is not regarded as necessarily creative.
> (Clark et al. 1987, p. 134)

What is evident here is a shift in the conceptualisation of creativity from the inherent ordinary everyday ability of individuals to the potential ability of someone who has a particular level of knowledge or expertise in their field. This dichotomy is similar to that occurring in the research on creativity.

In British education, a similar critique of creative free expression was taking place in the 1980s, primarily shaped by the Gulbenkian report

The arts in schools: Principles, practice and provision by Ken Robinson (1982, 1989). According to Robinson:

> We do not, however, share the view of some past advocates of the arts that this amounts to a need to encourage 'free expression'; that any response is acceptable from pupils because it is their response; that anything produced is worthwhile simply because it has been produced. (Robinson 1989, p. 30)

A central aim of Robinson's Gulbenkian report was a rejection of the conceptualisation of creativity as the innate ability of a few talented individuals, or as a separate mental faculty that could be measured. Instead it reconceptualised creativity as the result of a type of intelligence viewed in relation to specific disciplinary activities, which like any other mode of thinking, could be acquired through discipline and education. For Robinson, an increase in the creative intelligence of students would have a positive societal outcome and hence he advocated that a focus on developing creative intelligence should be a fundamental component of the school curriculum.

However, the Gulbenkian report did not reject free expressions outright; synonymous with the freedom/constraint dichotomy discussed in the previous section, Robinson acknowledged that a delicate balance between self-expression and institutional authority was central to the facilitation of creative work:

> The role of the teacher in the arts is at once vital and complicated. The task is not simply to let anything happen in the name of self-expression or creativity. Neither is it to impose rigid structures of ideas and methods upon the children. The need is for a difficult balance of freedom and authority.[1] (Robinson 1982, p. 31)

In England, the increasing conceptualisation of art and design creativity as something that could be learnt, rather than simply an innate ability or the result of free expression, coincided with the release of the first national curriculum in 1988. The national curriculum prescribed the specific content required to be taught along with the methods for assessment in a range of different subject areas, including art and design. Steers (2009) argues that this codification of the curriculum with its emphasis on key skills and what he refers to as an 'industrial input/output model' (p. 128) resulted in the eventual decline of any focus on creativity in art and design education. Perhaps also contributing to the decline was, as mentioned above, the ever-growing influence of postmodern critical theory on art practice in both schools and university departments, and the related shift in focus of student and contemporary artworks towards concerns of politics, gender, culture, oppression, and the environment (Emery 2002).

As the twentieth century approached, the place of creativity in education came into favour again. As mentioned earlier, this was largely a consequence of policy initiatives in developed Western countries where the newly titled creative industries became aligned with economic progress. In the United Kingdom, for example, the creative products and intellectual property rights emerging from sectors such as advertising, architecture, design, fashion, film, software, music, the performing arts, and television were progressively viewed as a key form of competition against the developing economies of Brazil, Russia, India, and China. Consequently, British government policy—supported by a task force, creativity committees, and numerous influential reports—pushed for an increased focus on creativity and innovation in industry. In order to build the type of workforce necessary for this new creative economy, an emphasis on creativity in education was promoted, and relevant university degree courses, including those in art and design, were encouraged to foster links with industry (Schlesinger 2007). A noticeable result of this renewed interest in creativity and its connection with industry can be seen in the reorganisation and retitling of university faculties. Examples include the Faculty of Design and Creative Technologies and Faculty of Creative Arts and Industries. These new academic clusters were to involve disciplinary fields representing the sciences, as well as the visual and design arts.

Out of this new wave of creativity, a number of studies examining the nature of creativity and the characteristics of creative behaviour have emerged from scholars working in the art and design fields. Unlike much of the social and cognitive psychological research described above, these new studies are largely qualitative, involving interviews with those involved in areas of creativity, or reflective, where researchers draw upon values and experiences gained through the art and design educative context. While the majority of these studies are still framed by an essentialist and external notion of creativity as involving novelty and usefulness, they nevertheless tend towards a more dynamic and multifaceted conceptualisation of creativity, which in many instances includes a focus on inner psychological criteria. Reid and Solomonides (2007), for example, suggest that students' individual emotional commitment or 'sense of being' (p. 30) is a significant factor for creative engagement in the art and design educative environment, while Kleiman (2008), based on interviews with academics, organises creativity into five key categories, some reproducing essentialist conceptions of creativity, while others conceptualising creativity as a personal fulfilment or a transformation-focused experience. Kleiman's study concurs with the work of Dineen, Samuel, and Livesey (2005), who find that, while there is some degree of correlation between essentialist descriptions of creativity and what students and teachers identify as creative, in the educative art and design environment creative success is often measured as individual growth and learner independence. Similarly Freedman's (2010) conceptualisation of creativity in the new educational context of the creative economy defines it as 'an open concept' (p. 10), and like the studies above, he argues that it emerges through internal processes of critical reflection, personal interest, self-motivated learning, and leadership. Nevertheless, Freedman still adds other external criteria such as 'functional' or 'useful' (p. 12), mirroring earlier cognitive psychological definitions of creativity.

Towards Creativity as a Discursive Construct

These overviews show that not only are there distinctly different conceptualisations of creativity in creativity research, but that the role and significance of creativity in the educative context is continually shifting. Although they are relatively infrequent, some studies have begun to reconsider the established views of creative behaviour as a fixed set of personal or culturally attributable qualities, or as a reflection of existing inner psychological states. Sternberg (2005), as well as Hennessey and

Amabile (2010), for instance, have suggested that creativity may in fact be multiple or multidimensional in nature and specifically dependent on the domain or field in which it occurs. Similarly, Carter (2004), who makes reference to the various conceptualisations and changing dynamics of creativity throughout time, across cultures, and within specific domains, concludes that creativity cannot be identified by a set of preconceived values. He suggests that 'what is valued as creative is itself highly variable' (p. 30), and furthermore, that even an attempt to explain creativity with reference to the social or cultural is too exclusive or essentialist. Lubart (1999), although unfortunately limiting his discussion to the effect of bilingualism on creativity, importantly mentions the role played by language in the constitution of creativity:

> Related to the effects of culture on creativity, described earlier, is the channeling influence of language on creativity. Whorf (1956) proposed that language shapes thought. Language structures categories and expresses a culture's understanding of the world (Lakoff and Johnson 1980). Language, as a vehicle of culture, can therefore be expected to shape creativity. (Lubart 1999, p. 344)

Not unlike Lubart, and as exemplified in the discussion at the beginning of this chapter, this book takes the view that language does in fact shape creativity and is facilitative of creative practice. However, rather than seeing the language of any particular culture as an already existing and reified homogenised code that (as Lakoff and Johnson have tended to argue) structures our thinking, language here is viewed as the communication between individuals, where meaning is constantly negotiated, relevant to the needs, constraints, and affordances of the particular context in which it occurs. What this means in terms of our discussion on communication and creativity is that the ongoing interactions between artists and their peers, between art critics' reviews and their readers, between curators' wall panels and gallery visitors, or even between art students and their tutors, do not simply facilitate creative activity nor provide interpretations of creative works as mentioned earlier, but that they shape the very nature of what is considered to be creative for any particular context in which creativity is deemed to take place. Of course, due to certain positions of influence or power, the way that creativity or creative practice is conceptualised in certain contexts can influence the way it is understood in other contexts. Statements made today about the nature and processes of contemporary design practice are still, in part, informed by the spoken interactions and written texts of the Bauhaus masters and their peers, who at the time were establishing a new design approach in response to the cultural shifts of the early twentieth century. And as will be explained in Chap. 6, the interactions of the Bauhaus masters themselves, most likely drew upon the nineteenth-century discourses of the culture of exploration, which at the time pervaded scientific, aesthetic, literary, economic, religious, and political life. Therefore, rather than being a essentialist or universalist phenomena with a set of fixed attributes, or even the reflection of existing inner psychological states, creativity is a contextually oriented and negotiated response to the existing amalgam of previous statements, utterances, and written texts produced about creativity or creative practice. Of course, over time new statements, utterances, and written texts are added to those already in existence and these contribute to ongoing shifts in the understanding of what is perceived as being creative for any particular context.

In essence then, this book takes the view that creative activity is discursively facilitated and that the nature of creativity is discursively constituted. In this view, and as will be seen throughout this book, the statements, utterances, and written texts about creative practice are collectively referred to as *discourse*. The term *discourse* usefully captures the way that language use actively contributes to shaping, social practices, processes, and identities in particular contexts. This constitutive process occurs at the *micro level*, through the words, sentences, genres (and other non-verbal forms such as gesture and gaze) used by individuals to communicate with one another. It also occurs at the *macro level*, through the ideological positions, knowledge, or values that—because of social, institutional, or professional constraints and affordances—regulate which words, sentences, and genres (and other non-verbal forms) we can use to communicate, or even think about, something. Due to different professional interests and allegiances, for example, a computer scientist is likely to bring a very different set of values and beliefs to a discussion about creativity in comparison to an arts examination board representative. Students who are said to be revealing an internal psychological passion to produce something original with a lasting impact (as in Reid and Solomonides 2007) may in fact be drawing upon wider modernist discourses of originality (Krauss 1985), or contemporary discourses of celebrity (Marshall 1997). As pointed out in a comment by educationalist Dennis Atkinson, even the declining interest in creativity in the 1980s, mentioned earlier, could be understood as the result of certain discursive shifts:

> [A]rt education came to be framed within a different discourse concerned with measurement and audit. The metaphors had changed from key concepts such as 'uniqueness', 'authenticity', 'creativity, 'expression' to ones relating to assessment and measurement. (Atkinson, cited in Steers 2009, p. 128)

Similarly, Schlesinger (2007) points out that the conception of the creative economy, widely adopted as a doctrine in the United Kingdom and other advanced free-market countries, was discursively engineered into being by the respective governments of these countries, through the use of marketing, branding, policy reports, and the media.

In order to find out more about the discursive constitution of creativity and the way that communication facilitates creative practice, the next chapter looks at how communication in creative settings might be analysed from a discourse-based perspective. The chapter will draw upon many of the conclusions made above about the nature of creativity and creative practice, not only regarding the role played by the communicative interaction of those involved in creative activity, but the role of language (for instance, the use of metaphor) as a resource for the framing of creative activity. It will consider the way that social and institutional histories are often repeated, recontextualised, or recycled in both the creative practices of the students and the pedagogical practices of the tutors, and it will consider how the personal dispositions and lived experiences of creative individuals, educators, and even creativity researchers, also contribute to their understanding of what it is to be creative.

Notes

1. According to Atkinson, this tension is still very active today and is largely manifested in the views of those who believe that art education should involve the teaching of skills and techniques, versus those who believe that an art curriculum should be concerned with challenging and resisting such traditions so as to facilitate the exploration of new meanings, both personal and social (Atkinson 2002, 2006).

References

Amabile, T. M. (2014). Big C, little C, Howard, and me: Approaches to understanding creativity. In M. L. Kornhaber & E. Winner (Eds.), *Mind, work, and life: A festschrift on the occasion of Howard Gardner's 70th birthday* (Vol. 1, pp. 5–25). Cambridge, MA: CreateSpace Independent Publishing Platform.

Antaki, C., & Widdicombe, S. (1998). Identity as an achievement and as a tool. In C. Antaki & S. Widdicombe (Eds.), *Identities in talk* (pp. 1–14). London, UK: Sage Publications.

Atkinson, D. (2002). *Art in education: Identity and practice.* Dordrecht, Netherlands: Kluwer Academic Publishers.

Atkinson, D. (2006). *School art education: Mourning the past and opening a future. Journal of Art and Design Education, 25*(1), 16–27.

Bhatia, V. K. (2004). *Worlds of written discourse.* New York, NY: Continuum.

Boden, M. A. (2004). *The creative mind: Myths and mechanisms* (2nd ed.). London, UK: Routledge.

Bourdieu, P. (1993). *The field of cultural production: Essays on art and literature.* New York, NY: Columbia University Press.

Burton, J. M. (2009). Creative intelligence, creative practice: Lowenfeld redux. *Studies in Art Education, 50*(4), 323–337.

Candlin, C. N., Bhatia, V. K., & Jensen, C. H. (2002). Must the worlds collide? Professional and academic discourses in the study and practice of law. In P. Cortese & P. Riley (Eds.), *Domain-specific English textual issues: From communities to classrooms* (pp. 110–114). Tübingen, Germany: Peter Lang.

Candy, L. (2007). Constraints and creativity in the digital arts. *Leonardo, 40*(4), 366–377.

Carter, R. (2004). *Language and creativity: The art of common talk.* New York, NY: Routledge.

Clark, G., Day, M., & Greer, W. D. (1987). Discipline-based art education: Becoming students of art. *Journal of Aesthetic Education, 24*(2), 129–193.

Craft, A. (2002). Little c creativity. In A. Craft, B. Jeffrey, & M. Leibling (Eds.), *Creativity in early years education: A lifewide foundation* (pp. 45–61). London, UK: Continuum.

Csikszentmihalyi, M. (1999). Implications of a systems perspective for the study of creativity. In R. J. Sternberg (Ed.), *Handbook of creativity* (pp. 313–335). Cambridge, UK: Cambridge University Press.

Cuff, D. (1991). *Architecture: The story of practice*. Cambridge, MA: Massachusetts Institute of Technology.

Danto, A. C. (1994). *Embodied meanings: Critical essays and aesthetic mediations*. New York, NY: Farrar, Straus and Giroux.

Davies, M. (2010). *The Corpus of Historical American English: 400 million words, 1810-2009*. Retrieved from http://corpus.byu.edu/coha/

Deleuze, G. (2004). *Difference and repetition*. London, UK: Continuum.

Dineen, R., Samuel, E., & Livesey, K. (2005). The promotion of creativity in learners: Theory and practice. *Art, Design and Communication in Higher Education, 4*(3), 155–172.

Duncum, P. (2001). How are we to understand art at the beginning of the twenty-first century? In P. Duncum & T. Bracey (Eds.), *On knowing: Art and visual culture* (p. 163). Christchurch, NZ: Canterbury University Press.

Efland, A. (1990). *A history of art education: Intellectual and social currents in teaching the visual arts*. New York, NY: Teachers College Press.

Emery, L. (2002). *Teaching art in a postmodern world: Theories, teacher reflections and interpretative frameworks*. In L. Emery (Ed.), *Teaching art in a postmodern world: Theories, teacher reflections and interpretative frameworks* (pp. 1–14). Altona, Australia: Common Ground.

FitzGerald, M. C. (1995). *Making modernism: Picasso and the creation of the market for twentieth-century art*. Berkeley, CA: University of California Press.

Fleming, M. (2010). *Arts in education and creativity: A literature review*. London: Creativity, Culture and Education. Retrieved from http://www.creativitycultureeducation.org/wp-content/uploads/arts-in-education-and-creativity-2nd-edition-91.pdf

Freedman, K. (2010). Rethinking creativity. *Art Education, 63*(2), 8–15.

Friedenthal, R. (1963). *Letters of the great artists: From Blake to Pollock*. New York, NY: Random House.

Gantefùhrer-Trier, A. (2004). *Cubism*. London, UK: Taschen.

Getty Centre for Education in the Arts. (1985). *Beyond creating: The place for art in America's schools*. Los Angeles, LA: J. Paul Getty Trust.

Gilot, F., & Lake, C. (1964). *Life with Picasso*. New York, NY: Anchor Books.

Greer, W. D. (1984). Discipline-based art education: Approaching art as a subject of study. *Studies in Art Education, 25*(4), 212–218.

Hackley, C. E. (2005). *Advertising and promotion: Communicating brands*. London, UK: Sage.

Hennessey, B. A., & Amabile, T. M. (1988). The conditions of creativity. In R. J. Sternberg (Ed.), *The nature of creativity* (pp. 11–38). New York, NY: Cambridge University Press.

Hennessey, B. A., & Amabile, T. M. (2010). Creativity. *Annual Review of Psychology, 61*, 569–598.

Johnson-Laird, P. N. (1988). Freedom and constraint in creativity. In R. J. Sternberg (Ed.), *The nature of creativity: Contemporary psychological perspectives* (pp. 202–219). Cambridge, UK: Cambridge University Press.

Kahnweiler, D. H. (1949). *The rise of Cubism* (H. Aronson, Trans.). New York, NY: Wittenbom, Schultz.

Kaufman, J. C., & Beghetto, R. A. (2009). Beyond big and little: The four C model of creativity. *Review of General Psychology, 13*(1), 1–12.

Kaufman, J. C., & Sternberg, R. J. (Eds.). (2010). *The Cambridge handbook of creativity*. Cambridge, UK: Cambridge University Press.

Kester, G. H. (2011). *The one and the many: Contemporary collaborative art in a global context*. Durham, NC: Duke University Press.

Kleiman, P. (2008). Towards transformation: Conceptions of creativity in higher education. *Innovations in Education and Teaching International, 45*(3), 209–217.

Kozbelt, A., Beghetto, R. A., & Runco, M. A. (2010). Theories of creativity. In J. C. Kaufman & R. J. Sternberg (Eds.), *Cambridge handbook of creativity* (pp. 20–47). New York, NY: Cambridge University Press.

Krauss, R. (1985). *The originality of the avant-garde and other modernist myths*. Cambridge, MA: MIT Press.

Kuhn, T. (1959). The essential tension: Tradition and innovation in scientific research. In C. W. Taylor (Chair) *Symposium conducted at the meeting of the The Third University of Utah Research Conference on the Identification of Creative Scientific Talent*. Salt Lake City, UT: The University of Utah Press.

Kuhn, T. S. (1977). *The essential tension: Selected studies in scientific tradition and change*. Chicago, IL: University of Chicago Press.

Lakoff, G., & Johnson, M. (1980). *Metaphors we live by*. Chicago, IL: University of Chicago Press.

Locher, P. J. (2010). How does a visual artist create an artwork? In J. C. Kaufman & R. J. Sternberg (Eds.), *The Cambridge handbook of creativity* (pp. 131–144). Cambridge, UK: Cambridge University Press.
Lowenfeld, V., & Brittain, W. L. (1964). *Creative and mental growth* (4th ed.). New York, NY: Macmillan.
Lubart, T. (1999). Creativity across cultures. In R. J. Sternberg (Ed.), *Handbook of creativity* (pp. 339–350). Cambridge, UK: Cambridge University Press.
Marshall, P. D. (1997). *Celebrity and power: Fame in contemporary culture.* Minneapolis, MN: University of Minnesota Press.
Mayer, R. E. (1999). Fifty years of creativity research. In R. J. Sternberg (Ed.), *Handbook of creativity* (pp. 449–460). Cambridge, UK: Cambridge University Press.
McDonnell, J. (2012). Accommodating disagreement: A study of effective design collaboration. *Design Studies, 33*(1), 44–63.
Moeran, B. (2006). *Ethnography at work*. New York, NY: Berg.
Moeran, B. (2009). *Cultural production, creativity and constraints* (Number 35). Copenhagen Business School Working Paper.
Oak, A. (2009). Performing architecture: Talking 'architect' and 'client' into being. *CoDesign: International Journal of CoCreation in Design and the Arts, 5*(1), 51–63.
Pennycook, A. (2007). 'The rotation gets thick. The constraints get thin': Creativity, recontextualisation and difference. *Applied Linguistics, 28*(4), 579–596.
Plucker, J. A., Beghetto, R. A., & Dow, G. T. (2004). Why isn't creativity more important to educational psychologists? Potentials, pitfalls, and future directions in creativity research. *Educational Psychologist, 39*(2), 83–96.
Pope, R. (2005). *Creativity: Theory, history, practice.* New York, NY: Routledge.
Reid, A., & Solomonides, I. (2007). Design students' experience of engagement and creativity. *Art, Design & Communication in Higher Education, 6*(1), 27–39.
Richards, R. (2007). *Everyday creativity and new views of human nature: Psychological, social, and spiritual perspectives.* Washington, DC: American Psychological Association.
Robinson, K. (1982). *The arts in schools: Principles, practice and provision.* London, UK: Calouste Gulbenkian Foundation.
Robinson, K. (1989). *The arts in schools: Principles, practice and provision.* London, UK: Calouste Gulbenkian Foundation.
Rugg, H., & Shumaker, A. (1928). *The child-centered school: An appraisal of the new education.* New York, NY: World Book Company.

Schlesinger, P. (2007). Creativity: From discourse to doctrine? *Screen, 48*(3), 377–387.

Simonton, D. K. (1999). *Origins of genius: Darwinian perspectives on creativity.* New York, NY: Oxford University Press.

Simonton, D. K. (2007). The creative process in Picasso's Guernica sketches: Monotonic improvements versus nonmonotonic variants. *Creativity Research Journal, 19*(4), 329–344.

Slutskaya, N. (2006). Creativity and repetition. *Creativity and Innovation Management, 15*(2), 150–156.

Smith, P. (1996). *The history of American art education: Learning about art in American schools.* Westport, CT: Greenwood Press.

Steers, J. (2009). Creativity: Delusions, realities, opportunities and challenges. *Journal of Art and Design Education, 28*(2), 126–138.

Sternberg, R. J. (2005). Creativity or creativities? *International Journal of Human-Computer Studies, 63*, 370–382.

Stokes, P. (2006). *Creativity from constraints: The psychology of breakthrough.* New York, NY: Springer.

Tannen, D. (1989). *Talking voices: Repetition, dialogue and imagery in conversational discourse.* Cambridge, UK: Cambridge University Press.

Thorson, E., & Duffy, M. (2011). *Advertising age: The principles of advertising and marketing communication at work.* Mason, OH: South Western, Cengage Learning.

Tomes, A., Oates, C., & Armstrong, P. (1998). Talking design: Negotiating the verbal visual-translation. *Design Studies, 19*(2), 127–142.

Weisberg, R. W. (2006). *Creativity: Understanding innovation in problem solving, science, invention, and the arts.* Hoboken, NJ: John Wiley and Sons.

West, M., Sacramento, C., & Fay, D. (2006). Creativity and innovation implementation in work groups: The paradoxical role of demands. In L. L. Thompson & H. S. Choi (Eds.), *Creativity and innovation in organizational teams* (pp. 137–159). Mahwah, NJ: Lawrence Erlbaum Associates.

Whorf, L. (1956). *Language, thought and reality.* Cambridge, MA: MIT Press.

Winkleman, E. (2015). *Selling contemporary art: How to navigate the evolving market.* New York, NY: Allworth Press.

2

Investigating Communication in Creative Practice

Introduction

In Chap. 1, it was argued that art and design creativity is a discursively constituted practice involving a complex interaction of spoken and written communication between creative individuals (e.g. artists and designers), their various professional or personal acquaintances, and their viewing public. Chapter 1 also framed creative communication as discourse, meaning that any instance of language use in a creative setting—for example, a studio discussion or a written design brief—is not only an often generically and interactionally organised collection of statements, but is also a set of ideological values and beliefs that are, in part, reproduced through, but also constrained by, these statements. Taking this view as a starting point, Chap. 2 looks at the ways that communication in creative settings might be analysed from such a discourse-based perspective to find out more about creativity and creative practice. In order to first establish this analytical process, I will return to the well-known context of the early modernist painters, including Pablo Picasso and George Braque, to show that the complex, dynamic, and situated nature of their respective creative practices can be discursively examined and

D. Hocking, *Communicating Creativity*, Communicating in Professions and Organizations, https://doi.org/10.1057/978-1-137-55804-6_2

understood through a set of differently focused analytical lenses and related methodological resources. The chapter will conclude by providing an approach for investigating the discursive construction of student creativity and creative practice in the university art and design studio that dynamically integrates these different lenses and methodologies and in doing so, acknowledges the interdependence between micro-scale language use and broader macro-relations of power and ideology.

A Focus on Interaction

As pointed out in Chap. 1, Picasso and Braque are renowned for their collaborative development of cubism, a movement widely viewed as having revolutionised Western painting and sculpture. It also stated that crucial to their cubist project were the many spoken and written interactions that the two painters had with one another. Some of these interactions focused on the evaluation of works recently completed or in progress. On 10 July 1912, for example, Picasso wrote to Braque:

> Kahnweiler told me you've seen my paintings from Céret. You must tell me what you think of them, especially of the biggest one, the one with the violin, whose intentions I'm sure you've understood. (Picasso, cited in Rubin 1989, p. 399)

In response to Picasso's desire for a critical evaluation of his recent paintings, Braque responded that they were 'very handsome' and reserved special mention for the work *Violin: "Jolie Eva"*, which he described as 'outstanding' (p. 399). In all probability, such a positive endorsement from Braque contributed to legitimising the direction that Picasso's work was taking at the time, and in many ways *Violin: "Jolie Eva"* can be viewed as indicative of this process. It was produced in the summer of 2012, a year suggested as marking a shift between analytical and synthetic cubism. Among the painting's rigidly geometric abstractions, which are characteristic of analytical cubism, one can also observe a number of easily recognisable forms, such as the printed paper and wood panelling. A focus on these new literal forms would become an increasingly distinctive component of Picasso and Braque's subsequent synthetic cubist works.

Comments that indicate the importance of critical appraisal for their respective creative practices are also evident in Picasso and Braque's correspondence. On 6 November 1911, Braque wrote to Picasso, stating:

> I am also at present working on the pretty Woman Reading, of which, I believe you saw the beginning. I was very happy that the large still life made a good impression on you. (Picasso, cited in Rubin 1989, pp. 383–384)

Similarly in a letter to his dealer Kahnweiler, Braque wrote in October 1913:

> [Y]our opinion about my paintings caused me great pleasure, and I was all the more sensitive to it as it is the only one I have gotten here where isolation leads to a loss of all critical sense … . (Braque, cited in Rubin 1989, p. 423)

In this second extract, Braque clearly indicates the importance of discussing his work in progress and that it affords him a critical understanding of its merits. This reliance on the opinion of others is also evident in Picasso's comment in Gilot and Lake (1964) that he and Braque met daily to critique each other's work and would not view a canvas as complete until both had agreed. Given their close relationship, it is highly likely that the type of constructive criticism that took place in the studio frequently involved offering advice or making recommendations about each other's work. There are few explicit details of Picasso and Braque's studio interactions, so it is difficult to know exactly how such appraisals took place; however, the letters of Vincent van Gogh offer some insight into the nature of the interaction between artists around the turn of the last century, and they show that advising and recommending were commonplace. In a 1983 letter to his friend Anthon van Rappard, Van Gogh, for example, discusses one of the regular visits to his studio by the Dutch painter, and his regular acquaintance, Van der Weele:

> [H]e said of the Sand quarry that there were too many figures in it. The composition wasn't simple. He said, look, draw that one little fellow with his wheelbarrow on a dyke in the evening set against the light sky, how

> beautiful that would be, for instance … . (Van Gogh 1983, cited in Jansen et al. 2009, letter 354)

Similarly in another letter to his brother Theo, written later in the same year, Van Gogh states:

> I discussed everything again with Van der Weele. He spent an afternoon at the studio and saw my studies one by one. Together we repainted several of them to show me some things to do with technique. Anyway, he showed me some useful things. Also, before I go, in the next few days in other words, he'll give some more of his time to tell me a thing or two. (Van Gogh 1983, cited in Jansen et al. 2009, letter 380)

As with the use of any communicative function, offering advice or making recommendations impact on the way any interactive encounter is structured, especially in creative contexts such as the studio interaction between Van der Weele and Van Gogh where the latter would have had an emotive personal connection to the work being discussed. Indeed, Van Gogh stated that he was 'mightily sensitive' to what was said about his work (letter 397), and in order to mitigate any possible offense, it is feasible that this sensitivity was taken into consideration by those offering him advice or making recommendations about his work. To achieve this, a number of interactional strategies—including the use of qualifications and hedges, over-personalisation, or positive-before-negative evaluations—may have been used. Such strategies are evident in the transcript of a studio tutorial from the interactional data collected for the study in this book.

Extract 2.1: Studio Tutorial

Anna (tutor): I think there are just a couple of things
that you could think about
that could um you know
just unclutter it you know
that bit-
Student 3: yeah yeah.
Anna: cause at the moment

what I do is
when I look at that
I look straight at-
the wallpaper's fantastic
but it's very full on
and it actually takes over.

In Extract 2.1, the tutor, Anna, moderates her critical appraisal of the student's work by first emphasising that her recommendations are minimal (*just a couple of things*, line 1), and then subsequently hedging these using the modal *could* (lines 2 and 3). A succession of first-person pronominal forms (*I think*, line 1; *what I do*, line 8; *when I look*, line 9; *I look*, line 10) shows a repeated use of over-personalisation throughout the tutorial, and this works to strategically frame the recommendations as nothing more than Anna's subjective views. Furthermore, before the negative evaluation is given (lines 12–13), it is mitigated by being prefaced with a positive evaluation (*the wallpaper's fantastic*, line 11). The deployment of these communicative strategies suggests that the practice of interacting around an art or design work, something that has been identified here as a historically pervasive and crucial component of creative activity, is a very structured kind of practice. Hence, not only are the content and functional elements of such interactions crucial to the constitution of creative practice, but also the way that such interaction strategically unfolds. An absence, for instance, of such appraisal strategies might result in a breakdown of the type of interpersonal relationship necessary for the production of creativity-facilitating interaction.

Clearly the interaction that occurs in creative contexts can provide an important resource for understanding more about the way that creative practice is discursively constituted. While such social interactions are often seen as routine, taken for granted, or involve discursive practices that often go unnoticed by those involved (Candlin and Crichton 2012), certain discourse analytical procedures—such as conversation analysis, linguistic ethnography, membership categorisation analysis, or genre analysis—can shed light on the way that aspects of interaction can contribute to the discursive construction of creative practice.

In brief, conversation analysis (Sacks 1992; Antaki 2011) examines the underlying way in which naturally occurring talk between individuals unfolds in a recurring, systematic, and organised way. Linguistic ethnography (Copland and Creese 2015; Rampton 2007; Tusting and Maybin 2007) draws upon the analytical resources of conversation analysis, but includes an ethnographic focus on the socio-cultural contexts and personal experiences that participants bring to, and take from, the communicative encounter. Membership categorisation analysis (Sacks 1992; Antaki and Widdicombe 1998) views a group or an individual's identity as their particular orientation through the local, situated, and emergent properties of their interaction, to the membership to certain categories (e.g. tutor, student, visual artist, designer), as well as to the actions and characteristics typically ascribed to these categories. Genre analysis (Swales 1990; Bhatia 1993) focuses on investigating the way that certain forms of spoken and written discourse have become regularised due to specific recurring needs in particular contexts. As indicated in Chap. 1, the brief, the artist's statement, or the studio tutorial are all examples of generic forms in the art and design context. Some of the areas focused on in genre analysis are the use of particular linguistic forms, rhetorical structures, and subject matter, as well as the way a genre is typically produced, distributed, and received. Finally, interaction, of course, is not simply verbal (i.e. spoken and written), but also involves non-verbal communicative modes such as gesture, head movement, posture, and gaze, among others. Thus, a method such as multimodal (inter)action analysis (Norris 2004, 2011), which provides insights into how people construct their social or professional worlds and identities through these other modes of communication, can also offer the analyst something for the investigation of communication in creative settings.

A Focus on Semiotic Choice

While an investigation of spoken and written interaction occurring in creative contexts can tell us something about the nature of creativity, so will a focus on the specific lexical (and at times, phonological, gestural, or graphological) choices that are made at each stage in the interaction. For example, and as evidenced in the three extracts below, the word *study* (étude in French) was routinely used by the early modernists to metaphorically describe the practice of drawing or painting, regardless of whether it referred to the process of creating a work or to the finished work itself. The first extract is from a letter Picasso wrote to Gertrude and Leo Stein in 1909, while the second and third are from a letter Van Gogh wrote to his brother Theo in 1889:

> I still don't know when I'll be back in Paris. I'm still doing *studies*, and am working fairly regularly. (Picasso 1909, cited in Rubin 1989, pp. 362–363, italics added)

> [F]or really I must do more figure work. It's the *study* of the figure that *teaches* one to grasp the essential and to simplify. (Van Gogh 1889, cited in Jansen et al. 2009, letter 805, italics added)

> I would like to have all of this, at least the etchings and the wood engravings. It's a *study* I need, for I want to *learn*. (Van Gogh 1889, cited in Jansen et al. 2009, letter 805, italics added)

In these extracts, the use of the word 'study', most probably colonised from the field of music where it once referred to a composition designed to advance a student's technical skills, constitutes the artists' creative practice as an educational pursuit. Van Gogh's close collocation of *study* with the verbs *teaches* and *learn*, words both semantically related to education, further exemplifies this educative framing of his creative practice. Interestingly, by the mid-twentieth century and due to certain cultural shifts happening at the time, the use of the word *study* to describe the creative practices of Western artists and designers was replaced by the word *explore*, thus differently constituting the nature of creative practice. This will be discussed further in Chap. 6.

What is evident from this example is that rather than necessarily providing a fixed and homogenised code that simply represents the existing realities of our contextual worlds, language (and other non-linguistic resources) can actively shape the way our worlds are conceptualised. In other words, it is, in part, through the linguistic choices that we make from the shared sets of resources available, that our worlds and their associated practices are brought into being. In another example, Vauxcelles' famous categorisation of Braque's new works as 'bizarreries cubiques' (cubic oddities), for example, had an important impact on the way the emerging style of painting would be perceived by the viewing public. Once Vauxcelles had publically described Braque's paintings as made up of geometric cubes, it was difficult for his new works, along with the similarly categorised works of Picasso, to be understood in any other way. The subsequent development and acceptance of the term cubism (le cubisme in French) also constituted the canvases of Braque and Picasso as belonging to a distinctive movement, which due to their increasing influence was inevitably embraced by a number of other artists. Over time, a close-knit group of painters emerged whose creative practices and identities as creative practitioners were made possible by their adherence to what they would eventually develop and formalise as a cubist dogma.

A number of analytical approaches can be used to investigate the shared semiotic resources that certain social, institutional, or professional groups draw upon and how the particular choices they make from these resources contribute to shaping their particular worlds and practices of those who use them. These include corpus analysis, systematic functional linguistics, and multimodal social semiotics. The corpus analysis of discourse (Baker 2006) can help the analyst quickly sift through large collections of spoken or written texts to find frequently occurring words and significant collocations or concordances which can provide information about the salience or 'aboutness' of a group of texts and the contexts in which they are used. Systemic functional linguistics (Halliday and Matthiessen 2004) can help the analyst identify how, within any communicative context, the specific language choices made by the speaker or writer from the wider set of socially and historically available language resources function to construct certain experiences of the world, certain types of social relations, and the structure of the communicative encounter itself. Multimodal social semiotics (Hodge and Kress 1998; Kress and Van Leeuwen 2001, 2006) expands the approach of systematic functional linguistics so that it can take into account the deployment of other nonverbal resources, including images, gesture, action, music, and sound.

A Focus on the Accounts and Lived Experiences of Individuals

While an examination of both the interactions and the semiotic choices made in these interactions can capture the nature of creative practice, they nevertheless only reveal part of the overall picture, one that could be viewed as leaning towards the often-detached interpretations of the analyst. As a way of addressing this imbalance, the interpretative accounts and lived experiences of creative practitioners and their professional or personal acquaintances can provide further insights into the subjective meanings and perceptions that they attach to their practices.

Throughout the twentieth century, both Picasso and Braque were interviewed on numerous occasions about their respective creative practices. In some instances their accounts have weakened scholarly observations made about their work, and in others they have supported research or provided opportunities for new areas of scholarly interest. The earlier extract from Braque's interview with Dora Vallier in 1954, where he refers to the significance of his communication with Picasso, provides a case in point relevant to the study in this book. Braque also made similar comments in another interview conducted by Jacques Lassaigne in 1961:

> Picasso and I had daily exchanges; we discussed and tested each other's ideas as they came to us, and we compared our respective works. (Braque 1961, cited in Rubin 1989, p. 358)

The written accounts of Fernande Olivier, who was in a close relationship with Picasso throughout the early years of his career, provide further insights regarding the interaction between the two painters. Referring to their early discussions about cubism, Olivier states:

> Braque did not adopt cubism without a display of typical Norman defiance and rebelliousness. The first time he discussed the subject at the studio, although Picasso was arguing his case very reasonably and clearly, Braque remained unconvinced. 'In spite of the way you explain your painting, it's as though you want to make us eat tow or drink kerosene.' (Olivier 2001, p. 259)

She goes on to say that while Braque was initially sceptical, he secretly developed a large canvas in the new style, which he subsequently exhibited at the Salon des Indépendants, much to the indignation of Picasso. While Olivier's emphasis on 'arguing' and 'explaining' corroborates the view that interaction was fundamental to the development of the two artists' work, her first-hand account also combines with other evidence to shed further light on the specific nature of these interactions and contributes to providing a more complete picture of Picasso and Braque's emergent creative practices. Interestingly, Olivier's account of the period when she lived with Picasso also makes reference to the art critic Vauxcelles' particular role in the development of cubism:

> The new development owed its name to Vauxcelles, who irritably declared that these artists were no more than 'Patagonian cubists.' Vauxcelles seemed to think it was his task to destroy all new developments, until they were crowned with success, at which point he would rally to their support.[1] (Olivier 2001, p. 260)

Olivier's account suggests that Vauxcelles' less than positive response towards Picasso and Braque's works, which as mentioned above contributed to the framing of a new movement, was the result of his own particular hostile disposition towards developments in the arts. However she adds to this her belief that such hostility was also an attribute of the French, who she noted were 'slow to accept what they can't instantly understand and only mollified by success' (p. 260).

As evidenced in the quotations above, the interview or the narrative (articulated through a personal journal or diary) are probably the most versatile tools for capturing the interpretative accounts and lived experiences of those associated with a particular discursive practice. Both are frequently used in qualitative research approaches, and both typically involve thematic analysis to inductively code and establish recurring themes and patterns in the data (see Dörnyei 2007; Creswell 2013). A more traditional ethnographic focus (Hammersley and Atkinson 2007) that looks for salient and recurring patterns within and across the participants' interactions, their choice of semiotic resources, and their narrative accounts is another useful methodological resource for understanding how individuals and groups conceptualise their worlds and the practices within them.

A Focus on Historical Context

Each instance of communication in creative practice can also be understood as a part of wider socio-economic, political, and institutional processes. As an illustration, the spoken and written interactions between Picasso and Braque, and even Vauxcelles' reviews for the *Gil Blas*, could be argued as shaped by the late 1800s relocation of the contemporary art market from London to Paris. According to Robertson (2005), this shift was due to the changes in English economic laws (no doubt the result of interactional encounters between those in power at the time), which resulted in a late nineteenth-century collapse of the prices of contemporary English painting. The wealthy English patrons of contemporary art subsequently failed to embrace the emerging and increasingly important Impressionist movement that was taking place in Paris and was a precursor to Picasso and Braque's cubism. Importantly, the French Impressionists' increasing success occurred outside the powerful institutional authority of the Académie des Beaux-Arts, which, at the time, was still largely responsible for setting artistic standards and establishing the reputations of individual artists (FitzGerald 1995). Instead, interest in the Impressionist's work was generated through the popular Salon des Indépendants (the subject of Vauxcelles' previously mentioned review), an annual exhibition set up by a leading group of artists to exhibit works excluded from the official Salons of the French Academy. Furthermore, and in contrast to the statues of the academy, which dismissed commercial success as detrimental to the intellectual standing of art, the Impressionists also actively and successfully collaborated with the increasingly tenacious Parisian dealers of the period to sell their paintings, one of whom, Kahnweiler, would eventually represent both Picasso and Braque. As a consequence, commercial success, rather than acknowledgement by the academy, became increasingly viewed as indicating the aesthetic and critical quality of an artist's work.

It was within the social context of this emerging twentieth-century art market for the avant-garde that many of Picasso's views towards his creative practice were formed. Kahnweiler (1949) frequently mentioned Picasso's aspiration for wealth and commercial success, and Picasso himself also admitted this intention, as evidenced, for example, in his later conversations with the photographer Brassaï (1999). In a commentary accompanying a reproduction of his pastel *Intimacy*, Picasso openly acknowledges his creation of the work for financial reasons:

> I was living on the rue Champollion. I wanted to do something to make some money. I'm a little ashamed to admit it, but that's how it was. So I did this pastel. I rolled it up and carried it to Berthe Weill. (Picasso, cited in Daix and Boudaille 1967)

Weill was one of Picasso's first dealers, and according to FitzGerald (1995), Picasso specifically created the work to suit the tastes of one of her regular clients, the influential art investor André Level. Picasso was acutely aware that his reputation and career would be enhanced should Level acquire the work for his investment consortium, an outcome which came to eventuate a few years later. Hence, it is inevitable that Picasso's spoken and written interactions, including his conversations with his close companion Braque or the surrounding network of professionals that organised his commercial affairs, would have included topics involving commercial success, the emergent avant-garde art market, and their particular roles within it. As indicated in the commentary for his work *Intimacy*, these interactions, shaped by the social values and practices of the time, made an impact on the particular choices made by Picasso in his creative practice.

What might be gleaned from the discussion above is that discourse, both at the micro and macro level, is produced in and through social interaction, and it shapes, but is also shaped by, the social practices in which these interactions take place. It is shaped by social practice, because over time certain recurring activities within certain contexts give rise to, or transform, certain sets of linguistic and non-linguistic resources. It shapes social practice, because the existing resources, and the meanings they encompass at any particular time, are what social actors draw upon to produce the spoken, written, and visual texts that constitute their everyday social, institutional, and professional practices. To produce his

1909 review of the Salon des Indépendants for the *Gil Blas*, Louis Vauxcelles would have drawn upon his mostly tacit knowledge of the lexico-grammatical and structural conventions of art criticism, as well as the art review genre. As Vauxcelles wrote his review, he was inevitably reproducing the conventions of art criticism and the art review, yet at the same time he was introducing subtle variations to these conventions. These changes may have been informed by his personal dispositions (Bourdieu 1993), including his identity as a quality journalist (Gee 1993), or the editorial requirements of the *Gil Blas*, notably its witty yet accessible in-house style (Schiau-Botea 2013). Indeed, Gee (1993) states that Vauxcelles brought a kind of journalistic urbanity and lightness to his art reviews, which he and others in his position developed in opposition to the prevailing and more pedantic academic art criticism of the time. Gee also suggests that Vauxcelles' contribution to the discourse of art criticism and the exhibition review genre is reproduced in the texts of many late twentieth-century art critics, including those written by the celebrated Australian critic Robert Hughes. Undoubtedly, in his 1909 review, Vauxcelles' description of the work being produced by Picasso and Braque as 'bizarreries cubiques' (cubic eccentricities), and his earlier reference to Henri Matisse's paintings as 'les fauves' (wild beasts), were motivated by his particular journalistic context. And as mentioned earlier, his use of these expressions brought the art categories cubisme (cubism) and fauvisme (fauvism) into common usage, forever discursively framing the creative practices of two significant approaches to early twentieth-century creative practice.

Many of the discourse analytical methods mentioned above already acknowledge that the discourses and discursive practices of the present are embedded in and related to wider historical contexts. The discourse-historical approach (Reisigl and Wodak 2009; Wodak 2001), however, takes this relationship as its central concern. In the discourse-historical approach, information about historical contexts, including an analysis and interpretation of relevant historical utterances, texts, genres, and discourses, is integrated into the analysis of the present-day phenomenon being investigated. The discourse-historical approach draws upon two important concepts, *intertextuality* and *interdiscursivity*, both of which are also of central importance to this book. While these concepts are often defined in slightly different ways, in general, intertextuality refers to the way that any text overtly draws upon and references other texts, as typically evidenced in the use of quotations and citations. Interdiscursivity, in contrast, refers to the way that any text will typically involve the articulation, to varying degrees, of the stylistic, lexico-grammatical, structural, and multimodal conventions of different genres, including the activities typically associated with the production and interpretation of those genres. Such interdiscursivity was evidenced earlier regarding the way that Vauxcelles' 1909 review of the Salon des Indépendants reproduced both the generic conventions of the art review genre, as well as those specifically representative of the *Gil Bas* periodical. Interdiscursivity, however, also refers to the way that any text will also draw upon prevailing macro-level discourses, as seen earlier in the way that Picasso's commentaries on his work, and even the work itself, are representative of the avant-garde discourse of entrepreneurship that emerged in the visual arts towards the beginning of the twentieth century. In the discourse-historical approach, ethnographic explorations, textual analyses, and extensive literature searches are typically used to establish intertextuality and interdiscursivity across texts and contexts.

Making Connections

The four foci described in the sections above can be seen as representing different lenses or perspectives, which can help us to understand the nature of site-specific discursive practices such as art and design creativity. It seems evident, then, that a more complete understanding of the relationship between communication and creative practice in a particular setting, one that captures the relationship between the micro and macro levels of discourse, can be produced by bringing together the different findings that emerge from an analysis of data representing these different perspectives. The Venn diagram in Fig. 2.1, which is adapted from Crichton (2004, 2010) and Candlin and Crichton (2011, 2012, 2013), shows how these different perspectives can be dynamically integrated, and in doing so provides a model for carrying out multi-perspectival dis-

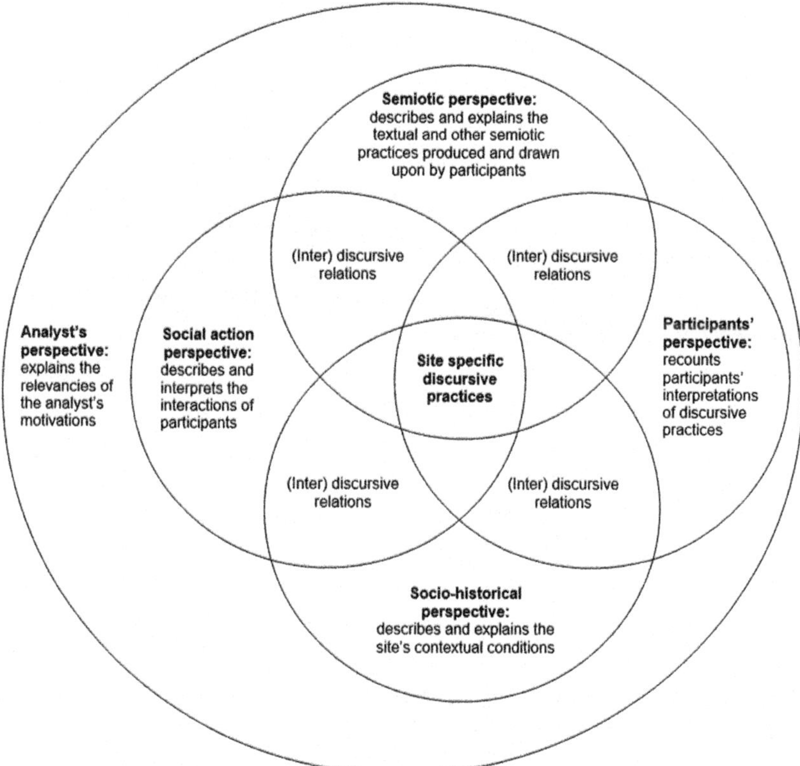

Fig. 2.1 A model for a multi-perspectival analysis of discourse (adapted from Crichton 2004, 2010, and Candlin and Crichton 2011, 2012, 2013)

course analysis in a principled and systematic way. The *social action perspective* in the model focuses on interpreting the participants' social interaction as they carry out their practices. The *semiotic resource perspective* focuses on analysing the textual and other semiotic choices made by the participants as they create or construe situated meaning in interaction. The *participants' perspective* involves investigating the discursive event from the subjective and lived experiences of the social actors involved, and the *socio-historical* perspective identifies the analysis of the wider social, institutional, and historical resources as providing further explanatory potential for the discursive practices occurring at the site of engagement.

An important feature of the Venn diagram in Fig. 2.1 is the overlapping boundaries of the four inner perspectives. As was demonstrated in the discussion of the early modernists' creative practice above, these overlapping boundaries characterise site-specific discursive practice as constituted through the nexus of semiotic and interactional resources and processes, socio-histories, and lived experiences. However, the overlapping circles also suggest that the boundaries between the four inner perspectives are not so clear-cut, allowing data initially viewed as representing one perspective to be approached as representing another, and thus subject to different methodological tools. What this means is that the interactions of participants could be approached, for example, not only as interactional data and investigated using conversation analytical tools, but also from a semiotic perspective which focuses on quantifying the linguistic choices made by the participants during their interactions. Thus, a particular methodological resource, such as corpus analysis, which as mentioned is particularly suitable for analysing data from the semiotic resource perspective, can also be useful for analysing data originally collected to represent the other perspectives. This use of a range of methods to examine diverse sets of data representing different perspectives has been described by Scollon (1998) as methodological interdiscursivity. Scollon argues that in order to fully understand the interdiscursive relationships that shape and can provide an understanding of the dynamic complexity of practice, a degree of methodological interdiscursivity must always be achieved.

Surrounding the four inner overlapping circles in the Venn diagram is the *analyst's perspective*. This outer perspective indicates that the selection of data, methodological resources, and specific choice of tools, as well as the different weightings given to each of the perspectives, are all subject to the particular research interests, backgrounds, and purposes of the analyst, as well as their understanding of the research context. This reflexive engagement with the analysis also includes acknowledgement of the particular macro-level discourses that underpin the research orientation itself. The three studies of Picasso's creativity, discussed in Chap. 1, provide a case in point. At a disciplinary level, they draw upon the disciplinary discourse of cognitive psychology, in which the individual is conventionally abstracted as an isolated unit, meaning is conceptualised in terms of individual cognition (Malson 2003), and attention is given to context-independent abstract concepts, rather than to context-sensitive linguistic constructs (Lemke 1994). To various degrees they also draw upon the romantic discourse of creative genius, which is prevalent in many studies of creativity (Banaji and Burn 2006, 2007), and has been defined as the belief that creativity is the 'special quality of a few highly educated and disciplined individuals (who possess genius)' (2007, p. 62). While it has been identified as emerging during the Renaissance, Banaji and Burn suggest, however, that it was not until the eighteenth century that the discourse of creative genius was used to conceptualise the personalities of celebrated artists. They cite Kristeller (1990), who states:

> The artist was guided no longer by reason or by rules but by feeling and sentiment, intuition and imagination; he produced what was *novel and original*. And at the point of his highest achievement he was a genius. (Kristeller 1990, p. 250, cited in Banaji and Burn 2006, p. 7, italics added)

The study of creative practice and creativity in this book is, for the most part, grounded in a social-constructionist discourse, which like much recent discourse analytical research (Jørgensen and Phillips 2002), holds that knowledge and identity is discursively constituted, largely through the historically and culturally situated social interactions of individuals and groups as they attempt to structure their experiences of the world (Burr 2003). Therefore, and as argued in the previous chapter, creativity and creative practice are not viewed throughout this book as an external reality resulting from an essentialist set of criteria or an objective psychological state, but as a historically situated and socially embedded phenomenon which is discursively accomplished and constituted through text, talk, and other semiotic forms.

Structuring the Study

The focus on multiple data sets representing different perspectives, and the requirement that these are approached using different methodological resources, presents a significant challenge for the analyst. In order to help structure and cohere such a multi-layered analytical process, this study established a set of themes or concepts around which the analysis could be oriented. These themes not only provided a useful means for both commencing and structuring the complex, dynamic, and explorative process of multi-perspectival research, but they also provided the basis for developing the theoretical framework through which the discursive interdependence of the semiotic, social action, social-historical, and lived-experiential perspectives could be explained.

Orienting themes have been previously recognised as useful structuring devices in both social science and discourse analytical research, in particular Derek Layder's (1998) notion of the *orienting concept*, Roberts and Sarangi's (2005) notion of the *focal theme*, and Candlin and Crichton's (2012, 2013) notion of the *conceptual construct*. According to Layder (1998), an orienting concept can provide a heuristic anchorage point to provide the analyst with theoretical guidance and methodological direction in the preliminary stages of a multi-strategy study. He suggests that it should be established by the analyst using a creative and intuitive search of 'words, ideas, accounts, frameworks, phrases' (p. 104) in existing theoretical or non-theoretical literature in both the field of research and adjacent fields. Rather than dominating the analysis, however, Layer states that the orienting concept should be flexibly employed and where necessary reframed, or even discarded, as new evidence appears. Roberts and Sarangi's theme-oriented discourse analysis involves focusing on a particular focal theme (e.g. decision making, diagnostic reasoning in the discipline of health) relevant to the discipline being studied and linking it with discourse analytic themes (e.g. frames and footing, contextualisation clues) to reveal insights in the use of disciplinary discourse. Similarly, Candlin and Crichton (2012, 2013), have identified a set of conceptual constructs—*characterisation*, *responsibility*, *identity*, *relationships*, *capacity*, *recognition*, *agency*, and *membership*—which they suggest can provide an orienting framework for investigating discursive phenomena, particularly in professional and institutional settings where such concerns are salient. They suggest that these conceptual constructs can help guide the analyst towards particular research questions, methodological choices, and relevant theoretical resources to facilitate both the exploration and explanation of the discursive practice under examination. The difference between the conceptual construct and Layder's orienting concept is perhaps that the latter emerges in response to the phenomena being studied, while the former provides a pre-existing set of constructs already valued as useful for framing the analysis of discursive practice.

The multi-perspectival study of student creative practice in this book is framed by six distinct orienting focal themes: *work*, *agency*, *motivation*, *exploration*, *ideas*, and *identity*. Each of these themes provides a distinct and bounded conceptual framework that enables a coherent investigation of the semiotic, social action, social-historical, and lived-experiential perspectives of student creative practice and the discursive relationships between these perspectives. The orienting focal themes that frame the central chapters of this book are represented in Fig. 2.2. As indicated by

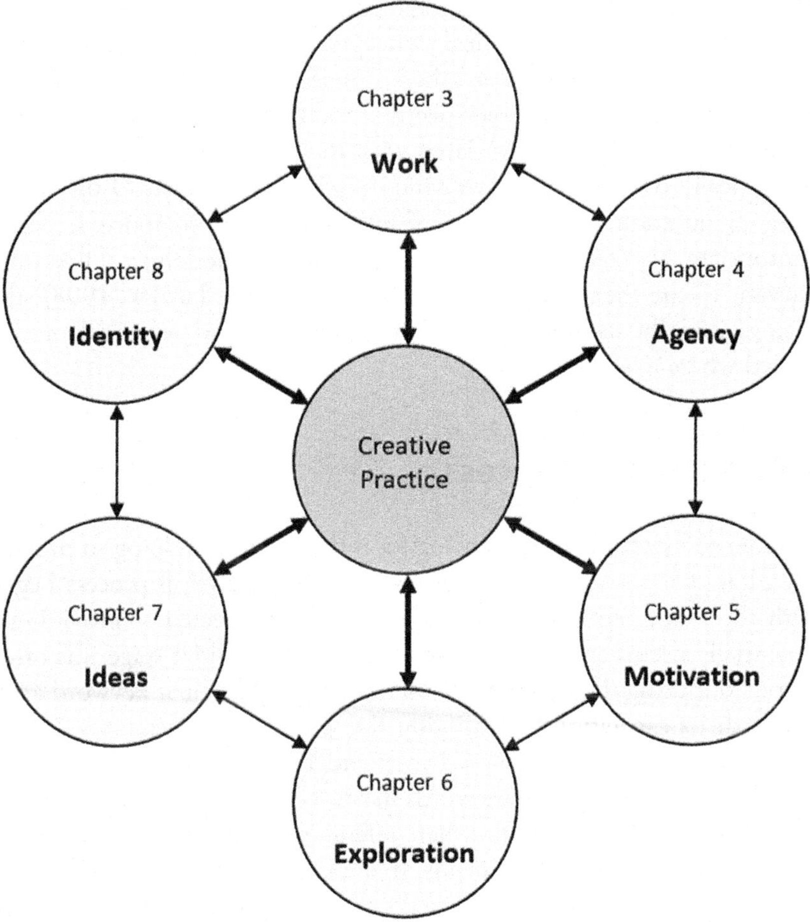

Fig. 2.2 The focal themes forming the organisational framework for the central chapters of this book

the double-headed arrows, the themes are interdependent and are therefore regularly referenced to each other throughout the book. As also indicated in the figure, each of the central chapters in this book focuses specifically on one of the six themes.

Rather than establish the orienting themes through a creative and intuitive search of the literature or through the use of pre-determined conceptual constructs, the approach taken throughout this book was to allow orienting themes to emerge through preliminary examinations of the data. Of course, like all actions in multi-perspectival research, the analysts' perspective, including their prior theoretical assumptions and knowledge of extant theoretical concepts, shapes the recognition and choice of certain themes over others. Once each orienting focal theme was established, the various perspectives and their data sets were explored for patterns of evidence associated with that theme in order to build a thematically oriented narrative which responded, in part, to the initial research question. This process of exploration was supported, where appropriate, by reference to the theoretical and methodological literature relevant to the theme. Importantly, as suggested by Layder (1998), the themes initially selected were flexibly employed and reframed or discarded where relevant.

The Analytical Process

In order to establish each orienting focal theme, and in doing so provide the catalyst for each stage of the research, the analytical process began with the examination of an individual data set selected as providing a potentially useful entry point into the data. This initial stage was often carried out using the tools of corpus analysis, in particular keyword analysis with its capacity for identifying the 'presence of discourses' (Baker 2006, p. 121) or the 'aboutness' (Scott and Tribble 2006, p. 79) of a collection of texts. Keywords are words in one corpus whose frequencies are identified as unusually high when referenced with the frequencies of words occurring in another corpus. If an orienting focal theme of significance emerged, it was used to facilitate other points of entry into the data, involving either data sets from the same or different perspectives, and deploying relevant methodological tools. This procedure was continually repeated and emergent findings were continually scrutinised alongside existing findings in order to augment or extend the ongoing analysis.

As an example, in Chap. 3, an initial keyword analysis of the corpus of student briefs, referenced against both the Wellington Corpus of Written English and a corpus of professional briefs, drew attention to the cognates *work*, *works*, and *working*. Since the noun *work* is traditionally used to refer to the art or design artefact, the keyness of these cognates was not, in the first instance, considered of particular significance. However, a subsequent concordance analysis of the cognates in their immediate textual context indicated that *work*, *works*, and *working* were frequently used in the student briefs as material processes verbs to construe successful creative practice in the studio as demanding a degree of physical labour.

Hence, this first set of findings, which emerged from the use of corpus analytical tools to examine a data set from the semiotic resource perspective, revealed the concept of *work* as a potential orienting theme. The next data set to be examined, primarily because of its close relationship with the student brief genre, involved the tutors' interactions in the brief writing meeting. Representing the social action perspective, this subsequent analysis deployed the tools of linguistic ethnography and revealed that, through the unfolding interaction of the brief writing meeting, the tutors discursively co-constructed successful student creative practice as involving 'hard work'. The analytical process then moved to the socio-historical context where the relevant historical literature was examined to identify the possible socio-historical discursive formations of creativity as work. In another example, in Chap. 5 interactional data from the tutors' meetings revealed that the motivation of students was a central rationale behind the inclusion of this critique session section in the brief. Combined with extant theoretical knowledge that motivation is frequently linked with creativity in art and design educational studies, motivation emerged as a potential orienting focal theme for this component of the study. As motivation had also materialised as a discourse in the investigation of agency and modality in Chap. 4, it was eventually formalised as a conceptual construct to frame the analysis in Chap. 5.

On occasion, in multi-perspectival research, the investigation of a specific data set using a particular methodological orientation produces findings that fail to provide any useful insights or relevant information about the specific focal theme under study at that time. However, and as indicated above, insignificant findings or unproductive data sets can often become of interest once successive analyses have been carried out. This is because the cumulative results of consecutive searches into different data sets can produce an increasingly comprehensive and insightful picture of the phenomena being studied; one that inevitably requires the re-examination of earlier data sets, perhaps involving the use of different methodological resources. As a result, multi-perspectival research requires an iterative and abductive analytical approach involving a constant to-ing and fro-ing between the different perspectives, methodological resources, and theoretical frameworks. As appropriately pointed out by Crichton (2010):

> [T]he perspectives are contingently engaged and 'in play'. This means that … the resources drawn on to operationalize the perspectives are held lightly, are responsive to incoming data and analysis, and are open to findings that emerge from the ongoing interplay between the perspectives. (Crichton 2010, p. 34)

What Crichton means here is that in multi-perspectival research, the analyst is accorded the freedom to continually reassess the incoming data and emergent findings, and as a result, make methodological decisions to re-enter, and in some cases expand, previously examined data sets in different and opportune ways. It should be noted that this iterative, exploratory, and non-linear analytical approach is found elsewhere in social- and discourse-related research. For example, Layder's (1993) multi-strategy approach, which seeks to convey 'the "textured" or interwoven nature of different levels and dimensions of social reality' (p. 7), is largely achieved using a flexible research model which, although grounded in methodological systematicity, promotes discovery and theory construction, rather than a tightly planned and rigid processes of data collection, analysis, and presentation. Similarly, Wodak (2001) has pointed out that a central characteristic of the discourse-historical approach is its abductive nature; that is, 'a constant movement back and forth between theory and empirical data is necessary' (Wodak 2001, p. 70).

The decision regarding which of the perspectives to begin investigating is usually influenced by the analyst's perception of a data set's relevance and position to the other data sets collected for the study. For this investigation of communication in creative practice, the student brief was viewed as a text around which the other activities of the art and design studio were centred, and hence a decision was made to examine data from the semiotic perspective of the student brief as the first analytical stage of the research process. Methodological considerations, notably the capacity of corpus analysis to identify keywords in the brief texts, also contributed to this decision. Alternatively, one might have argued that the social action perspective of the tutors' interaction in the brief writing meetings was responsible for constituting the structure and contents of the brief, and that instead the transcription and analysis of the interaction in these meetings might have been viewed as a more suitable entry point for the analysis.

It is also important to note that no perspective has primacy, and as evidenced in Crichton's (2010) study into the impact of commercialisation discourses on the practices of English language teachers, a successful multi-perspectival analysis does not necessarily require the collection and analysis of data from all perspectives. Furthermore, there is also no requirement to begin with an examination of the local and situated discourse of participants and then broaden the analysis to wider socio-historical contexts. In certain instances, emergent findings from an analysis of the utterances, texts, genres, and images representative of the wider socio-historical context can provide the catalyst for, or be corroborated by, an examination of the local, situated interactional, and semiotic context. There is also no requirement to move systematically from one perspective to the next. Instead, the analyst might repeatedly move back and forth between selected perspectives, making only cursory examinations of the respective data to elucidate the relevance of ongoing observations. Decisions regarding entry into the data might also be motivated by the analyst's interest in a particular methodological resource, perhaps due to its particular analytical foci, for example, membership categorisation analysis and its emphasis on identity. In such a case, data from all perspectives might be approached using this methodological resource and notable correlations or tensions noted.

In this study, the socio-historical perspective involved open and variable sets of data, such as institutional documents, historical texts, books, databases, and similar data sets that were often easily accessible via the internet. These included, among others, the British National Corpus, the Corpus of contemporary American English (Davies 2008), interviews with artists, the letters of Van Gogh (Jansen et al. 2009), and the websites of art and design institutions. Table 2.1 provides an overview of the data collected for this study relevant to the four inner perspectives. Specific details regarding the methodological tools and analytical approaches used will be discussed at the beginning of individual chapters.

Theory development in multi-perspectival research generally takes place as the analyst attempts to explain the convergences or tensions that emerge across the semiotic, social action, socio-historical, and lived-experiential perspectives of the discursive phenomena being studied. This often involves drawing upon extant theory; for example, in Chap. 4, Bourdieu's (1990, 1993) concepts of habitus, field, and practice help provide an explanatory connection for the different forms of modality found across the perspectives. Furthermore, the process of articulating the dynamic interdiscursivity occurring between and within the different layers of practice as a coherent explanatory and thematically bounded written narrative can contributes to the development of theory. Green (2009), who remarks on the interdependence between research and writing, makes the point that the process of writing up research is an integral part of the discovery process; one which he states is revealed through the aphorism 'How do I know what I mean until I see what I say?' (p. 13).

The Organisation of *Communicating Creativity: A Discursive Facilitation of Creativity in Arts*

Each of the six orienting themes that structure the central chapters of this book are essentially an examination of the way in which certain discourses, both at the micro level (the words, texts, and genres used in

Table 2.1 Data collected for the four perspectives for the analysis of the educational perspective

Perspective	Data collected
Semiotic resource	Student Brief Corpus: A 36,731-word corpus of 33 student brief texts sourced from four art and design institutions. Students' contextual statements The students' creative artefacts (completed works as well as preliminary sketches) Student workbooks Student formative assessment sheets
Social action	*Audio recordings of*: Meetings where tutors interacted to draft the student briefs (2) Brief launches (2) Tutorials between students and tutors (5) *Audio-visual recordings of*: Students working in studio (2) *Observation and field notes of*: The drafting of the brief genre (2) The brief launch (2) Students working in the studio (2) The assessment process (1)
Participants'	*Semi-structured interviews with*: Art and design students (4) Art and design tutors (4)
Socio-historical	Professional creative brief corpus: A 37,136-word corpus of 40 creative briefs sourced from the internet. Professional design brief corpus: A 72,673-word corpus of 20 design briefs sourced from the internet. The British National Corpus The Corpus of Historical American English The Wellington Corpus of Written English The published letters of Van Gogh Interviews with artists. Sourced from published books and the internet Exhibition catalogues Exhibition catalogue essays Published theoretical books Gallery visit guidelines Legal contracts Artists' statements Websites of art and design colleges

spoken and written communication) and at the macro level (socially constructed formations of knowledge), are facilitative of creative practice in the university art and design studio, and how in doing so, they constitute the phenomenon understood as creativity within that particular context. Hence, together, the six themes, *work*, *agency*, *motivation*, *exploration*, *ideas*, and *identity* could be categorised as a network of discourses which are interdiscursively connected to facilitate creative practice and constitute the nature of creativity in the educational context. Using a phrase adapted from Foucault (1971), Fairclough (1992) refers to such socially connected networks of discourses and their associated genres as *orders of discourse*. He states that orders of discourse define the 'totality of discursive practices within an institution or society, and the relationships between them' (p. 43). As will be seen in this multi-perspectival study of creative practice, Fairclough (1992, 2010) states that the analysis of interdiscursivity can provide insights into the way that particular groupings or networks of discourses and their associated genres are collectively drawn upon in dynamic ways to shape the structures, values, ideological positions, discursive resources, and identities of a particular social practice (see also Foucault 1972). It is also important to note that while orders of discourse delimit the discursive practices that frame a particular social practice, they are also capable of change, particularly when discourses and genres from other orders of discourses are strategically drawn upon to meet the ongoing challenges and shifting requirements of newly evolving practices (Candlin 2006; Carter 2004). Sometimes change occurs within an order of discourse due to the presence of competing discourses that have emerged from the struggles and changing dynamics of power (Lee 1992; Jones 2009). These competing discourses can result in hybrid generic forms or discursive tensions. An example was seen earlier in Picasso's commentary regarding his delivery of the pastel *Intimacy* to Berthe Weill, where a conflict exists between his commercial aspirations, most likely informed by the emerging modernist discourse of entrepreneurship in the arts, and his opposition to this discourse, the prevailing view of the period and one reproduced through the statutes of the powerful European arts academies. Hence, any order of discourse provides a socially ordered set of resources which can be drawn upon in diverse ways, dependent on the position and motivation of the social actor. As mentioned, the central Chaps. 3–8 in *Communicating Creativity: A Discursive Facilitation of Creativity in Arts* can be viewed as representing such a network of discourses, which collectively (though not exclusively) give rise to, and are part of, the order of discourse of art and design education. These discourses provide a set of resources which facilitate, but also delimit, creative activity in the context of the university art and design studio.

Chapter 3 begins by examining the discourse of work and how it constitutes what the tutors perceive as successful creative behaviour. The chapter argues that the discourse of work is the result of emergent twentieth-century social and economic structures, and suggests that it has superseded the previously dominant Western discourse of creativity as involving individual creative genius and an emphasis on traditional artistic skill. Chapter 4 shows how the students' creative activity is driven by a hypothetical orientation to the future; one which typically involves a series of affordances and constraints. These future-oriented affordances and constraints are discursively constituted by the tutors through the use of the linguistic modal system (the use of verbs, such as *might*, *can*, and *will*), which, as well as pragmatically functioning to both constrain and facilitate personal volition, is also linked to futurity.

Chapter 5 focuses on the discourse of motivation. The chapter shows how, in response to their construction of the students as unmotivated, the tutors collaboratively put together a discursive strategy to motivate the students into creative action. Underpinning the justification for this strategy is the tutors' belief that motivated students should be consistently producing work as the result of an ongoing explorative process; a view seemingly in conflict with the students' own creative motivations, which appear more closely related to their identities, desires, and ideal future-selves. Chapter 6 looks at how the discourse of exploration is used to both characterise and facilitate the creative activity that takes place in the university art and design studio. The chapter goes on to examine how this discourse has its roots in the European art and design schools of the early twentieth century, notably the Bauhaus, who responded to the political and industrial advances of the time by reframing creative practice through the language associated with nineteenth-century travel and exploration.

Chapter 7 shows that the primary means by which the participants make sense of their creative actions as ordered and intelligible is through the notion of idea transference; that is, the metaphorical transference of an 'idea' from the brief to the students' minds, and then to the work of art. The chapter examines how the discourse of the idea has its origins in the conceptual art of the 1960s. Chapter 8 focuses on the discourse of identity. It investigates how both the written and interactional texts occurring in the studio orient the students towards one of a set of institutionally constrained, though more locally shaped and exploited, art and design disciplinary identities. The chapter then goes on to show how students perform their chosen disciplinary identities in the studio setting through certain interactional modes, such as gaze, posture, head movement, and layout.

Chapter 9 focuses on the relationship between the world of the academy and the professional world. It argues that the effects of the categorisation and identity work carried out in the university art and design studio become structured in the habitus (Bourdieu 1993) of the students, and is inevitably reproduced in their future creative (inter)actions and professional practices. To show this, the chapter examines how the discourses central to the preceding chapters are manifest in the practices of two professionals, both of whom, like many others, attended institutions similar to the one which is the focus of this study.

The final chapter discusses the implications of the study for those involved in art and design education, both as educators and researchers. It also identifies the implications of the study for creativity research. Ultimately, the proposed book will provide art and design educators and researchers with an understanding of creativity as a discursively and historically situated phenomenon, and hence provide deeper insights into the relationship between student creative activity and the communication that takes place in and around the studio context.

The organisation of the six central chapters in this book is not unlike the structure of the literary genre of the composite novel, which Dunn and Morris (1995) describe as 'a literary work composed of shorter texts that—though individually complete and autonomous—are interrelated in a coherent whole according to one or more organising principles' (p. xiii). According to Dunn and Morris, the emphasis of the composite novel is 'upon a whole text rendered coherent through a dynamic interaction with and among its parts' (p. 12). As a result, none of Chaps. 3–8 necessarily serve as a starting point for the analysis from which the other chapters incrementally develop, and each could be read as a stand-alone response to the question of the discursive facilitation of creativity. The reader, therefore, is welcome to dive immediately in to any of the central six chapters that they find of particular interest.

Notes

1. Benjamin (2000) also attributes a 'Patagonian cubists' remark to critic Raymond Bouyer (1911, p. 134).

References

Antaki, C. (Ed.). (2011). *Applied conversation analysis: Intervention and change in institutional talk*. Basingstoke, UK: Palgrave Macmillan.

Antaki, C., & Widdicombe, S. (1998). Identity as an achievement and as a tool. In C. Antaki & S. Widdicombe (Eds.), *Identities in talk* (pp. 1–14). London, UK: Sage Publications.

Baker, P. (2006). *Using corpora in discourse analysis*. London, UK: Continuum.

Banaji, S., & Burn, A. (2006). *The rhetorics of creativity: A review of the literature*. London, UK: Arts Council England.

Banaji, S., & Burn, A. (2007). Creativity through a rhetorical lens: Implications for schooling, literacy and media education. *Literacy, 41*(2), 62–70.

Benjamin, R. (2000). Ingres chez les fauves. *Art History, 23*(5), 743–771.

Bhatia, V. K. (1993). *Analysing genre: Language use in professional settings*. London, UK: Longman.

Bourdieu, P. (1990). *The logic of practice*. Stanford, CA: Stanford University Press.

Bourdieu, P. (1993). *The field of cultural production: Essays on art and literature*. New York, NY: Columbia University Press.

Bouyer, R. (1911). Expositions et Concours. *Bulletin de l'art ancien et moderne, 502*, 133–134.

Brassaï. (1999). *Conversations with Picasso*. Chicago, IL: University of Chicago Press.

Burr, V. (2003). *Social constructionism.* New York, NY: Routledge.
Candlin, C. N. (2006). Accounting for interdiscursivity: Challenges to professional expertise. In M. Gotti & D. S. Giannoni (Eds.), *New trends in specialized discourse* (pp. 21–45). Bern, Switzerland: Peter Lang.
Candlin, C. N., & Crichton, J. (2011). Introduction. In C. N. Candlin & J. Crichton (Eds.), *Discourses of deficit* (pp. 1–22). Basingstoke, UK: Palgrave Macmillan.
Candlin, C. N., & Crichton, J. (2012). Emergent themes and research challenges: Reconceptionalising LSP. In P. Margrethe & J. Engberg (Eds.), *Current trends in LSP research: Aims and methods* (pp. 277–316). Bern, Switzerland: Peter Lang.
Candlin, C. N., & Crichton, J. (2013). From ontology to methodology: Exploring the discursive landscape of trust. In C. N. Candlin & J. Crichton (Eds.), *Discourses of trust* (pp. 1–18). Basingstoke, UK: Palgrave Macmillan.
Carter, R. (2004). *Language and creativity: The art of common talk.* New York, NY: Routledge.
Copland, F., & Creese, A. (Eds.). (2015). *Linguistic ethnography: Collecting, analysing and presenting data.* London, UK: Sage.
Creswell, J. W. (2013). *Research design: Qualitative, quantitative, and mixed methods approaches.* Thousand Oaks, CA: Sage.
Crichton, J. (2004). *Issues of interdiscursivity in the commercialisation of professional practice: The case of English language teaching* (PhD thesis). Macquarie University, Sydney.
Crichton, J. (2010). *The discourse of commercialisation.* Basingstoke, UK: Palgrave Macmillan.
Daix, P., & Boudaille, G. (1967). *Picasso: The blue and rose periods: A catalogue raisonné, 1900–1906.* (P. Pool, Trans.). Greenwich, CT: Evelyn Adams & Mackay.
Davies, M. (2008). *The Corpus of Contemporary American English: 425 million words, 1990–present.* Retrieved from http://corpus.byu.edu/coca/
Dörnyei, Z. (2007). *Research methods in applied linguistics.* Oxford, UK: Oxford University Press.
Dunn, M., & Morris, A. (1995). *The composite novel: The short story cycle in transition.* New York, NY: Twayne.
Fairclough, N. (1992). *Discourse and social change.* Cambridge, UK: Polity Press.
Fairclough, N. (2010). *Critical discourse analysis: The critical study of language* (2nd ed.). Harlow, UK: Pearson.
FitzGerald, M. C. (1995). *Making modernism: Picasso and the creation of the market for twentieth-century art.* Berkeley, CA: University of California Press.

Foucault, M. (1971). The order of discourse. In R. J. C. Young (Ed.), *Untying the text: A post-structuralist reader* (pp. 48–78). London, UK: Routledge.

Foucault, M. (1972). *The archaeology of knowledge.* (A. M. Sheridan Smith, Trans.). London, UK: Tavistock.

Gee, M. (1993). The nature of twentieth-century art criticism. In M. Gee (Ed.), *Art criticism since 1900* (pp. 3–21). Manchester, UK: Manchester University Press.

Gilot, F., & Lake, C. (1964). *Life with Picasso*. New York, NY: Anchor Books.

Green, B. (2009). Introduction: Understanding and researching professional practice. In B. Green (Ed.), *Understanding and researching professional practice* (pp. 1–18). Rotterdam, Netherlands: Sense.

Halliday, M. A. K., & Matthiessen, C. M. I. M. (2004). *An introduction to functional grammar* (3rd ed.). London, UK: Arnold.

Hammersley, M., & Atkinson, P. (2007). *Ethnography: Principles in practice* (3rd ed.). London, UK: Routledge.

Hodge, R., & Kress, G. (1998). *Social semiotics.* Cambridge, UK: Polity Press.

Jansen, L., Luijten, H., & Bakker, N. (Eds.). (2009). *Vincent van Gogh: The letters.* Version: December 2010. Amsterdam and The Hague: Van Gogh Museum & Huygens ING. Retrieved from http://vangoghletters.org

Jones, A. (2009). Business discourse as a site of inherent struggle. In A. Mahboob & C. Lipovsky (Eds.), *Studies in applied linguistics and language learning.* Cambridge, UK: Cambridge Scholars Publishing.

Jørgensen, M., & Phillips, L. (2002). *Discourse analysis as theory and method.* Thousand Oaks, CA: Sage.

Kahnweiler, D. H. (1949). *The rise of Cubism.* (H. Aronson, Trans.). New York, NY: Wittenbom, Schultz.

Kress, G. R., & Van Leeuwen, T. (2001). *Multimodal discourse: The modes and media of contemporary communication.* London, UK: Edward Arnold.

Kress, G. R., & Van Leeuwen, T. (2006). *Reading images: The grammar of visual design* (2nd ed.). London, UK: Routledge.

Kristeller, P. (1990). Afterword: 'Creativity' and 'Tradition'. In *Renaissance thought and the arts: Collected essays* (pp. 247–258). Princeton, NJ: Princeton University Press.

Layder, D. (1993). *New strategies in social research.* Cambridge, UK: Polity Press.

Layder, D. (1998). *Sociological practice: Linking theory and social research.* London, UK: Sage.

Lee, D. (1992). *Competing discourses: Perspective and ideology in language.* London, UK: Longman.

Lemke, J. (1994). Semiotics and the deconstruction of conceptual learning. *Journal of the Society for Accelerative Learning and Teaching, 19*(1), 67–110.

Malson, H. (2003). *The thin woman: Feminism, post-structuralism and the social psychology of anorexia nervosa*. New York, NY: Routledge.

Norris, S. (2004). *Analyzing multimodal interaction: A methodological framework*. New York, NY: Routledge.

Norris, S. (2011). *Identity in (inter)action: Introducing multimodal (inter)action analysis*. New York, NY: De Gruyter Mouton.

Olivier, F. (2001). *Loving Picasso: The private journal of Fernande Olivier*. New York, NY: Abrams.

Rampton, B. (2007). Neo-Hymesian linguistic ethnography in the United Kingdom. *Journal of Sociolinguistics, 11*(5), 584–607.

Reisigl, M., & Wodak, R. (2009). The discourse-historical approach. In R. Wodak & M. Meyer (Eds.), *Methods for critical discourse analysis* (2nd ed., pp. 87–121). London, UK: Sage.

Roberts, C., & Sarangi, S. (2005). Theme-oriented discourse analysis of medical encounters. *Medical Education, 39*(6), 632–640.

Robertson, I. (2005). Art, religion, history, money. In I. Robertson (Ed.), *Understanding international art markets and management* (pp. 37–61). New York, NY: Routledge.

Rubin, W. (1989). *Picasso and Braque: Pioneering cubism*. New York, NY: Museum of Modern Art.

Sacks, H. (1992). *Lectures on conversation: Volumes I and II*. Oxford and London: Blackwell.

Schiau-Botea, D. (2013). Performing writing; Le Chat Noir (1881–95); Le Courrier français (1884–1913); Gil Bias illustré (1891–1903); and Les Quat'z'arts (1897–8). In P. Brooker, S. Bru, A. Thacker, & C. Weikop (Eds.), *The Oxford critical and cultural history of modernist magazines: Europe 1880–1940* (Vol. 3, pp. 38–59). Oxford, UK: Oxford University Press.

Scollon, R. (1998). *Mediated discourse as social interaction: A study of news discourse*. New York, NY: Longman.

Scott, M., & Tribble, C. (2006). *Textual patterns: Key words and corpus analysis in language education*. Amsterdam, Netherlands: John Benjamins.

Swales, J. M. (1990). *Genre analysis: English in academic and research settings*. Cambridge, UK: Cambridge University Press.

Tusting, K., & Maybin, J. (2007). Linguistic ethnography and interdisciplinarity: Opening the discussion. *Journal of Sociolinguistics, 11*(5), 575–583.

Wodak, R. (2001). The discourse-historical approach. In R. Wodak & M. Meyer (Eds.), *Methods of critical discourse analysis* (pp. 63–94). London, UK: Sage.

3

Work

Introduction

The British Turner Prize is one of Europe's most prestigious contemporary art awards; however, like the Salon des Indépendants held in the early twentieth century (see Chap. 2), it regularly attracts widespread criticism. This is due to the often-controversial nature of the nominees and winners' works, examples of which are shown during the award at the Tate Britain art museum. The exhibited work of the 1995 winner, Damian Hirst, for instance, involved four glass tanks of formaldehyde containing the bisected halves of a cow and calf, while the exhibited work of the 2001 winner, Martin Creed, involved an empty room in which the lights repeatedly turned on and off. In her exploration of creativity, Jeanes (2006) makes reference to the Turner Prize and the British tradition of conceptually provocative artists, whose work she believes is supported and motivated by the award's bias towards the controversial. Jeanes suggests that the conscious desire of these artists to generate innovative and provocative creative outcomes, perhaps with an eye to winning the Turner Prize, inevitability results in repetitive works which she views as 'clichéd' and 'passé' (p. 131). Instead, Jeanes contends that creativity should

D. Hocking, *Communicating Creativity*, Communicating in Professions and Organizations, https://doi.org/10.1057/978-1-137-55804-6_3

involve 'a process of personal and perpetual crisis', where the artist is persistently '*working* on the continually evolving, unfinished and "unfinishable" project' (p. 131, italics added). Alluding to the conceptually motivated British artists, she suggests that:

> By trying to be creative, in a very conscious way, rather than merely *working* at some idea or problem, they are by that very act being uncreative. (Jeanes 2006, p. 131, original italics)

While Jeanes provides a thought-provoking critique of the discourse of creativity as innovation, she appears to embrace another creativity discourse, that of creativity as a process of working. It is the examination of this discourse of creativity as work, the way that it facilitates creative practice in the university art and design studio, as well as its wider socio-historical context, which forms the focus of Chap. 3.[1] A further focus on conceptual art, including the work of Damian Hirst, will take place in Chap. 7.

Perspectival and Methodological Foci

The examination commences at the semiotic resource perspective with a corpus analysis of the student briefs. The student brief corpus consists of 33 student briefs, which were sourced from four different art and design university institutions. As indicated in Chap. 1, student briefs are central to the creative process in art and design education, as they facilitate student creativity by setting out, in textual form, the conceptual and technical parameters for each project. These formal guidelines are most often the result of interactions carried out in the brief writing meeting among the students' tutors, who draw upon their collective interpretations of the values and expectations of their institution, as well as the contemporary art and design world. Thus, it might be expected that both underlying institutional and social discourses regarding creativity are reproduced in the text of a brief. The results of this preliminary corpus analysis suggest that student creative action is discursively conceptualised through a discourse of working.

In order to corroborate and extend the results of the corpus analysis, the social action and participants' perspective is then examined. Here, the analysis draws upon linguistic ethnography (Copland and Creese 2015; Rampton 2007), in that a close analysis of the tutors' unfolding interactions in the brief writing meeting is carried out to see how they jointly construct the creative practices of their students through a discourse of work. It also draws more broadly upon ethnography (Hammersley and Atkinson 2007), whereby the participants' interpretations and explanations of their practice is examined for evidence of salient themes related to the creativity as work discourse. The chapter's final analytical focus involves a discussion of relevant socio-historical texts and contexts (Reisigl and Wodak 2009; Wodak 2001), focusing, in particular, on the cultural shifts taking place in the Western art world during the mid-twentieth century. The aim here is to identify the wider historical discourses that may have shaped present-day beliefs and values regarding the constitution of the artist's identity as worker. Table 3.1 indicates the methodological resources used in this chapter with respect to the data collected from the different perspectives.

Simply Working on Something

The first stage focuses on an analysis of *keywords* from the corpus of student briefs. Keywords are words in a target corpus whose frequencies are identified as unusually high when compared with the frequencies of the same words occurring in another corpus. If this second corpus is a specialised *reference corpus*—that is, one that has been designed to contain a wide-ranging and balanced collection of different texts and genres—then the resultant keywords are said to provide insights into the 'presence of discourses' (Baker 2006, p. 121) or the 'aboutness' (Scott and Tribble 2006, p. 79) of the target corpus. Moreover, if the target corpus is referenced with one representing the same type of texts from another context, then the keywords that emerge can often indicate something discursively salient about the particular context being studied. In carrying out these analytical procedures, corpus software tools such as Wordsmith (as used throughout this book) will determine a *keyness* value for each word in the

Table 3.1 The data analysed and methodological foci for each of the perspectives

Perspective	Data	Methodological orientation	Tools
Semiotic resource perspective	A 36,605 word corpus of 33 student briefs	Corpus analysis	Keyword analysis Concordance analysis
	The text of the Binary Opposites brief, including extracts from the requirements section and the assessment criteria	Systematic functional analysis	Thematic structure Transitivity
Social action perspective	Audio recording of the first brief writing meeting, where the tutors co-establish the text of the Binary Opposites brief. The tutors, Anna and Mike, are participants in this meeting	Linguistic ethnography	Micro analysis of the participants' unfolding interactions.
Participants' perspective	Semi-structured interviews with tutors about the student brief and their studio teaching Semi-structured interviews with students about the student brief and their creative work	Ethnographic analysis	Observation of salient themes in the participants' interactions.
Socio-historical perspective	Theoretical and historical literature regarding creativity and art production	Discourse-historical analysis	An account of wider socio-political and historical contexts to identify how these have shaped the phenomena and context under analysis Thematic analysis Interdiscursivity

Table 3.2 Top 20 keywords of student briefs from the educational context, when compared to a corpus of briefs from a professional context and the Wellington Corpus of Written English

	Using a corpus of professional briefs as reference				Using the Wellington Corpus of Written English as reference			
	Keyword	Freq	Freq Ref.	Keyness	Keyword	Freq	Freq WCC	Keyness
1	your	499	125	859.38	your	499	894	1787.4
2	you	419	192	533.34	studio	186	32	1143.1
3	work	333	127	471.69	work	333	1025	916.18
4	studio	186	22	398.2	brief	141	58	766
5	week	130	6	321.93	design	157	131	727.35
6	start	127	20	253.46	drawing	106	48	565.47
7	drawing	106	8	246.34	you	419	3358	543.76
8	art	128	31	222.46	research	133	186	523.27
9	research	133	57	175.84	etc	72	0	511.94
10	assessment	82	11	170.41	start	127	192	485.41
11	presentation	57	5	129.19	week	130	322	400.77
12	ideas	80	24	127.24	materials	83	60	399.13
13	artists	55	5	123.88	art	128	324	390.33
14	possibilities	47	1	123.72	assessment	82	65	385.02
15	critique	41	0	115.91	project	90	126	353.86
16	working	96	52	108.57	visual	71	45	352.51
17	paper	60	15	102.95	ideas	80	93	335.38
18	Thursday	41	2	100.85	will	257	2093	327.02
19	directed	43	4	96.439	presentation	57	19	320.89
20	works	68	26	95.9	working	96	282	270.59

target corpus. The higher the keyness value, the more significant the word concerned is likely to be. An example of these two different types of keyword analysis can be seen in Table 3.2.

The left hand side of Table 3.2 shows the keywords of the student brief corpus when it was referenced with a 113,802 word corpus containing 60 creative briefs and design briefs representative of professional contexts. The right hand side of Table 3.2 shows the keywords of the student brief corpus when it was referenced with the 1,234,111 word reference corpus, the Wellington Corpus of Written English. While there are a number of keywords that might merit further investigation, it is particularly interesting that the words *work*, *working*, and *works* appear in the third, sixteenth, and twentieth places, respectively, in the left hand list, and *work* occurs in third place and *working* in twentieth place in the right hand list. This suggests that while there is a strong use of *work* cognates in the student brief, these appear much less frequently in either the creative briefs typically used in advertising agencies or in the design briefs typically used in construction. It also shows that *work* cognates occur significantly more frequently in the student brief texts than they do in everyday written texts. It should be pointed out that only those words appearing in at least one third of all student briefs were included as keywords, thus avoiding the occurrence of keywords resulting from items such as proper nouns which might repeatedly appear in a single brief. It is not surprising that *work* appears as key in the student brief corpus when compared with the reference corpus. The noun *work* has referred to artistic labour from the thirteenth century and was first recorded as referring to a creative artifact in 1774. However, given the occurrence of the verb *working* in both lists, and the fact that the three cognates, *work, working,* and *works* do not appear with the same level of frequency in the professional brief corpus, a focus on *work* and its cognates is warranted at a closer, more contextualised level of analysis.

To achieve this closer level of analysis, *concordances* of the words *work, works, and working* from the collection of brief texts were examined. Concordances are all instances of a selected word presented in its immediate textual context, usually a few words to the right and a few words to the left. They can provide more specific information about the meaning of a word and its particular use. While a concordance analysis shows that the lexical item *work* and the plural *works* are often conventionally used in the student brief texts to denote the object produced as a result of art or design activity, for example, *work of art, a body or work, practical work, design work, art work,* and so on, the concordance list in Table 3.3 also indicates that the verb *work* is regularly used in the education briefs to describe the *material processes* of the students. The term *material process* derives from systemic functional linguistics (Halliday and Matthiessen 2004) and refers to the carrying out of concrete, tangible actions.[2] The relative keyness of the material process *work*, rather than, for example, *create*, *make*, or even *study*, suggests that creative practice in the university studio may be primarily conceptualised as a form of labour.

Table 3.3 Examples of work used as a material process in the corpus of briefs from an educational context

1	You are encouraged to	work	within personal areas of interest. You
2	significantly as you	work	through the project –100 words—why
3	In other words to	work	with an awareness of what you did
4	expected that you will	work	on your studies a minimum of 40 hours
5	expect that you will	work	in studios. For those of you who need to
6	or mode you choose to	work	in is up to you. Remember the emphasis
7	inserting as you	work	towards creating spatial possibilities.
8	Objectives: To	work	in a self-initiated framework. To explore
9	much more! Enjoy,	work	hard and most of all: Have Fun!

Table 3.4 Work semantically related to quantity, production, and time

1	produce sufficient quantities of	work	to effectively engage with the
2	papers it is expected that you will	work	on your studies a minimum of 40
3	the work. It is expected that you	work	in studio and make between 5 and 10
4	at least 20 developed prints to	work	from. Please have them on your
5	- This is your final chance to	work	on-site. Use this time well!
6	High Standard. Develops a good	work	habit by attending consistently
7	using tape to do so. The aim is to	work	quickly, finding ways to inhabit

The extent of this conceptualisation is evidenced in Table 3.4 (lines 1–4) where concordances with *work* (both as a noun and a verb) are semantically related to quantity, and the belief that the students' creative practices should involve the production of significant output of material goods. Other concordances in the table relate work to temporal issues and imply that the work ethic should be habitual or that periods involving work should be used effectively (lines 5–7).

The conceptualisation of art and design production as habitual, routine-based, and occurring in often pre-designated and concentrated time periods can be observed further in a representative selection of concordances with *working* (Table 3.5). Notable is again the perception that students are not creating, developing, or generating art and design at the beach, but are instead *working* (line 5). Interestingly, in an example comparable to Jeanes' (2006) comment that the essence of creativity should involve 'merely working at some idea or problem' (p. 131), concordance line 8 states that an aim of the brief is *to simply get students working on*

Table 3.5 Concordances with working, semantically related to the habit and routine of working

1	will form a regular part of your	working	life formulating a
2	Working in Studio. July 27—9am start	working	in studio Wk 3: Aug 1
3	12.30 Lunch Self-Directed: Continue	working	10.00–12.00 Drawing
4	duration of this project you will be	working	individually on site
5	will need:—appropriate clothing for	working	at the beach.—wet
6	pieces of masking tape Exercise:	working	within the given time
7	the importance of understanding good	working	Habits—to develop an
8	thoughts 4) To simply get everyone	working	on something. After

something (line 8). What is foregrounded in these concordance lines is the importance that processes of labour are actively taking place.

To further investigate the discursive construction of creative activity as work, I will now turn to the other perspectives identified in the multi-perspectival model (see Chap. 2), focusing firstly on the social action perspective of the brief writing meeting, where the tutors work together to draft the contents of a student brief, one which they have given the title Binary Opposites. This brief encourages students to create works around the theme of binary oppositions or contrasting conceptual categories.

The Numbers Game

In most student briefs there is a section that indicates the number of creative artifacts that students are required to produce for the final studio assessment related to that brief. The final assessment typically involves each student displaying a small selection of what they believe are their strongest works produced for that brief on the studio wall, while leaving most other works in a folder or workbook beside this display. Extract 3.1 provides an example of an interaction between two tutors, Anna and Mike, from a brief writing meeting. In this interaction, they are discussing the number of individual creative artifacts that students will need to produce to constitute an acceptable output for the final assessment of work for the Binary Opposites brief, and how this directive will be presented in the written text of the brief itself.

Extract 3.1: First Brief Writing Meeting

1	→	Mike:	I'm just using very [broad language here.
2	→	Anna:	[hmm . hmm
3			and I think it has it has to be pretty pretty broad umm
4	→		because we're covering so ma:ny different things
5			because the specifics will then come in to .hh um
6	→		.hh remember when we had that discussion about the numbers
7	→		the numbers game.
8	→	Mike:	how do you mean.
9	→	Anna:	five on the wall
10	→		twenty-one support works
11	→		or whatever we decide on that.
12	→	Mike:	you don't have to have that but [but but
13	→	Anna:	[no:
14	→	Mike:	and I worked on the programme
15	→		when they didn't do that [but
16	→	Anna:	[exactly yeah
17	→	Mike:	as I- you know I used that- you know
18	→		and there was very little done.
19	→	Anna:	hmm mm mm
20	→	Mike:	in fact very very little done
21		Anna:	okay
22	→	Mike:	you know students were were presenting. minimal work

In the extract, Anna is initially sceptical of Mike's emphasis (which she acknowledges in line 6 as having been discussed previously) on identifying the number of works required in the brief (lines 9–10), which she negatively categorises as *the numbers game* (line 7). Mike however refers back to his experience with prior briefs to support his argument (lines 14–15), suggesting that when output numbers were omitted, the students failed to produce an acceptable quantity of work (lines 17–18, 20, and 22). Mike's emphasis here is solely on the quantity of production, and there is no explicit discussion in the meeting about the relationship between quantity and quality, or why quality cannot be achieved in a single work. In Extract 3.2, Anna eventually shows agreement with Mike's position (line 9 and 13). Even when Mike concedes that 2 or 3 works might in fact be appropriate (line 26), there is now a consensus that these should involve *a lot of work* (line 29).

Extract 3.2 First Brief Writing Meeting

1	→	Mike:	twenty items↑ *writing*
2	→	Anna:	yep
3	→	Mike:	I'm sorr- ((*raising voice*))
4	→		I I I know [I (feel like) a bit of a pain.
5	→	Anna:	[to come up with nu:mbers isn't it
6			yeah yeah yeah.
7	→	Mike:	well … you know it could be . umm,
8			it just puts a bit of pressure [on them to fulfil . ah rather than
9	→	Anna:	[I think it's good I agre:e you know
10			because if you put nothing in there
11			then they just might [you know
12	→	Mike:	[you're going to get nothing.
13	→	Anna:	yep yep.
14	→	Mike:	you know if you [don't ask for it they're not going to do it
15	→	Anna:	[and we know that if it's a good quality
16			twelve works or something
17			that's also going to be fine isn't it.
18	→	Mike:	well that's right.
19	→	Anna:	yep.
20	→	Mike:	you can you can then judge on their performance [can't you
21	→	Anna:	[mm mm

→	Mike:	and, and the amount of engagement
		that was required
→	Anna:	yep
→	Mike:	within what they do present↑
→		it might only be two or three pieces in the end
→	Anna:	mm mm
→	Mike:	but if it involves you know
→	Anna:	a lot of work

The decision regarding the quantity of works that the students must produce for the brief and the final assessment is ultimately dialogic in nature (Linell 1998), and unfolds through the ongoing interaction of the brief writing meeting. The tutors' awareness of the intersubjective nature of the decision making process is explicitly acknowledged in comments seen in the earlier Extract 3.1, *whatever we decide on that* (line 11) and *you don't have to have that* (line 12), although Anna, who is the course coordinator, takes the more consensual stance, evidenced through her regular use of the personal pronoun *we* (Extract 3.1, lines 4, 6, and 11). In contrast Mike, while expressing a stronger point of view overall, seen through his use of repetition (Extract 3.1, lines 18, 20 and 22), short direct utterances (line 8), and recourse to prior experience (lines 14–15), is nevertheless cognisant of Anna's final authority, seen through his use of the personal pronoun *you* (Extract 3.1, line 12 and 3.2, line 20) and his apology and somewhat self-deprecatory stance (Extract 3.2, lines 3–4).

Returning to the *semiotic resource perspective*, the discursive construction of the creative act as involving work is reinforced in the three assessment criteria that comprise the final section of the brief (Extract 3.3). Although the tutors make subtle changes to this section for each new brief, it is mostly reproduced from previously used briefs, and its original form was the outcome of a similar type of meeting.

Extract 3.3: Assessment Criteria 1 and 3

→ 1. Employs a systematic process of making work,
accompanied by processes of

2 → visual experimentation and analysis. Uses a variety of media and technical
3 processes appropriate to the work produced. Uses media to explore, develop and
4 → communicate ideas/issues being addressed. Produces work that meets the
5 → requirement of the brief

6 → 3. Develops a good work habit by attending consistently, organising resources
7 → (i.e. equipment and materials), and producing work that effectively meets the
8 → requirements of the brief. Works cooperatively, with respect for others and
9 observes all Art and Design School protocols.

Again, drawing upon systemic functional linguistics, and focusing in particular on the structural placement of information, we find that the process of making work is fronted in the main clause of the first criterion (lines 1–2). The theme of this clause, *employ*, is used here as a synonym of *use*, however *employ* has a strong semantic association with the concept of paid work. The first criterion ends with a focus on the production of work, and its ability to meet the requirements of the brief (lines 4–5). The main clause of the third criterion also foregrounds a view of creative success as based on the habitual action of work (line 6), which is defined in the subsequent clauses (lines 6–7) and is again related to meeting the requirements of the brief (lines 7–8). The verb *works* is placed in the thematic position of the final sentence of the third criterion, which emphasises the importance of working cooperatively (line 8). In general, throughout these criteria, there is a focus on systematicity and a work-like, regular, orderly, and methodical approach to creative activity in the university studio.

The requirements section of the Binary Opposites brief, which both criteria refer to, is reproduced in Extract 3.4. This requirements section entextualises the consensus reached by the tutors in the brief writing meeting, in particular, the requirement that the students produce a minimum of twenty works throughout the assessment event (line 4).

Extract 3.4: Requirements Section of the Binary Opposites Brief (Original Bold)

1 On Friday August 15 by 10am. You will present the following:

2 **Five items of work you consider are the most successful** (Presentation method
3 will be by negotiation).

4 → **At least twenty exploratory supporting items of work** (Placed on the floor
5 beside or beneath the presentation work).

It may have been noticed that there has been no mention of the concept 'creativity' in the extracts presented above, and in fact it was absent from much of the ethnographic data collected for this study. When questioned about the absence of the concept in their particular educative context, or about their own conceptualisations of creativity with respect to the university art and design studio environment, the tutors' responses were multifarious, perhaps showing evidence of the conflicting and contested discourses of creativity identified in Chap. 1. The tutor, Anna, for example, suggested that creativity was very important in the educative environment and initially aligned creativity with innovation, which she described as coming from the few students who had something 'new to offer'. In this comment, Anna is reproducing the widely accepted discourse of creativity as the production of ideas or products that are novel. She went on to admit, however, that creativity was a 'hard thing to define' and then struggled to construct a definition of creativity that was exclusive from the notion of *hard work* (Extract 3.5):

Extract 3.5: Interview with the Tutor Anna

Anna: … some people can be really hard workers and be really good designers, you know, and not necessarily … oh, well, yeah, I suppose you've still got to be sort of quite creative, um, sometimes maybe through the hard work the creativity comes out.

Anna reproduces these values in her presentation of the Binary Opposites brief to students in the brief launch (Extract 3.6), where she emphasis the point (*draw your attention to the fact*, line 1) that the studio work expectations are equivalent across the different disciplinary areas, for example, visual arts, graphic design, spatial design (*it doesn't mean that you've got more or less work to do*, line 3). This utterance, and the emphasis Anna places on it, perhaps identifies a presupposition that students select their disciplinary areas according to perceived workload.[3] Anna reinforces the work discourse through her following utterance stating that the students are expected to be *working really hard* (line 5).

Extract 3.6: Brief Launch

1	→	Anna:	um just also wanted to just draw your attention to the fact that umm
2			if you are doing one area: . rather than another
3	→		it doesn't mean that you've got more or less work to do:
4			the expectations. for each brief. is about the same↑
5	→		so we expect you guys to be working really hard .hh

Competing discourses, evident in the interview with Anna, are also apparent in an interview with the tutor, Mike. When asked about the importance of creativity in the studio, Mike suggested that creativity is a 'hoary word' and 'inappropriate' for the art and design educative context. Here, Mike is possibly reproducing the discourse prevalent since the late 1980s which viewed art and design practice not as the result of creative self-expression, but as something that could be taught (see Chap. 1). Extract 3.7 reproduces his response to a question on this point.

Extract 3.7: Interview with the Tutor Mike

Mike: Well, it's tangled and fraught, and, and the mere mention of it, we use words like coming from left field or lateral, or thinking

> outside the square, as being better descriptors for what traditionally we may have called creativity.

In this extract, Mike, however, is still assigning value to notions of transformation and divergence, but he is perhaps trying to avoid associating these with traditional creativity discourses, which he refers to in the interview, as the ability 'disposed upon a few that excel'. When questioned further on his comments, he suggest that concepts, such as 'lateral', are more appropriate because the boundaries of meaning associated with the 'problematic' words creative or creativity are in a constant state of flux, which he argues depends on the 'fashions' of the time. Here, Mike is revealing an awareness of creativity as a discursively and historically constituted phenomenon.

The next stage of the analysis involves an examination of the socio-historical context to establish the existence of wider socio-historical discourses which have shaped the discursive construction of creativity as work in the context of the university art and design studio. This process is largely carried out through an investigation of published literature on creativity and art practice.

The Rise of the Art Worker

Banaji and Burn (2007) trace the romantic view of the individual creative genius, one that they suggest has shaped orthodox views of creativity, to the writings of the influential German philosopher, Immanuel Kant. In his seminal text *Critique of Judgment*, which was first published in 1790, Kant asserts that the production of what he refers to as 'beautiful' works of art do not result from the teaching or learning of rules, but from the innate and mysterious abilities of a few gifted individuals with a particular talent for imagination and originality. *Critique of Judgment* is also notable for Kant's related views on aesthetic taste, which he asserts that, although subjectively determined, is nevertheless universal in nature. This is because, for Kant, our personal appreciation of a beautiful work of art typically occurs without regard to any other social, moral, or sensual purpose that the work might have, and as a result, it differs from the type of appreciation or desire that we develop for objects which have a more definite purpose (he gives the example of a horse). Kant argues that due to this disinterest or detachment, individuals are therefore more than likely to share, or at least negotiate, similar kinds of responses to similar kinds of creative works. Hence, he contends that aesthetic taste is legitimated through universal consensus.

According to Banaji and Burn (2007), the twentieth-century cultural theorist and sociologist Pierre Bourdieu provided an influential critique of Kant's aesthetic philosophy in his 1979 work *Distinction: A Social Critique of the Judgement of Taste* (first published in English in 1984) in which he opens up a more democratic discourse of creativity. In *Distinction*, Bourdieu draws upon empirical evidence to show how the type of disinterested universal taste referred to by Kant actually represents the taste of an educated and privileged social class. Bourdieu argues that, in fact, a certain level of cultural competence is necessary before it is possible to engage in any form of aesthetic judgment. The literary theorist Pope (2005) suggests that another influential critique of nineteenth-century romantic notions of creativity came from the Marxist literary critic Pierre Macherey, an influential figure in the development of post-structuralism. Macherey argued that the conceptualisation of the writer or artist as creator belonged to a humanist ideology, and as a result, the centrality of *work* or the *process of making* was overlooked in theories of creativity. Consequently, in his seminal 1966 text on literary theory *A Theory of Literary Production,* he consciously avoided using the word 'creation' and systematically replaced it with the word 'production'. Interestingly, the cover of recent editions of *A Theory of Literary Production* contains the images of many iconic tools of labour, including a hammer, a hacksaw, and a screwdriver.

The increasing shift in the late twentieth century towards a discourse of creativity as production can further be seen in the following quotation from Rosenberg (1983), which refers to a dialogue that influential artist Marcel Duchamp had with Pierre Cabanne in 1971:

> People like to think that art is the mystery of creation, but, Duchamp pointed out, the artist, as a person active in society, is a 'man like any other. It's his job to do certain things'—in the case of the painter, 'things on a

> canvas, with a frame'. Duchamp said that he had always been drawn to the notion of the artist as a craftsman – a term more venerable than 'artist' This was a revision to the traditional idea of making, and it provided him with a stand against the romanticism of his friends the Surrealists. (Rosenberg 1983, pp. 3–4)

Like Macherey, Duchamp dismisses the romantic and individualist discourse of creativity, simultaneously repositioning the act of painting as a trade signified only by its tools, the canvas, and the frame, thus constituting creativity as a more egalitarian discourse of production or making work.

Further insights regarding the increasing pervasiveness of the creativity as work discourse in the twentieth century are provided by Molesworth (2003) in her essay, included with the catalogue for an exhibition titled *Work Ethic*. According to Molesworth, as artists in the twentieth century moved away from both the traditional skills and materials associated with the 'visual pleasure and seduction of mimetic representation' (Molesworth 2003, p. 17), they turned towards other criteria that would be valued by their audiences. This largely involved constituting themselves as workers, and 'replacing the skills of art with the activities of work' (p. 25), which she views as an appropriate response to the rise of twentieth-century capitalism and the resulting professionalisation of the artist. Molesworth makes the point that artists' conscious portrayal of themselves as workers, particularly during the 1960s, can be evidenced in the many photographs or documentaries where they appear hard at work in their studio, dressed in the work shirt and blue jeans attire normally associated at the time with the working classes. One revealing example of the discourse of creativity as work colonising visual arts during the mid-twentieth century is a quotation by the abstractionist Frank Stella who states that 'it sounds a little dramatic, being an "art worker". I just wanted to do it and get it over with so I could go home and watch TV' (Stella, cited by Molesworth 2003, p. 35). For Steinberg (1972), a significant consequence of the reconceptualisation of creativity as work, particularly in the United States, is that artistic culture has shifted from its traditional associations as a pleasurable leisure activity of aristocracy to that of the practical and economic. As a result, the act of being creative could be justified by the notion that work was being done. In some cases, the discourse of creativity as work became the central focus of many artists. One example, pointed out in Molesworth (2003), is Tehching Hsieh's performance piece *One Year Performance*, where he punched a time clock in his New York City studio every hour on the hour from 11 April 1980 until 11 April 1981.

Concluding Comments

In this chapter, it has been suggested that the emerging social and economic structures of the twentieth century are responsible for the discursive reconstitution of creative activity as work. This seems to have occurred initially in the field of visual arts production, where the dominant discourse of the individual creative genius, coupled with the emphasis on traditional artistic skill, was largely relinquished and replaced with a discourse of work; a discourse which, as observed in the institutional setting of this study, continues to articulate the practice of art and design and the attributes of what is perceived as creative behaviour. The student brief plays a major role in formalising this creativity as work discourse (among others) into the regulatory language of the institution, thus structuring the creative processes and activities of the students and tutors.

However, it could be argued that certain complications can arise with the discourse of creativity as work in the university art and design environment. Firstly, it often competes with discourses of a more traditionalist nature that students may have previously encountered and internalised. In the ethnographic accounts of this study, it was regularly noticed that students were anxious about their drawing abilities, believing that their tutors were looking for displays of a particular artistic quality, rather than evidence of regular studio attendance and adherence to a habitual work ethic. Many students enter the university art and design environment expecting to be taught traditional fine art skills in a more formal tutor-oriented setting, but in the contemporary university environment students are more likely to be provided with a studio space, a brief, and expected to begin working.

Like other workers in the contemporary labour market, students are given designated work hours and their attendance during these hours is regularly monitored. Any indication that the required work ethic is lacking can negatively affect a student's final results. Furthermore, the studio hours (9am–3pm in the context studied) are longer than most students' previous experiences of short focused periods (approximately one hour) of art and design instruction at a secondary institution, where the final product is potentially more important than the process of working.

Secondly, it is perhaps difficult to clearly constitute a work ethic as underpinning creative activity in the minds of students. The abstract nature of creativity as work makes it difficult for tutors to specify exactly what working entails in a way that is meaningful to the students. Therefore, to facilitate creative action as work, tutors resort to 'the numbers game', as evidenced in the data collected for this study. Tutors encourage students to work hard by requiring them to produce a certain number of preliminary drawings and final works, but as a consequence, students ironically begin to focus on the product rather than the process. The section of the brief that students gave the highest priority to was the section indicating the number of creative outputs required. Interestingly, the ambiguity evidenced here in the lack of clarity involving the discourse of creativity as work might also be viewed as a discursive strategy of power. By framing creativity through the abstract notion of work, the tutors are able to bring a level of personal connoisseurship to their validation of the students' creative output, while simultaneously enforcing students' commitment to regular attendance. Chapter 4 picks up on many of the issues introduced above, focusing, in particular, on the facilitation of creative activity in the university art and design studio through the regulation of student creative agency.

Notes

1. This chapter is based on Hocking, D. (2011), 'The discursive construction of creativity as work in a tertiary art and design environment'. *Journal of Applied Linguistics and Professional Practice*, *7*(2): 235–255. © Equinox Publishing Ltd 2011.

2. Systemic functional linguistics views different verbs as representing different types of processes. The tendency of an individual or a group to use certain verb processes over others in a particular communicative context can often provide an analyst with information about how that individual or group construes the reality of that context.
3. This presupposition also provides insights into the tutors' conceptualisation of the students' motivation, and their own role as 'student motivators', which will be discussed further in Chap. 5.

References

Baker, P. (2006). *Using corpora in discourse analysis.* London, UK: Continuum.

Banaji, S., & Burn, A. (2007). Creativity through a rhetorical lens: Implications for schooling, literacy and media education. *Literacy, 41*(2), 62–70.

Bourdieu, P. (1984). *Distinction: A social critique of the judgement of taste.* Cambridge, MA: Harvard University Press.

Copland, F., & Creese, A. (Eds.). (2015). *Linguistic ethnography: Collecting, analysing and presenting data.* London, UK: Sage.

Halliday, M. A. K., & Matthiessen, C. M. I. M. (2004). *An introduction to functional grammar* (3rd ed.). London, UK: Arnold.

Hammersley, M., & Atkinson, P. (2007). *Ethnography: Principles in practice* (3rd ed.). London, UK: Routledge.

Jeanes, E. L. (2006). 'Resisting creativity, creating the new': A Deleuzian perspective on creativity. *Creativity and Innovation Management, 15*(2), 127–134.

Kant, I. (1790). *The critique of judgement.* (J. C. Meredith, Trans.). Oxford, UK: Clarendon Press.

Linell, P. (1998). *Approaching dialogue: Talk, interaction and contexts in dialogical perspectives.* Philadelphia, PA: John Benjamins.

Macherey, P. (1966). *A theory of literary production.* London, UK: Routledge and Kegan Paul.

Molesworth, H. (2003). *Work ethic.* In H. Molesworth (Ed.), *Work ethic* (pp. 25–51). University Park, PA: Pennsylvania State University Press.

Pope, R. (2005). *Creativity: Theory, history, practice.* New York, NY: Routledge.

Rampton, B. (2007). Neo-Hymesian linguistic ethnography in the United Kingdom. *Journal of Sociolinguistics, 11*(5), 584–607.

Reisigl, M., & Wodak, R. (2009). The discourse-historical approach. In R. Wodak & M. Meyer (Eds.), *Methods for critical discourse analysis* (2nd ed., pp. 87–121). London, UK: Sage.

Rosenberg, H. (1983). *Art on the edge*. Chicago, IL: University of Chicago Press.

Scott, M., & Tribble, C. (2006). *Textual patterns: Key words and corpus analysis in language education*. Amsterdam, Netherlands: John Benjamins.

Steinberg, L. (1972). *Other criteria: Confrontations with twentieth-century art*. Oxford, UK: Oxford University Press.

Wodak, R. (2001). The discourse-historical approach. In R. Wodak & M. Meyer (Eds.), *Methods of critical discourse analysis* (pp. 63–94). London, UK: Sage.

4

Agency

Introduction

The tension between freedom of choice and constraint is perceived as crucial for the process of creativity (Chap. 1). For many theorists, however, this tension is delicately balanced, with either excessive freedom or excessive constraint perceived as resulting in creative inertia. In their interviews, the students frequently made reference to such a creative tension, particularly when asked about the purpose of their studio briefs (Extracts 4.1 and 4.2).

Extract 4.1: Interview with Student 1

Student 1: Well what I expect obviously just umm, a theme or some sort of options, of what you want to do your work in, because I think it's particularly hard to, like, with all that freedom, when there's too much freedom, you find it hard to like decide what you want to work on, you need some sort of guidance, like in a way like some sort of idea.

D. Hocking, *Communicating Creativity*, Communicating in Professions and Organizations, https://doi.org/10.1057/978-1-137-55804-6_4

Extract 4.2: Interview with Student 2

Student 2: I want it to be more straightforward, more thoroughly, like kind of give us clear guidelines of what we have to do, what we have to achieve, and what kind of objects we have to make or, but this is a creative course, so of course they're giving us a free space.

While the extracts show that the students prefer explicit details regarding the nature of their creative activities, they also acknowledge that such a requirement competes with wider discourses of creative free expression. Interestingly, the students' responses reflect the concerns of twentieth-century art education debates regarding the balance between free expression and the imposition of methods, skills, or techniques (e.g. Eisner 1972; Robinson 1982). Motivated by these concerns, this chapter focuses on student creative agency. It looks, in particular, at the language system of modality and the way that it is used to constitute the balance between creative freedom and constraint in the university art and design studio.

Perspectival and Methodological Foci

Commencing with the semiotic resource perspective, the chapter carries out a keyword analysis (see Chap. 3) of the combined brief corpora. As well as providing a useful entry point into the data, it leads to a more targeted concordance analysis of the student brief corpora. The results identify an emphasis on the use of the rare modal form *you* + *will* in the student brief. Following a discussion regarding the pragmatic function of this modal usage in the studio context (Coates 1983; Gotti 2003), the analysis turns to the social action perspective to further examine modality as it occurs across the trajectory of interactional studio genres, notably the brief writing meeting, the brief launch, the studio tutorial, and casual studio interaction. Drawing upon linguistic ethnography (Copland and Creese 2015; Rampton 2007), the focus in this perspectival phase is on the use of modal auxiliaries for negotiating the creativity-facilitating balance between freedom and constraint. Moreover, because modality is inherently linked to the future, this chapter will also examine how the hypothetical anticipation of future actions associated with the setting of freedom and constraint is an important constituent of creative practice. Throughout the analysis, extracts from the student brief will be referred to as support. Table 4.1 indicates the methodological resources used in this chapter with respect to the data collected from the different perspectives.

Table 4.1 The data analysed and methodological foci for each of the perspectives

Perspective	Data	Methodological orientation	Tools
Semiotic resource perspective	Three brief corpora (146,414 words total) (i) 36, 605 word student brief corpus (ii) 37,136 word creative brief corpus (iii) 72,673 design brief corpus	Corpus analysis	Keyword analysis Frequency analysis Concordance analysis Collocation
	The Binary Opposites brief, including extracts from the objectives section and the assessment criteria.	Pragmatics	Description and analysis of modal usage
Social action perspective	Audio recording of the first brief writing meeting Audio recording of a brief launch Audio recording of a studio tutorial where two students discuss their visual work with the tutor Anna Audio recording of casual studio interaction Extract from the documentary *The September Issue*	Linguistic ethnography Pragmatics	Micro analysis of the participants' unfolding interactions. Description and analysis of modal usage

(*continued*)

Table 4.1 (continued)

Perspective	Data	Methodological orientation	Tools
Participants' perspective	Semi-structured interviews with students	Ethnographic analysis	Observation of salient themes in the participants' interactions
Socio-historical perspective	Theoretical and historical literature on art and design education and anticipatory futures	Content analysis	Identification of salient themes in relevant theoretical and historical texts

The Modal *will* in the Brief Corpora

Table 4.2 shows the highest ten keywords of a corpus which combines the student briefs, professional design briefs, and professional creative briefs. The table also indicates the frequency of these keywords in each of the three individual corpora, and the number of brief texts they occur in. It is of interest that although *will* is regularly identified as being the most frequently occurring modal in English (Biber et al. 1999; Coates 1983; Kennedy 2002), it nevertheless still occurs as the third highest keyword when the corpora of combined briefs is referenced with the Wellington Corpus of Written English.

If we solely examine the student brief corpus, *will* has a frequency of 257. Interestingly, 31.5 per cent (a total of 81) of all instances of the modal *will* occur immediately after the pronoun *you* in the student briefs. To provide an example, Table 4.3 lists the first 30 concordances found in the student brief corpus that contain the collocation *you will,* and it is clear that in most of these concordance lines, the modal is used to express necessity or obligation. What is of note, is that, firstly, this particular function of the collocation *you* + *will* only occurs four times in the two professional brief corpora, which comprise 60 individual brief texts and total just over 100,000 words. Secondly, it is described by Coates (1983) and Gotti (2003) as a particularly rare modal form. As a result, it could be argued that *you will* is somewhat marked for the student brief genre, with the pattern *you* + *will* + V [inf] (e.g. *You will do something different*

Table 4.2 Combined keyness of the three brief corpora, using the Wellington Written Corpus as a reference corpus

			Student briefs		Prof. design briefs		Prof. creative briefs	
	Word	Overall keyness	Freq	Texts (*t*=33)	Freq	Texts (*t*=20)	Freq	Txts (*t*=40)
1.	design	2376.35	157	23	458	19	67	14
2.	be	1487.41	353	29	1396	19	403	40
3.	will	1458.46	257	28	668	19	259	35
4.	brief	1245.07	141	25	111	19	87	37
5.	your	918.98	499	32	25	5	100	21
6.	site	898.92	49	14	172	13	94	15
7.	project	895.15	90	20	179	15	42	19
8.	space	761.14	64	16	203	14	12	10
9.	etc	745.24	72	21	54	10	41	20
10.	studio	741.61	186	21	16	2	6	2

afterwards; see also concordances 4, 7, 8, 10, 16, 17, 18, 19, 20, 21, 22, 25, 26, 27, 30) as the most prominent in Table 4.3, closely followed by *you* + *will* + be + V-ed (e.g. *You will be expected to present a body of work which …;* see also concordances 3, 5, 9, 11, 24, 28).

In studies where the analysis of corpora has been used to identify the pragmatic characteristics of modals, *will* is described as being associated with either deontic volition, as in *I might/may/will do it tomorrow*, or epistemic prediction, as in *he may/might/will be there by now* (Biber et al. 1999; Coates 1983; Verplaetse 2003). However, these two functions are seen as regularly overlapping, with Biber et al. stating that 'the distinction between volition and prediction is often blurred' (p. 496). For example, utterances such as *Raymond Baxter and I will describe the scene* or *I will decide what to do with her later, he imagined* (Coates 1983, p. 179) are examples of prediction, which according to Coates are also shaded with volition.

Interestingly, in most studies on modality, the collocation of the pronoun *you* with the modal *will* is largely under-examined, especially with regards to the type of usage frequently found in the student brief corpus. For example, while Coates states that in *You will decide what to do with her later, he imagined*, the modal *will* is associated with prediction, I would

Table 4.3 First 30 concordances (overall total = 81) with the collocation *you will* found in the student brief corpus

1	efore and with the knowledge that	*you will*	do something different afterwards. In this wa
2	is assignment on Thursday, 6 April.	*You will*	be expected to present a body of work which
3	dy of works along a *line of enquiry*.	*You will*	be asked to talk about the different ways you
4	The brief. As a starting point	*you will*	make only physical bodily connections with a
5	rials, technologies and techniques.	*You will*	be asked simply to make rather than attempti
6	s, by the morning of Friday 20 July	*you will*	have collected and brought to the studio a su
7	1. On Thursday 16 August at 12pm	*you will*	present the following: 1. 19 works or docume
8	corners. If you have made work. 2.	*You will*	also present evidence of the remainder of wo
9	jects you combine, but at this stage	*you will*	be asked to reduce the material elements you
10	arity. Another consideration is how	*you will*	present. Understanding a piece of art work is
11	ape as a central focus in their work.	*You will*	be asked to produce—Workbooks containing
12	the work constructed at Kare Kare	*you will*	have to submit a series of small painted studi
13	on Mondays Thursdays and Fridays	*you will*	be painting in your studio spaces.
14	be given to the environment which	*you will*	be working in if are to make practical decision
15	ughout the duration of this project	*you will*	be working individually on site gathering infor
16	Be prepared !! When at the beach	*you will*	need :—appropriate clothing for working at th
17	aims of the project will be, what	*you will*	need to bring , where to meet the van on Tue
18	s … as well as on site requirements	*you will*	need to organise your studio space at …… Ho
19	ur workbook of visual material that	*you will*	need to gather in the following week. WEEK
20	oup discussion of your speculation.	*You will*	need to use the slides for this purpose and to
21	by Damien Hirst 1966. In this brief	*you will*	investigate the relationship between inside sp
22	e space. The private and the public.	*You will*	get to learn about the space between.
23	ted with spatial and interior design.	*you will*	discover new ways of articulating your taste a
24	a message on …. ….'s voice mail).	*You will*	be expected to establish contact with the clas
25	erations and new disciplines/ areas	*you will*	rotate around. * Finish off.
26	ting point. Over the next five weeks	*you will*	individually respond and develop a series of e
27	gnage, architecture, and short film.	*You will*	require at least 20 developed prints to work fr
28	nd 3 week block of the brief where	*you will*	be asked to extend your body of work in relati
29	Communication	*You will*	be: Researching and resourcing ideas, m
30	or critique and formative feedback.	*You will*	have: Group and individual critiques, present

suggest that in a different context, particularly one involving a differential power relationship (e.g. *But the Boss expects that you will decide what to do next and that these decisions will be reasonable.*) the modal *will* could be seen as marking necessity, or a lack of volition on the part of the addressee. Coates (1983) does make a brief comment on this latter usage of *will*:

> There is a (rare) use of WILL which can be compared with the Root [i.e. deontic] MUST. (…) An utterance like *You will finish your homework* is structurally parallel to a command like *You must finish your homework*, and pragmatically stronger (since WILL here implies the speaker's determination to see the action referred to in the proposition fulfilled). (Coates 1983, p. 183)

Coates also points out that the modal *will* asserts a particularly strong relationship between futurity and modality, stating that the 'the meaning of *You will be here at three o'clock* is essentially the same, whether it is used as a prediction or as a directive' (p. 233). Gotti (2003) also identifies this unusual imperative function of *will*, which he states is found in 'non-interrogative sentences, especially when the addressee is a subordinate person'. He provides *You will do as I say* (I want you to do as I say) as an example, and adds that this particular deontic value of *will* as necessity can also be evidenced in prescriptions such as *The successful candidate will have a university degree and be fluent in French* (The successful candidate is required to have a university degree and be fluent in French) (p. 288).

As a result, I would suggest that in the context of the student brief the frequent use of *you* + *will* + V [inf] (e.g. *You will also bring a folder of your research material*) can be described as a directive or a command and marks necessity or obligation. However, this necessity or obligation is occluded using a modal form 'will', which typically marks the less obligative function of volition or prediction. Perhaps the use of this particular grammatical choice in the art and design studio context results from the conflict discussed earlier between the commonly perceived discourse of creative action as the individualistic action of the creator, and one that is constituted through external obligation and necessity. Furthermore, *will* marks a strong relationship between modality and futurity. Many studies argue that the verbal anticipation or construction of future visions are powerful and creative forces for influencing the future as they are often self-fulfilling (de Saint-George 2003; Encisco 2007; Ross and Buehler 2004), a point which I believe is central to creative action. These ideas will be explored in more detail in the sections below.

Modality in the Brief Writing Meetings

The rest of this chapter will examine a number of interrelated issues—the role of authority in the art and design tertiary environment, its often-occluded nature, and its role in constructing creativity forming hypothetical futures. Drawing on the findings of the previous section, this examination will continue to focus on the linguistic area of modality, as I believe it is a pervasive feature of both the interactional and textual data collected for this study, and is pragmatically responsible for both constituting and occluding authority, as well as constituting the various degrees of hypotheticality necessary for creative action. To begin this section, I am going to look at a component of the student brief that I have termed the *objectives* section, and examine how it is co-constructed by the tutors in the brief writing meeting. The *objectives* section outlines the general aim or direction of the creative project, and it immediately precedes the *requirements* section that was discussed in the previous chapter.

Extract 4.3 shows an objectives section from the completed visual arts version of the Binary Opposites brief. In the first brief writing meeting (Extract 4.4), it is being used by the tutors Anna and Mike as a model for the draft of a new objectives section which will be given to those students specifically wanting to work in the 3D and spatial design areas.[1]

Extract 4.3: Objectives Section of the Visual Arts Version of the Binary Opposites Brief (Bold and Underlining are as in the Original Document)

<u>Visual Arts</u>

Read the brief **Binary Opposites** carefully. Having done this you are to **<u>develop and explore visual interpretations of</u>**

4 **<u>contrary conceptual categories</u>**. Your interpretations may take
5 any form you feel appropriate. You may use any media.

In the brief writing meeting (Extract 4.4), it appears that the tutors believe the current form of this objectives section, especially the clause *take any form you feel appropriate* gives the 3D and spatial design students too much freedom in the creative process. In order to constrain the choices that will be made available to the students, and therefore establish how they might redraft this section of the brief for the 3D and spatial students, the tutors' interaction involves conceptualising what it is that they think the students should be able to produce for this brief.

Extract 4.4: First Brief Writing Meeting (the Modal *Could* is Marked in Bold)

1	→	Anna:	yeah yeah cos I've worked a little bit on the spatial one
2			and I thought
3	→		maybe it could be something like
4	→		((*reads*)) develop 3D conceptual models of your initial ideas
5	→		but it **could** be models, or ((*two seconds of silence*))
6	→		well models [are quite general isn't it, you know.
7	→	Mike:	[I don't think, well . I don't think
8	→		well models **could** be part of what some of them do↑
9			I, I-
10	→	Anna:	well maybe 3D concepts.
11	→	Mike:	yes.
12	→	Anna:	yeah.
13	→	Mike:	cos they might want to make sculpture.
14	→	Anna:	yep yep.
15	→	Mike:	you know [u:m.
16	→	Anna:	[and it **could** be . if it . doesn't have to be
17	→		necessarily [models.
18	→	Mike:	[or it **could** be clothes, you know=
19	→	Anna:	=exactly.

→ Mike: you know. [and it-
→ Anna: [or it **could** be models of architecture.
→ Mike: or it **could** be spatial, you know
where it where it's ridiculous
you can't . you can't realize ... full-size.
→ Anna: yep yep
→ Mike: but some of it **could** be.
→ Anna: yeah.
→ Mike: you know, cos it **could** be installation work.
→ Anna: yeah
→ Mike: which **could** a:h.
→ Anna: keeps it quite sort of broad, yeah u:m↑

In Extract 4.4, the tutor Anna initially conceptualises the only options available to the 3D and spatial students as *conceptual models* or *models* (lines 4 and 5). However, she indicates some uncertainty with this view which she signals by the use of the conjunction *or,* and the following long pause (end of line 5). This might be because she has recognised that an exclusive focus on models may overly constrain the future creative processes of students, which could explain why she subsequently suggests that the word *models* has the potential to be defined more generally (line 6), and also because she is attempting to elicit a response from Mike regarding her views. This expression of uncertainty is repeated at the end of line 6, through the use of a tag question and the sentence-ending expression *you know* (Holmes 1986). Mike responds to Anna's signal of uncertainty by interrupting her turn and envisaging other potential creative options besides those defined by the word *models* (line 7). In doing this, Mike has contributed to broadening Anna's visualisation of the students' future options, evidenced in her subsequent turn, *well maybe 3D concepts* (line 10), and her subsequent rejection of her exclusive emphasis on *models* (lines 16 and 17). Once this broader visualisation of the students' creative potential has been established, the two participants work together to envisage a range of potential future options for the students (seen in the sequence 13–31). These include *clothes* (line 18), *models of architecture* (line 21), *spatial* (line 22), and *installation work* (line 28).

Extract 4.5 presents the final draft of the 3D and spatial objectives statement that was written following the tutors' interactions in the first brief writing meeting.

Extract 4.5: New Objectives Section for 3D and Spatial Version of the Binary Opposites Brief (Bold and Underlining are as in the Original Document)

> Your interpretations **must deal with three dimensional and or spatial elements**, but otherwise may take any form you feel appropriate.

It is evident that the tutors have simply replaced the first two sentences of the earlier visual arts version (Extract 4.3) with the new sentence, 'Your interpretations must deal with three dimensional and spatial elements'. While this addition seems not to have achieved much beyond including reference to the two art and design discipline areas, *3D* and *spatial design*, the interaction in Extract 4.4 that preceded the writing of this new objectives section enabled the two tutors to intersubjectively co-construct a common understanding of what it is that the 3D and spatial students are authorised to produce in the studio. So, while the information presented in the brief might not explicitly state what these creative outputs might be, the result of this collaborative writing process is that the tutors' future interactions with students related to this brief will be more or less synchronised. This can be seen in a short extract from the brief launch (Extract 4.6), where Anna introduces the brief to her group of students. Anna explains that *models* (line 1) and *clothes* (line 3), one of the Mike's suggestions in Extract 4.4, could be the focus of the spatial students' creative processes.

Extract 4.6: Brief Launch (The Modal *Can* is Marked in Bold)

→ Anna: and the spatial people **can** make models
they **can** make objects
→ they **can** make clothes
anything in that kind of spatial form.

It is through the dialogic interaction, then, that occurs in the brief writing meeting that the individual tutors' various and incomplete perceptions are brought together, and collaboratively synchronised. Linell (1998) points out the principal role of dialogue for 'building and using fragments of understanding and contexts' (p. 198), because, as individuals, 'our realities are only partially shared and fragmentarily known' (p. 198). He goes on to state that:

> Under many circumstances, people undoubtedly have different knowledge of, perspectives on and opinions about the world and the specific situations they are in. Dialogue and discourse can then be used to develop a common view, a shared understanding for current purposes (and sometimes common understandings that last much longer).[2] (Linell 1998, p.198)

The high repetition of the syntactic form *it could be* in the brief writing interaction above (Extract 4.4, lines 3, 5, 16, 18, 21, 22, 26, and 28) provides the interactional cohesion (Johnstone 1987; Tannen 1987) for this synchronisation of fragments of understanding. The cohesive work carried out by this repetition is further supported by the high frequency of alignment tokens—for example, *yes* (line 11), *yeah* (lines 12, 27, 29), *yep yep* (line 14, 25), and *exactly* (line 19)—used by the participants to signal conceptual consensus and to facilitate the continuation of the interactional work at hand (Lambertz 2011). Johnstone (1987) also raises the point that repetition is used by interlocutors to create categories, and in Extract 4.4, the participants use the repetition of the structure *it could be*, to create (at least for the time being) a category identifying the future creative options for the 3D and spatial students.

As a caveat to this discussion, Candlin (2002) evokes the concept of *alterity* in discourse to argue that such intersubjectivity is only ever temporarily achievable, and that instead differences in opinion routinely drive interaction forward to achieve resolution (see, for example, lines 5–8 in Extract 4.4 above). Candlin states that such resolution is often only momentary and transitory; a view which supports my observations of the art and design studio, where many of the agreements and understandings previously established at one brief meeting are renegotiated at the next. I would argue that the production of each new brief, then, facilitates the reduction of alterity and formalises a degree of resolution for the duration of the assessment event, thus temporarily synchronising the views of the tutors and enabling the creative process to take place without disjuncture for the present assessment event. I would also suggest that this is one reason why the tutors always choose to redraft a new set of briefs for every new assessment event, even when there is an opportunity to reuse older briefs from previous years. Perhaps the need to bring together and resolve opposing and dialogic voices from time to time is an important role of the student brief genre.

Modality and Future-oriented Interaction

In Extract 4.6 above, when Anna addresses the students in the brief launch and gives them permission, repeatedly using the modal *can* (lines 1, 2 and 3), to make certain objects, she is inevitably making reference to their future. Coates (1983) states that one of the conditions of using the root *can* (= permission) is that the 'speaker believes that the action referred to in the main predication has not already been achieved' (p. 233) and therefore refers to a future event. In fact she goes on to identify the general relationship between futurity and modality:

> It is acknowledged in most studies of the modals that tense and modality overlap where there is reference to the future, since the future, unlike the past is unknown. Reference to future events and states is a crucial aspect of the meaning of the modals. (Coates 1983, p. 233)

Coates concludes that 'commands, recommendations and permission-granting utterances all refer to an action which will be carried out at a time subsequent to the utterance' (p. 233).

Similarly, if we return to the interaction between Anna and Mike (Extract 4.4), it is evident that, as they determine the creative options of the students, they are inevitably interacting about the future; but they are doing more than simply making reference to future time, they are envisaging or imagining the future possibilities of the students through talk, and in a sense talking the students' creative futures into being. This is carried out through the use of the modal *could* (lines 16, 18, 21, 22, 26 and 28). *Could* is the most frequent modal in the two brief meetings recorded for this study (15, 280 words in total), occurring 90 times. In this interaction, *could,* as the remote of *can*, also simultaneously construes both permission, and hypothetical possibility (Coates 1983). We have now seen that these are two central functions of the tutors' interaction in the brief writing meeting (Extract 4.4).

Accordingly, a number of studies show how hypothetical or imagined futures are powerful and creative forces for influencing the future. Ross and Buehler (2004), for example, pointing to a number of psychological studies that examine the nature of predictions, conclude that 'peoples' thought and forecasts sometimes influence what actually transpires' (p. 36). Future-oriented talk has also been shown to invoke alterative realities enabling those involved to cope with potentially difficult situations (Peräkylä 1993), and enact social change (Thomson and Holland 2002). Mediated discourse analysis, in particular, shows how sequences of events, including negotiated acts of communication, can establish a commitment to future action (Jones 2008; Scollon and Scollon 2004), and how social actors assign meaning to their anticipated realities through discourse and in doing so ultimately shape their outcomes (S. Scollon 2001). De Saint George (2003), for example, provides evidence of how 'an overwhelming part of our everyday behaviour consists of, consciously or unconsciously, projecting outcomes and finding means for accomplishing them' (p. 2) and Al Zidjaly (2006) shows how 'hypothetical future-oriented narratives' (p. 102) can be used strategically to affect future change. (p. 36). Therefore, by projecting ourselves forward to the future, we are able to alter the present in preparation for the realisation of our imagined futures, a process which is paramount to creative action. Jackson (2002), for example, states that:

> Creativity involves first imagining something (to cause to come into existence) and then doing something with this imagination … (Jackson 2002, para. 1)

The work of Bourdieu (1990, 1993), in particular his concepts of habitus, field, and practice, also has much to offer this discussion. Bourdieu argues that practical action is necessarily future-oriented because the predisposition of the *habitus* in the (cultural) *field* is towards the generation and organisation of further practice. The habitus is always oriented towards practical action, because, as a product of the collective histories of the different institutions that it inhabits, it is also conditioned to reproduce these histories. For example, some students will necessarily orient to Anna's categorisation of *spatial people* (Extract 4.6, line 1) and accumulate membership of this category as a part of their habitus; a membership which is defined in the context of this study through the practice of *making* (Extract 4.6, lines 1–4). Bourdieu (1990) suggests, however, that the generation of practice is not a causal or rational process. The motivating structures and action of the individual's habitus, embodied with certain schemes of perception, classification, and appreciation is a 'world of already realized ends—procedures to follow, paths to take' (p. 53)—perhaps seen here in the options which the tutors have constituted as belonging to the category spatial design, which they themselves have drawn from their own collective experience. Bourdieu holds the view that what motivates practice, therefore, is an *anticipation of the future* based on the experience of the past. He states that the habitus 'at every moment, structures new experiences in accordance with the structures produced by past experiences' (Bourdieu, 1990, p. 60). The result is 'both original and inevitable' (p. 57). This is because although each individual habitus (in its capacity for generating practice) draws upon its own unique set of dispositions, it is inevitably synchronised with others within the institutional context; what Bourdieu perhaps refers to as the 'generative principle of regulated improvisations' (p. 57).

In a sense, it could be argued that the predisposition towards the coordinated generation of creative practice is, at least in part, constituted through the system of modality and its potential to both enable and place constraints on the future. The next section considers this notion further, by examining the use of modality in the studio tutorials.

Modality in the Studio Tutorials

In the studio tutorials the most frequent marker of modality, which functions to set creative freedoms and constraints, is the modal auxiliary *might*. Interestingly, the adverb *maybe*, a fifteenth-century composite of the lexical pattern *it may be*, is the second most frequent marker of modality in the tutorials. The use of *might* can be seen in Extract 4.7, where the tutor Anna is interacting with student 3 about their work in progress. Coates (1983) states that the pragmatically hypothetical root *might* 'is often used to indicate a course of action politely, without giving overt advice' (p. 161), and Halliday and Matthiessen (2004) place the modal auxiliary *might* at the low end of the spectrum of modal strength.

Extract 4.7: Studio Tutorial between the Tutor Anna and Student 3 (The Modal Might is Marked in Bold)

1	→	Anna:	so you **might** want to just have a look at your composition
2			there a little bit
3			and [see whether you could . um . perhaps actually-
4	→	S3:	[yea:h.
5	→	Anna:	what would happen here if we put our hand over the:re
6			if you took a little bit of the <u>top</u> off
7	→	S3:	[yea:h
8	→	Anna:	[so we're looking more down at . um . uh . the the
9			what the subject's really about . um
10	→		that actually **might**-
11	→		that **might** improve the: the … well the communication
12	→	S3:	Yea:h
13	→	Anna:	because we're sort of talking about communicating
14	→	S3:	yea:h
15	→	Anna:	um ideas quite a bit.
			(…)
16			I really like the way that you've used the . the wild wild →
17			west type [of ima:ge . um . oh text there
18	→	S3:	[yea:h
19	→	Anna:	but I think it **might**-
20	→		you **might** need to look at some other colours.

Lines 1, 19, and 20 provide evidence of what Coates (1983) refers to as the 'pragmatically specialized' (p. 168) use of *you* + *might* as a directive/advice, while lines 10 and 11 involve the epistemic use of might. In lines 1–6 Anna is directing student 3 to amend a component of her creative work. This can be seen by the use of the verb phrase *have a look at* (line 1), a metaphoric expression regularly used in the art and design tutorial environment, which in the context of this interaction means 'consider and adjust/redo'.[3] The same choice of metaphor is also used for the directive in line 20. However, Anna's choice of *might* (line 1), and her use of the diminutive *a little bit* (line 2), construes the directive as an option, which student 3 might or might not choose to take up in the future. In fact this ambiguity between obligation (what is permitted) and personal volition pervades the entire interaction. For example, as well as the modal auxiliary *might*, Anna uses the adverb *perhaps* (line 3), conditionals (line 5), and the vague expression *sort of* (line 13) which repeatedly construe her utterances as simply offering advice. However, at the macro level Anna is clearly the dominant speaker, holding much longer turns that the student, who is only allowed minimal responses (*yeah*, lines 7, 12, 14, and 18). Anna is also permitted to say what she likes or dislikes about the students' work, and identify potential changes. While significantly hedged, the obligative nature of Anna's turns is realised if we return to assessment criteria three, which is located in the brief (Extract 4.8).

Extract 4.8: Criteria 3 from the Binary Opposites Brief (Original Bold)

3 Actively discusses work with peers and tutors

Minimum Standard
Analyses own work and directions, discusses the appropriateness and effectiveness of the art/design processes being used. Participates in group analytical discussion and discusses work with tutors.
High Standard
Critically analyses and discusses own work and its directions in relation to concept, context, media and process. As a result of this, makes selective decisions in order to enhance focus of concept and effectiveness of process.

> Actively seeks critical feedback and engages with analytical/critical discussion in-group and with tutors

The criteria state that a student who '[c]ritically analyses and discusses own work and its directions in relation to concept, context, media and process' and '[a]s a result of this, makes selective decisions in order to enhance focus of concept and effectiveness of process' will achieve at a high standard. In the situated context of the art and design studio, this is understood as meaning that a student's success would be measured in part by their willingness to commit to the directives/advice provided by their tutors (*as a result of this … makes selective decisions*). The final statement in these criteria highlights the importance of interaction or dialogue to the process of creative action in the studio environment.

The next section focuses on the casual interaction that occurs in the studio environment in order to examine yet another important shift in modality across the genre system of the student brief.

Casual Studio Interaction

Extract 4.9 is a transcription from what I have referred to as casual studio interaction, because unlike the more formal studio tutorials where the focus is directly on the students' creative work and often related indirectly to assessment, casual studio interaction is not a formally planned or timetabled event, and the topics are multifarious. Furthermore, while the studio tutorials are usually between a single tutor and a single student, casual studio interactions might be between any number of students or tutors. Extract 4.9 contains two short sequences of casual studio interaction that occur around a worktable in the centre of the studio. In the first sequence of this interaction, two students are discussing with the tutor, Anna, their interest in putting together a formal exhibition of their work, while in the second sequence, which occurs after Anna has left the table, the same two students are talking about one of the student's creative ideas.

Extract 4.9: Casual Studio Interaction (*Want* is Marked in Bold)

1 → S8: there's like quite a few of us
2 → that **want** to do something.
3 → Anna: have a little show or something [like that ↑
4 → S9: [exhibition.
((*simultaneous unintelligible speech*))
5 → S8: yeah I really **want** to do something like tha:t.
6 → Anna: you know what we could do is um
7 is that gallery up on . edmonds street's not always booked up.
(…)
8 → S9: you could take some home and do it during the holidays
9 → S8: I **want** to do like for one page.
10 → I **want** to do like a giant fucken fuck off tree.
11 Like do another one
12 like bind another one to it
13 and bind another one to that page
14 so that's it's a huge wall . of like these sticks.
15 → S9: yep
16 → S8: that would be pretty cool eh↑
17 → S9: it would be immense.
18 → I reckon it would be so good.

What is evident here is that in these examples of casual studio interaction, there is a shift to a discourse of desire and strong creative agency, primarily expressed through the desiderative verb *want* (lines 2, 5, 9, and 10), which is frequently described as having modal qualities. The students also provide strong hypothetical support to their future desires by positively imagining the future results of their desires through a quick succession of adjectives and qualifiers: *pretty cool*, *immense*, and *so good* (lines 16–17). In many ways, this provides evidence of students assigning meaning to their anticipated realities through discourse (S. Scollon 2001), therefore contributing to the commitment needed to establish future (creative) action (Scollon and Scollon 2004; Jones 2008). A discourse of desire in such interactions is not limited to the educational context. The documentary *The September Issue* (Cutler 2009), which chronicles *Vogue* editor Anna Wintour's preparations for the 2007 September issue, contains a wealth of interactional data from professional designer–client meetings that mirror the casual studio interaction in Extract 4.9. For example, the celebrated fashion photographer Mario Testino, in a meeting with Wintour to discuss a brief for the cover of *Vogue*, states:

> I mean I *want* things that are quite spectacular and I *want* to do something to do with a Vespa in Saint Peter's Square and then I *wanted* something with horses and soldiers. I mean there is a lot of white, like I *love* that. (italics added)

Given the relative power of Wintour, it could be argued that Testino's recurrent use of desiderative (*want, wanted*) and emotive language (*spectacular, love*) reveals—as with the students in the educational context—not only a hypothetical orientation to his creative future, but an attempt to take control of his creative agency. This is, perhaps, supported by Oak (2009), who shows how the 'emotion' and 'personal engagement' (p. 53) are role-specific behaviours of designers in their meetings with clients.

Concluding Comments

In the situated context of this study it would appear that the students' creative activity is, in part, discursively facilitated through a hypothetical orientation to the future involving the setting and subsequent direction of a series of freedoms and constraints, often constituted by, and constitutive of, a particular art and design discipline or domain. However, as also evidenced in this chapter, creativity-forming freedoms and constraints are not the result of a rationally organised, static, or predetermined set of social or institutional rules, but are accomplished for each particular setting through interaction, such as that seen in the brief writing meeting. Central to this process is the linguistic form of modality, in particular the modal auxiliaries, which pragmatically function to both constrain and facilitate available options and therefore the nature of the students' agency. The modal auxiliaries are also linked to futurity; as Coates (1983) remarks, 'reference to future events and states is a crucial aspect of the meaning of the modals' (p. 233).

An examination of the use of modality throughout the various spoken and written genres that occur within the trajectory of the art and design assessment event reveals shifts in the nature of the students' creative agency. For example, in the brief writing meeting, the future is constituted as a set of possibilities (through the prominence of the modal *could*). These possibilities are entextualised in the brief as a future of obligation (seen in the prominence of the modal *will*), although as discussed in this chapter, *will* can also pragmatically function to mark volition. In the brief launch, the creative options set earlier by the tutors are revealed to the students using the modal *can*, which signifies both possibility and permission, and in the studio tutorials, the future is constituted as one of recommended options (seen in the prominence of the modal *might*), although the accompanying assessment criteria commits students to take up these options. In contrast, the students constitute their own creative futures through a modality of desire during casual studio interaction, seen in the prominence of the desiderative *want*.

In conclusion, while the tutors co-construct a common understanding as to the nature of students' future creative outputs, they avoid the use of explicit obligation to convey these to the students. Instead they draw upon the modal system which is simultaneously facilitative and constraining; that is, it brings hypothetical future options into existence, but at the same time limits what is possible. Ultimately, I would argue that the freedom/constraint, present/future dichotomies captured in the modal system are crucial for the facilitation of creative practice. Inevitably, however, the ambiguity that occurs between volition and authority can lead to conflict, especially in the situated context of this study where the students are relative novices to both institutional processes and the wider discipline of art and design. The next chapter will examine evidence of the potential conflict that may occur as a result of this ambiguity.

Notes

1. In the context of this book, *3D* loosely refers to work of a sculptural nature, while *spatial* loosely refers to work of an interior design or architectural nature.
2. He also makes the point that in certain contexts the positions of participants in a dialogue will be so disparate that no intersubjectivity is possible.
3. The conceptualisation of 'looking at' something can, within the historical context of art and design production, also be connected to the concept of the gaze (see Chap. 6).

References

Al Zidjaly, N. (2006). Disability and anticipatory discourse: The interconnectedness of local and global aspects of talk. *Communication and Medicine, 3*(2), 101–112.

Biber, D., Johansson, S., Leech, G. N., Conrad, S., & Finegan, E. (1999). *Longman grammar of spoken and written English*. Harlow, UK: Pearson Education.

Bourdieu, P. (1990). *The logic of practice*. Stanford, CA: Stanford University Press.

Bourdieu, P. (1993). *The field of cultural production: Essays on art and literature*. New York, NY: Columbia University Press.

Candlin, C. N. (2002). Alterity, perspective and mutuality in LSP research and practice. In M. Gotti, D. Heller, & M. Dossena (Eds.), *Conflict and negotiation in specialized texts* (pp. 21–40). Bern, Switzerland: Peter Lang Verlag.

Coates, J. (1983). *The semantics of modal auxiliaries*. London, UK: Croom Helm.

Copland, F., & Creese, A. (Eds.). (2015). *Linguistic Ethnography: Collecting, analysing and presenting data*. London, UK: Sage.

Cutler, R. J. (2009). *The September issue* [Documentary]. Australia: A&E IndieFilms and Actual Reality Pictures.

de Saint-George, I. (2003). *Anticipatory discourses: Producing futures of action in a vocational programme for long term unemployed* (PhD dissertation). Georgetown University, Washington, DC.

Eisner, E. W. (1972). *Educating artistic vision*. London, UK: Collier-Macmillan.

Encisco, P. (2007). Reframing history in sociocultural theories: Toward an expansive vision. In C. Lewis, P. Encisco, & E. B. Moje (Eds.), *Reframing sociocultural research on literacy: Identity, agency and power* (pp. 49–74). Mahwah, NJ: Lawrence Erlbaum.

Gotti, M. (2003). Shall and will in contemporary English: A comparison with past uses. In R. Facchinetti, M. Krug, & F. Palmer (Eds.), *Modality in contemporary English* (pp. 267–300). Berlin, Germany: Mouton de Gruyter.

Halliday, M. A. K., & Matthiessen, C. M. I. M. (2004). *An introduction to functional grammar* (3rd ed.). London, UK: Arnold.

Holmes, J. (1986). Functions of *you know* in women's and men's speech. *Language in Society, 15*(1), 1–21.

Jackson, N. (2002). A guide for busy academics: Nurturing creativity. Retrieved from http://www.heacademy.ac.uk/assets/documents/resources/database/id157_Guide_for_Busy_Academics_Nurturing_Creativity.rtf

Johnstone, B. (1987). Introduction: Perspectives on repetition. *Text, 7*(3), 205–214.

Jones, R. H. (2008). Good sex and bad karma: Discourse and the historical body. In V. K. Bhatia, J. Flowerdew, & R. H. Jones (Eds.), *Advances in discourse studies* (pp. 245–257). London, UK: Routledge.

Kennedy, G. (2002). Variation in the distribution of modal verbs in the British National Corpus. In R. Reppen, S. Fitzmaurice, & D. Biber (Eds.), *Using corpora to explore linguistic variation* (pp. 73–90). Amsterdam, Netherlands: John Benjamins.

Lambertz, K. (2011). Back-channelling: The use of *yeah* and *mm* to portray engaged listenership. *Griffith Working Papers in Pragmatics and Intercultural Communication, 4*(1/2), 11–18.

Linell, P. (1998). *Approaching dialogue: Talk, interaction and contexts in dialogical perspectives.* Philadelphia, PA: John Benjamins.

Oak, A. (2009). Performing architecture: Talking 'architect' and 'client' into being. *CoDesign: International Journal of CoCreation in Design and the Arts, 5*(1), 51–63.

Peräkylä, A. (1993). Invoking a hostile world: Discussing the patient's future in AIDS counselling. *Text, 13*(2), 291–316.

Rampton, B. (2007). Neo-Hymesian linguistic ethnography in the United Kingdom. *Journal of Sociolinguistics, 11*(5), 584–607.

Robinson, K. (1982). *The arts in schools: Principles, practice and provision.* London, UK: Calouste Gulbenkian Foundation.

Ross, M., & Buehler, R. (2004). Identity through time: Constructing personal pasts and futures. In M. B. Brewer & M. Hewstone (Eds.), *Self and social identity* (pp. 25–51). Malden, MA: Blackwell Publishing.

Scollon, R., & Scollon, S. W. (2004). *Nexus analysis: Discourse and the emerging internet.* London, UK: Routledge.

Scollon, S. B. K. (2001). Habitas, consciousness, agency and the problem of intervention: How we carry and are carried by political discourses. *Folia Linguistica, 35*(1-2), 97–129.

Tannen, D. (1987). Repetition in conversation: Towards a poetics of talk. *Language, 63*(3), 574–605.

Thomson, R., & Holland, J. (2002). Imagined adulthood: Resources, plans and contradictions. *Gender and Education, 14*(4), 337–350.

Verplaetse, H. (2003). What you and I want: A functional approach to verb complementation of modal *want to.* In R. Facchinetti, M. Krug, & F. Palmer (Eds.), *Modality in contemporary English* (pp. 151–190). Berlin, Germany: Mouton de Gruyter.

5

Motivation

Introduction

Chapter 4 explored the way in which both the tutors and students assign meaning to their anticipated realities through discourse, and in doing so, establish the commitment necessary for future creative activity. The chapter showed how the future visions of the tutors were realised through the setting of freedoms and constraints, while those of the students were articulated through a discourse of future desire. Imagined futures and desire are brought together in the work of Ushioda (2009) and Dörnyei and Ushioda (2011) under the important concept of *motivation*. They suggest that we create visions of our desired futures in order to establish the motivation necessary to get things done. Accordingly, motivation is viewed as a key concern in art and design educational studies and is often regarded as a requirement for effective creative activity. Perry (1987), for example, talks about creativity being 'primarily a motivational word' (p. 285) and claims that student success in the creative subjects needs a special motivational attitude. Likewise, Dear (2001) argues that it is motivation, rather than ability or socio-political effect, which is 'central to art as a practice' (p. 276).

D. Hocking, *Communicating Creativity*, Communicating in Professions and Organizations, https://doi.org/10.1057/978-1-137-55804-6_5

Studies that examine motivation in the context of art and design education largely focus on evaluating the relative effectiveness of intrinsic or extrinsic motivation. Intrinsic motivation is when a learner is driven by the personal satisfaction of carrying out the creative activity itself, while extrinsic motivation is driven by the need to achieve an externally imposed goal. Most studies conclude that creative success is linked to intrinsic motivation and learner independence (Dineen and Collins 2005; Dineen et al. 2005), and that consequently students should be encouraged 'to pursue lines of inquiry that are personally meaningful and relevant to them' (Reading 2009, p. 116). However, some studies also suggest that extrinsic motivation—driven, for example, by use of regular formative assessment (Hickman 2007), by the milestones set out in learning contracts (Jerrard and Jefsioutine 2006), positive feedback (Dineen et al. 2005), or by rewards that recognise creative achievement (Hickman 2010)—can also increase art and design creativity without necessarily detracting from any intrinsic stimulus. Given the importance attributed to motivation in the art and design educational context, this chapter focuses on the theme of motivation to establish the way in which motivated creativity is discursively facilitated. Importantly, however, the chapter will also examine what happens when the creativity-forming future desires of the students come into conflict with the tutors' own collective expectations of the students' creative activity and as a result, cause the students to be categorised as unmotivated.

Perspectival and Methodological Foci

The first phase of the analysis begins with an ethnographic examination (e.g. Hammersley and Atkinson 2007) of the interview, textual, and interactional data to identify salient themes regarding the tutors' perceptions of the relationship between motivation and student creative activity. The results of this preliminary examination provide the context for a more detailed focus on the social action perspective, which, drawing upon a linguistic ethnographic analysis (Copland and Creese 2015;

Rampton 2007) of unfolding interaction in the brief writing meeting, observes how the tutors jointly conceptualise and make sense of the concept of motivated creativity—and subsequently establish a strategy that will facilitate this conceptualisation.

The tutors' strategy for motivating the students is realised in the semiotic resource perspective, where the interactions of the brief writing meeting are entextualised within the brief in a formal attempt to extrinsically motivate student creative activity. Sung-Yul-Park and Bucholtz (2009) suggest that entextualisation within modern institutional settings is always involved in the construction of authority. This is because it typically involves the act of writing down—usually by those with the power to do so—the transient discourse produced in interaction, thus guaranteeing it a degree of institutional permanence. As a result, this stage of the study primarily employs the analytical resources of systemic functional linguistics (Halliday and Matthiessen 2004) to critically examine the tenor of the motivating strategy in the brief text and its potential effect on student creative agency.

Drawing upon the tools of multimodal (inter)action analysis (Norris 2004, 2007, 2011), the study returns to the social action perspective and examines the casual studio interaction of a tutor and two students. According to Norris, the analysis of non-verbal modes of communication can expand insights gathered from that of the verbal modes, particularly with regard to the identities of the interactants. In this phase of the analysis, it becomes clear that the tutors' conceptualisation of motivated creativity conflicts with the motivating potential of the students' ideal future self. Throughout the various phases of the analysis, and drawing upon the concepts of Membership Categorisation Analysis (e.g. Antaki and Widdicombe 1998; Sacks 1992), attention is also given to the way that the participant's draw upon their normative assumptions (both individually or collectively) to assign themselves and others to certain categories or identities, and how these are made relevant in the context of their interactions. Table 5.1 provides details of the methodological orientations and corresponding analytical tools used to examine the data collected for each of the four perspectives.

Table 5.1 The data analysed and methodological foci for each of the perspectives

Perspective	Data	Methodological orientation	Tools
Semiotic resource perspective	The text of the first assessment criteria of the learning outcomes section of the brief	Textual analysis Ethnography	Lexical choice Repetition Observation of salient themes
	The text of the *critique section,* a component of the brief used in the situated context under analysis	Systemic functional analysis	Mood Transitivity Thematic structure
Social action perspective	Audio recording of the second brief meeting, where four tutors, Anna, Mike, Claire, and Sam, collectively draft the text of the brief	Linguistic ethnography Membership categorisation analysis	Micro analysis of unfolding interaction Categories Category-bound activities and predicates
	Audio and video recordings of casual studio interaction, involving the tutor Anna and two other student participants	Ethnography Multimodal (inter)action analysis	Field notes Observation of salient themes Gaze Gesture Head movement
Participants' perspective	Semi-structured interviews with Claire and Mike	Ethnography	Observation of salient themes in the participants' accounts
Socio-institutional perspective	One-semester focused observation of a studio environment Insider knowledge of tutoring in a studio	Ethnography	Field notes Observation of salient themes in institutional life
	Theoretical and historical literature on motivation in art and design education	Content analysis	Identification of salient themes in relevant theoretical texts

Just Not that Motivated Creatively

In the student brief, the section referred to by the tutors as the *provocation* provides the stimulus for the students' creative work. The type of provocations included in the brief are varied and can include, for example, quotations by artists, extracts from short stories, or lists of key words. In the provocation section of the Binary Opposites brief, students are presented with three direct quotations, each describing the way in which binary oppositions are manifest in a different culture. These are followed by extracts from popular song lyrics that represent the notion of binary opposites. The brief then requires the students to 'develop and explore visual interpretations of contrary conceptual categories'. In his interview, the tutor Mike was asked about the function of the provocation section (Extract 5.1).

Extract 5.1: Interview with the Tutor Mike

→	Mike:	What might be a better idea is to think
		without a provocation what happens?
→	Int:	Right
→	Mike:	And often nothing.
→		It becomes a hiatus or a procrastinating period,
		where students aren't focused
		and haven't got something literally
		to get their teeth into,
		to get them, to get them, moving, to start the process …

Mike's response indicates that the tutors perceive the provocation as crucial for motivating the students' creative practice, and that without the stimulus of the provocation section students would procrastinate (line 5) and no creative activity would take place (line 4). The tutor Claire also refers to the students' lack of motivation (Extract 5.2). In her interview, she describes the students as *just not that motivated creatively* (line 3) and as a result *going through the motions* (line 11). Claire implies that having an *absolute desire* to create (line 5) or being *really excited* (line 9)—qualities absent from all but a few of the students (line 4)—are essential for motivated creativity.

Extract 5.2: Interview with the Tutor Claire

→ Claire: I think it might be a hangover from school.
→ They might be very literal perhaps, but also
→ they're just not that motivated creatively.
→ I find that they don't, very few of them have
→ that absolute desire to be creating,
you know, they seem to, I don't know, it's a very
different sort of mindset, and maybe, it might be
because they haven't really found what is that
→ they want to do and that they're really excited
about, so they're just kind of, you know
→ going through the motions.

Clare appears to relate this lack of motivation with literal creativity (e.g. simply using black and white colours to symbolise issues of race), something that she suggests is learned in secondary school (lines 1–2). In the context of this study, students who develop creative works using literal symbolism are often negatively regarded to be avoiding a more demanding and lengthier process of creative activity, which is seen as involving the continuous exploration of ideas by experimenting with different media, materials, methods, or technical processes. The tutors believe that this latter approach, which they value as requiring an increased level of work (see Chap. 3), will result in less literal and more engaging creative outputs.

While it will be discussed in greater detail in Chaps. 6 and 7, this emphasis placed on the process of exploration through experimentation can be evidenced in the first of three assessment criteria that are included in the brief (Extract 5.3). The assessment criteria have been developed and refined over the years by the tutors, and so are reused in successive student briefs. As a result, they can provide further insights into the tutors' collective conceptualisation of motivated creative activity, as well as Claire's comments in Extract 5.2.

Extract 5.3: Assessment Criterion 1

→ 1. Employs a systematic process of making work,
→ accompanied by processes of visual experimentation
→ and analysis. Uses a variety of media and technical
→ processes appropriate to the work produced. Uses media
→ to explore, develop and communicate ideas/issues being
addressed. Produces work that meets the requirement
of the brief.

In the criterion 1, the value of creative process is emphasised through the foregrounding of the word *process* in line 1, its subsequent repetition in lines 2 and 4, and use of the gerund *making* (line 1), which grammatically emphasises continuity. The types of processes foregrounded include exploration (*explore*) of *ideas/issues* (line 5), and *experimentation* (line 2) of *media* and *technical processes* (lines 3–5). Combined, these statements in the brief criterion metaphorically constitute creative activity in the studio as a repetitive and ongoing process of trial and discovery.

Extract 5.4 reproduces a short interactional episode from the second brief writing meeting where the tutors are discussing the draft of the Binary Opposites brief. This interaction is included here because it corroborates the observation in Extract 5.2 that literal representation is viewed negatively, but also provides evidence that the tutors view literality as a default mode of the students' creative practice. In this extract, the tutors are discussing how students might respond to the provocation of the Binary Opposites brief.

Extract 5.4: Second Brief Writing Meeting

→ Claire: you know they can use a [line from
→ Anna: [mmm mmm
→ Claire: one of the song lyrics
→ o:r the ide:a

5	→		from one of the:se … paragraphs
6	→		as a provocation for the work
8			((*3 seconds of silence*))
9	→		But are they going to <u>think</u>
10	→		that they can pick . <u>fi:ve .</u> [lines of—
11	→	Mike:	[Well the idea was
12	→		not even to pick the five.
13	→	Anna:	nobody's going to [pick anything.
14	→	Mike:	[they're just sort of provocations.
15	→	Claire:	right
16			[okay, alright
17			[((*unintelligible simultaneous speech*))
18	→	Mike:	it's it's <u>just</u> the <u>first one</u>
19	→		you know the . the the Alanis Morrissette so:ng
20	→		talks . they're . they're quite . you know
21	→		they do that
22	→		they do the sort of notion of
23	→	Claire:	mmm
24	→	Mike:	binary opposites in a very a:hh you know . .
25	→		literal way.
26	→	Anna:	yep.
27	→	Claire:	mmm.

In lines 1–10, Claire suggests that the students are likely to select a different individual line from the lyrics and quotations as a provocation for each of their five required works. Mike and Anna reply that the extracts are meant to be read together as a more general stimulus for the students' creative work, rather than as a collection of individual lyrics from which the students pick and represent literally in their work (lines 13–14). However, Mike, regularly pausing as he considers his remarks, does concede (lines 18–22) that contrary to these intentions, students will nevertheless orient towards making work that represents the notion of binary opposites captured in the song lyrics in a *literal way* (lines 24–25). Both Anna (line 26) and Claire (line 27) agree.

The sections below examine the tutors' response to their collective perception that the students' lack motivation in the art and design studio. The discussion begins by firstly examining how the tutors jointly construct, through the ongoing interaction of the brief writing meeting, a discursive strategy to more generally motivate the students. Following that, an extract from informal interaction in the studio demonstrates how a more experimental non-literal type of motivated creativity is encouraged.

Motivation and the 'Crit'

In Extract 5.5 from the second brief writing meeting, the tutors are continuing to draft the Binary Opposites brief. The assessment event facilitated by the brief will commence after the forthcoming mid-semester break. The tutors have agreed that distributing the brief to students before the break will motivate them to carry out some useful preliminary work before they return. The extract begins at the point where the tutors are discussing how they might encourage this to occur.

Extract 5.5: Second Brief Writing Meeting

→	Sam:	we could have
→		a crit first day back.
→		*everybody laughs*
→	Mike:	yeah, I've got that you know
→		[followed by a group critique.
→	Anna:	[some people are going oh.
→	Mike:	well I think it's really good
→		because you'll get
→		you'll get them
→	Anna:	it'll be a really good [start.
→	Mike:	[rea:lly rea:lly
→		[conscientious ones
→	Claire:	[yeah.

→ Anna: yeah [yeah yeah yeah
→ Mike: [who will do something
→ Anna: and then
→ it should make the others go a:w you know
→ I should have got going
→ because some people have gone
→ would have gone overseas
→ and not have worked as much.
→ I know there are a
→ couple of people going overseas
→ and going on holiday.

The tutor Sam introduces the notion of a *crit* on the first day after the mid-semester break (lines 1–2) as a potential way of motivating the students to carry out work over the break. A *crit* or critique refers to an individual studio tutorial where students are asked to dialogue about their work in process. The resultant laughter from the group (line 3), Mike's ironic acknowledgement *I've got that you know* (line 4), his humorous suggestion that the students engage in a group critique immediately after the crit (line 5), and Anna's anticipation of the students' concerns through direct reported speech (line 6), all work to foreground the tutors' collective understanding that this is a devious or underhand motivational strategy. However at line 7, signalled by the discourse marker *well,* Mike begins to reconceptualise the strategy as potentially effective (lines 8, 9, 11, 12, and 15), and constructs the hypothetical group, *conscientious* students (line 12), as positive recipients of the strategy to validate his new position. Successive backchannelling by Anna (lines 10 and 14) and Claire (line 13) shows increasing support for this strategy. Finally, Anna, in a longer and uninterrupted turn (lines 16–24), further rationalises what has now been reconceptualised as a potentially successful motivational strategy by directly reporting the anticipated response of another hypothetical student group—one she envisages will not complete the required work. For Anna, this idle cohort includes students who are abroad for the holiday period, both hypothetical (*would have gone,* line 20) and actual (*have gone,* line 19). By collectively constructing an imagined cohort of students as lacking the motivation for what at this stage is essentially an unspecified amount of work, the tutors have rationalised the 'crit' as an effective strategy for motivating this cohort into creative action.

Extract 5.6 is also from the same brief writing meeting and chronologically follows Extract 5.5. In this extract, a shift in the tutors' strategy to motivate the students is evident.

Extract 5.6: Second Brief Writing Meeting

→ Mike: you can you can critique
→ you ca:n critique
→ you've got ta have something to critique. *laughs*
→ Anna: mmm mmm.
→ Mike: you know uhh
I I think one critique in the in the middle week
is is . su:fficient.
→ Anna: [ah maybe that'll be fine.
→ Claire: [I think . I think it's good
→ Anna: mmm
→ Claire: asking them . to get some work up on the wall.
→ Sam: yeah.
→ Claire: cos it seems to have a very—
→ it seems to be a very kind of mo:tivating thing.
→ Anna: yeah, [otherwi:se—
→ Claire: [cos they can actually see what
→ they have and haven't done
and they get to [see what everyone else has done
→ Anna: [and puts them on the spot a bit.

Beginning at line 1, Mike reappraises the consensus to hold a critique session on the first day back. While emphasising that the critique is in fact possible (signalled through the elongated vowel in line 2), he now speculates that the students will not have completed any work during the break to make it a viable option (lines 1–3). His rationale for this shift now clearly predicates all students as lacking motivation. Following Anna's backchannelling, which facilitates the continuation of his turn, Mike reformulates the critique as needing to occur at a later stage in the project period—a strategy tentatively accepted by Anna and Claire (*maybe that'll be fine*, line 8; *I think it's good*, line 9). Importantly, Claire suggests that this middle-week critique should involve the additional strategy of students putting work produced *up on the wall* (line 11). She justifies this strategy with reference to its motivational function—*a very kind of motivating thing* (line 14). Justification for this 'up on the wall' strategy, and hence the unmotivatedness of the students, is further evidenced through Anna's incomplete turn *otherwise* (line 15), which might be completed as *they won't produce any work*, and Claire's reference to the creative work *they … haven't done* (lines 16–17), where she constructs a hypothetical category of non-existent student work. Similarly Anna's comment that the students will be put *on the spot* (line 19) implies a view that the students need to be humiliated into creative action. It is evident, then, that through the communicative interaction of the brief writing meeting—including the iterative sequential stages of strategy contribution, followed by justification for the strategy—the tutors jointly construct the students as unmotivated, and as a result co-construct their own roles as motivators, and the activities of the studio as designed to motivate.

Motivation and the Brief

Once the interaction of the brief writing meeting has constituted the student cohort as lacking motivation, and as a result has established a strategy—the critique session—as a way to motivate students, the interaction of the meeting moves to a focus on drafting the contents and rhetorical structure of a section in the student brief titled *critique sessions*. Extract 5.7 reproduces two paragraphs from the larger critique sessions section and provides an indication of how the unfolding flow of talk from the brief writing meeting, in particular the belief that students' creativity can be motivated extrinsically, is entextualised into the brief.

Extract 5.7: The Critique Sessions Section

Critique sessions are a common feature of university
study. If you are successful in gaining a place on a
[name of institution] undergraduate programme,
you can expect to make both formal and informal
oral presentations about your work and also critically
engage with the work of your peers. The
[name of programme] critique sessions have been
designed to prepare you for this.
→ Staff will select individual students for the critique
and a small group of students for each
→ 15 minute session. Students will be expected to make
a 3–5 minute oral presentation about their work in a
manner that addresses the brief and the [name of paper]
criteria. All other student members of a critique group
→ will be expected to comment and discuss the work.
→ Be ready for a longer than average day. The critique
→ sessions will begin at 9.15 sharp. Be prepared
→ and be on time.

A functional analysis of the second paragraph in Extract 5.7 reveals that the tutors' strategy to extrinsically motivate the students is clearly manifested through a strong contractual discourse of obligation or necessity, one that diminishes the agency of the students. At the level of interpersonal meaning, this is predominantly constituted through the use of the modulated finite modal *will* (lines 9, 11, 15, and 17), as well as through the passive expansion of the predicator (e.g. *be expected to make/comment/discuss* in lines 11 and 15). In fact the choice of the finite/predicator phrase *will be expected to*, used twice in this paragraph (lines 11 and 15), involves two consecutive forms of high-level modulation. Furthermore, the passive form found in this structure further strengthens the degree of obligation conveyed by potentially constructing the directives as incontestable regulations of the wider institution, rather than originating from the local context of the tutors. It should also be pointed out that the verb clause *will be expected to* is frequently found in legal or contractual genres (Bhatia et al. 2008; Orts Llopis 2009). The strong degree of obligation conveyed by the tutors can also be further seen in the imperatives, *be ready, be prepared*, and *be on time* (lines 16–18). The recurring use of circumstantial adjuncts, for example, *for a longer than average day* or *at 9.15 sharp* (lines 16–17), is also notable, in that the tutors are making demands on the circumstances of the students regarding the time, manner, and matter of their interactions.

Motivation and Casual Studio Interaction

Extract 5.8 demonstrates how motivated creativity, viewed as involving the continuous exploration of ideas by experimenting with different media and materials, is also facilitated through interaction in the studio. The extract focuses on an unscheduled communicative episode between Anna and student 9. Anna has noticed that student 9 has been continually stirring plaster in a bucket, a process that she may have evaluated as resembling the *going through the motions* attribute of the unmotivated student, as described by Claire in Extract 5.2.

Extract 5.8: Casual Studio Interaction

→ Anna: you could think about other sorts of things ↑
→ you know you might sort of ro:ll it out, you know
→ with a ro(h)lling pin
→ S9: yeah
→ Anna: and you know sort of experiment with . sort of
→ with rolling it up in some newspaper
→ and uh . maybe adding some some some paint to it
and you know.
→ go go and do some experimental things especially
you could take some of th- take some of them home
→ and you know maybe set up a little bit of a

→ a laboratory at home and you know
→ were you planning to do work at home.
→ S9: yeah yeah [during the holidays.
→ S8: [yeah yeah during the holidays.
→ Anna: yeah yeah yeah

Anna frames the topic for the interactional episode by stating that student 9 *think about other sorts of things* (line 1) that she could do. Anna then draws upon the discourse of creativity as experimentation to identify a number of other processes that the student might consider applying to the plaster, *roll it out … with a rolling pin* (lines 2–3), *rolling it up in some newspaper* (line 6), and *adding some paint to it* (line 7). She explicitly characterises these processes as experimental, for example, *sort of experiment with* (line 5), *go and do some experimental things* (line 9) and *set up a little bit of a laboratory at home* (line 11–12)—the latter evoking a metaphor of experimental science. Interestingly, Anna's earlier categorisation from Extract 5.5 (lines 18–24) of motivated students as those who continue with their creative activities outside normal studio hours is reproduced in the final lines of Extract 5.8, where she makes the suggestion that student 9 should work on her experimental processes *at home* (line 13)—a concern subsequently emphasised by an interrogative that seeks to confirm whether this will occur (line 14). Through the following enthusiastic affirmative responses and overlapping repetition of *during the holidays* (lines 14 and 15) both students project the motivated personas expected by Anna.

As indicated in the introduction to this chapter, art and design educational studies view motivation as a central requirement for student creative practice. Hence, it is not surprising that an important role of art and design tutors involves developing strategies to motivate students who are often seen as exhibiting a lack of intrinsic motivation. However, using multimodal (inter)action analysis (Norris 2004, 2007, 2011), the next section reveals that students can in fact be motivated, but in a way that relates more to their future dreams and desires as creative professionals, than to the more immediate concerns of the university art and design studio.

Motivation and the Ideal Future Self

The following extract and figures involve an episode of casual studio interaction that occurred just prior to Extract 5.8 above. As indicated previously, the focus of casual studio interaction is not always specifically on the students' creative work, and may involve a discussion of general matters related to art and design. Nevertheless, an analysis of such interaction can provide further insights into the nature of motivation in the art and design studio.

The interactional episode analysed largely involves student 8 discussing a building in the central city, which she imagines owning as a future art studio and gallery space. It commences with the student stating, *what I want like, this is my dream, my absolute dream, my absolute dream.* Figure 5.1 provides a visual reproduction of the (inter)action that takes place as this is uttered by student 8. The use of the desiderative *want*, the lexical repetition of the noun *dream*, which is collocated twice with the intensifier *absolute*, construes a strong discourse of desire. At the same time, the student's gaze is directed upwards towards the ceiling, potentially representing a hypothetical engagement with her desired future world. In contrast, the tutor Anna maintains her gaze at student 8, while student 9 focuses on her creative work at hand, stirring plaster in a bucket.

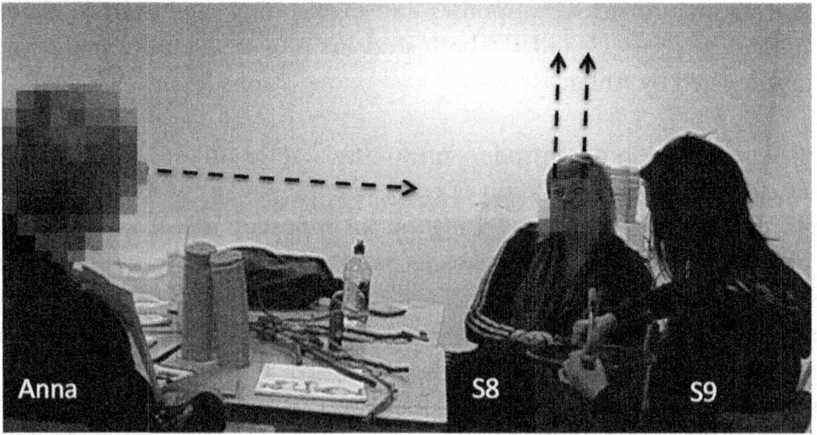

Fig. 5.1 Casual studio interaction

In the interaction that follows this opening utterance, student 8 predominantly discusses the ways in which she would like to renovate and organise the gallery space. Extract 5.9 contains a transcription of the verbal and other modes occurring in this sequence, following the conventions of Norris (2004). Importantly, this involves student 8 making accompanying 'iconic gestures' (p. 29) that visually represent what she communicates verbally (lines 4, 10, 14–16).

Extract 5.9: Casual Studio Interaction

1	→	S8:	Yeah, well I want that and
2			*brushes hair back with right hand*
3	→		I want to knock the wall in between, so [it's
4	→		*gestures from left to right with right hand*
5			*gazes towards Anna*
6	→	Anna:	[ye:(hh)ah
7	→		*nods twice*
8	→	S8:	a roundabout walk in gallery.
10	→		*makes a motion of 3 sides of a square in front of body*
11	→	Anna:	ye:ah
12			*nods twice*
13	→	S8:	and then you go straight upstairs to like my studios
14	→		*makes vertical movement with right hand*
15	→		*gazes upwards into space*
16	→		*gestures horizontally with right hand*
17			*twitches head*
18			and then the following floor would be like
19			*redirects gaze to Anna*
20			you and my design friend's and like our like little–
21			*brushes hair back with hands*
22	→	Anna:	*nods twice*
23	→	S8:	and then . [I want to have
24			*gazes at water bottle*
25			*fidgets with water bottle*
26	→	Anna:	[that would be s:o gre:at.
27	→	S8:	and I want to have that gallery space like
28			*fidgets with something on desk*

gazes at Anna
fidgets with water bottle
gazes at water bottle
and use it as a gallery space
gazes at Anna

Of note in this interaction, and as discussed in Chap. 4, is the students' repetitive use of the desiderative *want* (lines 1, 3, 23, and 27), which further emphasises the students' desire. Moreover, while the tutor, Anna, verbally embraces the student's visions (*Yeah*, lines 6 and 11; *That would be so great*, line 26) or simply nods (lines 7 and 22) to indicate attention, her gaze remains firmly fixed on student 8 and the present reality of the art and design studio context.

To compliment this written transcription, Fig. 5.2 provides a visual reproduction of the (inter)action that takes place between lines 13–16. As the student states *and then you go straight up to like my studios*, she first makes the vertical movement of going upstairs and then the horizontal movement of an upper floor. Again her gaze is directed towards the ceiling, imagining her ideal future world.

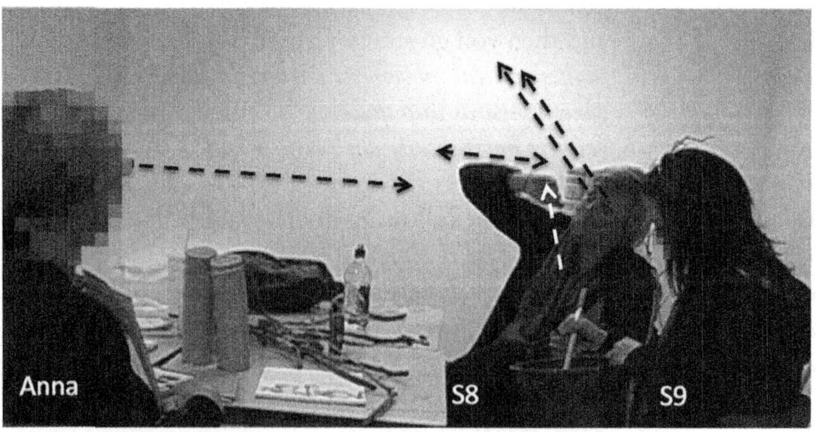

Fig. 5.2 Casual studio interaction

The motivation research of Ushioda (2009) and Dörnyei and Ushioda (2011) can perhaps offer some useful insights into the results of this multimodal analysis. Their conceptualisation of motivation attempts to capture the dynamic and mutually constitutive nature of the relationship between motivation, situated context, and self. Central to this conceptualisation is Markus and Nurius' (1986) concept of the *possible self*, which Dörnyei and Ushioda (2011) describe as 'visions of the self in a future state', representing 'individual's ideas of what they *might* become, what they *would like* to become, and what they are *afraid of* becoming' (p. 80, original italics). Importantly, they suggest that an individual's conception of their possible self is more than a simple contemplation of their future desires or wishes. It involves 'tangible *images* and *senses*' (p. 81, original italics). These are 'represented in the same imaginary and semantic way as the here-and-now self … they are a *reality* for the individual—people can 'see' and 'hear' a possible self' (p. 81, original italics).

Hence, it could be suggested that throughout the interactional episode transcribed in Extract 5.9, as student 8 expresses her future dreams or desires as a professional artist and gallery owner, she employs a combination of interactional modes, including gaze and gesture, to help conceptualise the hypothetical future space of the gallery as a 'tangible' (Dörnyei and Ushioda 2011, p. 81) phenomenon. Referring specifically to the educational context, Hadfield and Dörnyei (2013) point out that the construction of the ideal future self is inextricably linked to strategies of motivation, and that it is through the capacity to actualise their ideal future self in the here and now that a student is *motivated* to carry out the action necessary to achieve their future desires or wishes:

> … one type of possible self, the ideal self, appears to be a particularly useful concept, referring to the characteristics that someone would ideally like to possess. It includes our hopes, aspirations and wishes—that is, our dreams. It requires little justification that if someone has a powerful ideal self—for example a student envisions him/herself as a successful businessman or scholar—this self-image can have considerable motivational power, because we would like to bridge the gap between our actual and ideal selves. (Hadfield and Dörnyei 2013, p. 2)

Concluding Comments

Through the interaction that takes place in the brief writing meeting, the tutors collectively construct the students' as unmotivated, and as a result develop a motivating strategy that emerges as the critique sessions section in the brief. As a result, the structural and lexico-grammatical qualities of the brief have as much to do with motivating the students and constituting the nature of their creative identities, as they do with the more traditional role of the brief as 'a written description of a project that requires some form of design' (Phillips 2004, p. 1). The perceived nature of student motivation is also associated with a particular twentieth-century discourse of creative activity—that is, the exploration of ideas by experimenting with different media and technical processes. Other types of creative activity, such as the literal interpretation of ideas, are regarded as lacking motivated creativity. Furthermore, and following the work of Ushioda (2009) and Dörnyei and Ushioda (2011), who link motivation to desire through the concept of the possible self, the analysis of the multimodal (inter)actional data provides evidence that students do position themselves as motivated, but in a way that relates to their future identities as members of the cultural field, for example, as gallery owners, curators, or exhibiters of creative work. The intrinsic potential of the students' ideal future selves is perhaps overlooked by the tutors in their well-meaning attempts to facilitate a particular type of institutionally expected motivated creativity.

Interestingly, Webster (2003) links the perceived lack of student motivation observed by studio tutors in this study and in other similar contexts as related to what she refers to as the '"master-pupil" relationship' (p. 105). She argues that this relationship emerged in art and design education due to the institutional belief that the most effective pedagogical model, and one probably influenced by the nineteenth-century atelier system of the École des Beaux Arts in Paris, involves the employment of skilled professionals who legitimate the creative work of students through the setting of the studio tutorial. Nevertheless, Webster finds that tutors regularly find the use of tutorials frustrating and unproductive. However, when questioned:

> … tutors tended to blame students for their lack of motivation, lack of knowledge or lack of suitable skills. In contrast, tutors talked about positive tutorial experiences having occurred when the student was well motivated, had well-developed knowledge and skills, where teacher and student were thinking 'in the same plane', and when the student listened and was responsive to teacher prompts. (Webster 2003, p. 107)

The point that tutors' perceptions of students' motivation are fundamentally tied to the tutors' own perceptions of creative practice is implied here by Webster (2003) through her suggestion that motivation was only believed to be occurring by the tutors when students were perceived to be thinking 'in the same plane' (p. 107) as the tutors.

To conclude, the key points to emerge from this chapter demonstrate that creative motivation, like many other aspects of creativity, is discursively constructed, historically situated, and as discussed by Webster (2003), linked to relationships of power. Viewed as such, individuals and groups arguably structure their understanding of motivated creativity in different ways according to their particular habitus (Bourdieu 1993), their position within the cultural field (including cultural institutions), and how it is accounted for within any particular interactional moment. The next chapter will further investigate the focal theme of exploration, a recurring and prominent concept throughout this chapter.

References

Antaki, C., & Widdicombe, S. (1998). Identity as an achievement and as a tool. In C. Antaki & S. Widdicombe (Eds.), *Identities in talk* (pp. 1–14). London, UK: Sage Publications.

Bhatia, V. K., Candlin, C. N., & Engberg, J. (Eds.). (2008). *Legal discourse across cultures and systems*. Aberdeen, Hong Kong: Hong Kong University Press.

Bourdieu, P. (1993). *The field of cultural production: Essays on art and literature*. New York, NY: Columbia University Press.

Copland, F., & Creese, A. (Eds.). (2015). *Linguistic Ethnography: Collecting, analysing and presenting data*. London, UK: Sage.

Dear, J. (2001). Motivation and meaning in contemporary art: From Tate Modern to the primary school classroom. *Journal of Art and Design Education, 20*(3), 274–283.

Dineen, R., & Collins, E. (2005). Killing the goose: Conflicts between pedagogy and politics in the delivery of a creative education. *Journal of Art and Design Education, 24*(1), 43–52.

Dineen, R., Samuel, E., & Livesey, K. (2005). The promotion of creativity in learners: Theory and practice. *Art, Design and Communication in Higher Education, 4*(3), 155–172.

Dörnyei, Z., & Ushioda, E. (2011). *Teaching and researching motivation*. Harlow, UK: Pearson.

Hadfield, J., & Dörnyei, Z. (2013). *Motivating learning*. Harlow, UK: Longman.

Halliday, M. A. K., & Matthiessen, C. M. I. M. (2004). *An introduction to functional grammar* (3rd ed.). London, UK: Arnold.

Hammersley, M., & Atkinson, P. (2007). *Ethnography: Principles in practice* (3rd ed.). London, UK: Routledge.

Hickman, R. (2007). (In defence of) whippet-fancying and other vices: Re-evaluating assessment in art and design. In T. Rayment (Ed.), *The problem of assessment in art and design* (pp. 85–88). Bristol, UK: Intellect.

Hickman, R. (2010). *Why we make art: And why it is taught*. Bristol, UK: Intellect.

Jerrard, R., & Jefsioutine, M. (2006). Reflections on using online contracts for work-based learning and teaching in art and design. *Art, Design & Communication in Higher Education, 5*(1), 55–69.

Markus, H., & Nurius, P. (1986). Possible selves. *American Psychologist, 41*(9), 954–969.

Norris, S. (2004). *Analyzing multimodal interaction: A methodological framework*. New York, NY: Routledge.

Norris, S. (2007). The micropolitics of personal national and ethnicity identity. *Discourse & Society, 18*(5), 653–674.

Norris, S. (2011). *Identity in (inter)action: Introducing multimodal (inter)action analysis*. New York, NY: De Gruyter Mouton.

Orts Llopis, M. A. (2009). Legal genres in English and Spanish: Some attempts of analysis. *Ibérica, 18*, 109–130.

Perry, L. (1987). The educational value of creativity. *Journal of Art and Design Education, 6*(3), 285–296.

Phillips, P. L. (2004). *Creating the perfect design brief.* New York, NY: Allworth Press.

Rampton, B. (2007). Neo-Hymesian linguistic ethnography in the United Kingdom. *Journal of Sociolinguistics, 11*(5), 584–607.

Reading, C. (2009). Sources of inspiration: How design students learn from museum collections and other sources of inspiration. *Art, Design & Communication in Higher Education, 8*(2), 109–121.

Sacks, H. (1992). *Lectures on conversation: volumes I and II.* Oxford and London: Blackwell.

Sung-Yul Park, J., & Bucholtz, M. (2009). Introduction. Public transcripts: Entextualization and linguistic representation in institutional contexts. *Text and Talk, 29*(5), 485–502.

Ushioda, E. (2009). A person-in-context relational view of emergent motivation, self and identity. In Z. Dörnyei & E. Ushioda (Eds.), *Motivation, language identity and the L2 self* (pp. 215–228). Bristol, UK: Multilingual Matters.

Webster, H. (2003). Facilitating critically reflective learning: Excavating the role of the design tutor in architectural education. *Art, Design & Communication in Higher Education, 2*(3), 101–111.

6

Exploration

Introduction

In the previous chapter, it was observed that the tutors in this study associate motivated creativity with a particular type of activity, notably, the exploration of ideas through experimentation with different media, materials, methods, or technical processes. This chapter focuses more closely on the discourse of exploration and its role in the facilitation of creativity activity in the university art and design studio, and in doing so, also examines the wider socio-historical contexts in which this creativity as exploration discourse emerged. Of course, the view that creative activity primarily involves the process of exploration is not limited to the situated context of this study, and on further examination it can be identified as constituting the creative experience, practices, and values of many contemporary Western artists and designers. A selection of quotations attributed to contemporary artists provides evidence for this view.

Extracts 6.1–6.6: Artists' Quotations

Ex. 6.1: Joseph Plaskett: All that is happening in art is part of a process of exploration and discovery.

D. Hocking, *Communicating Creativity*, Communicating in Professions and Organizations, https://doi.org/10.1057/978-1-137-55804-6_6

Ex. 6.2: Tom Francesconi: I am mindful to allow for the joy of exploration and discovery within the framework of each of my works.

Ex. 6.3: Prunella Clough: Each painting is an exploration in an unknown country.

Ex. 6.4: Justin Beckett: The life of an artist is a continuous journey, the path long and never ending.

Ex. 6.5: Paul Foxton: You can accelerate your development by giving yourself a fresh set of challenges, or the same set viewed from a different angle, every day. Explore a different path—if it's a dead end, explore another.

Ex. 6.6: C. W. Mundy: An artist has to be a little like Lewis and Clark, always exploring in new, uncharted directions.

The description of art and design creativity as a process of exploration involves the deployment of *metaphor*, described by Burke (1969) as 'a device for seeing something *in terms of* something else' (p. 503, original italics). Such cross-mapping is evident in the way that images of discovery (Extracts 6.1 and 6.2), unknown countries (Extract 6.3), continuous journeys and never-ending paths (Extract 6.4), dead ends (Extract 6.5), and uncharted directions (Extract 6.6) are used by the artists in the quotations above to describe their creative practices. More recent theories of metaphor, however, suggest that metaphors do more than simply describe a particular process or domain in terms of another. Conceptual metaphor theory (Lakoff and Johnson 1980), for example, holds the view that generalised conceptual metaphors function at the level of thought to structure our knowledge and experience. It argues that metaphorical expressions represent the fixed and stable cognitive mappings between a literal domain (e.g. explorer) and a target domain (e.g. artist) and that such mappings are manifestations of our underlying conceptual systems and motivated by pre-linguistic image schemas. Charteris-Black (2004) extends the conceptual metaphor theory of Lakoff and Johnson by focusing on the more pragmatic, and therefore contextualised, factors of metaphor use. He argues that metaphors can be selectively deployed to arouse emotions and influence opinions, and that a strategic use of metaphor for persuasive effect can lead to the emergence of new conceptual frameworks, potentially playing a role in the development of ideology.

Accordingly, Charteris-Black examines metaphor use in the discourse of politics, press reporting, and religion 'to reveal the covert (and possibly unconscious) intentions of language users' (Charteris-Black 2004, p. 34).

More recently, Cameron (2007, 2010a) and Deignan (2005) have established what they refer to as a discourse dynamics approach to the understanding and analysis of metaphor. This approach focuses on the dynamic use of metaphor in social interaction, and identifies how people use metaphors in interaction to develop and explain ideas, express feelings, or show empathy to one another. Importantly, in the discourse dynamics approach, the deployment of metaphors is seen as influenced less by sets of pre-existing conceptual mappings, and more by the circumstances of the particular discourse environment, the personal histories of participants, as well as their membership of various socio-cultural groups. As a result, there are numerous reasons why metaphors come to be deployed in instances of spontaneous interaction, for instance, as a playful attempt to verbalise a particular idea, or as a conventional expression or formulae connected with a particular context. However, whether newly emerging in unfolding social interaction, or familiar and conventionalised, according to Cameron the analysis of metaphor can 'tell us something about how people are thinking, can indicate socio-cultural conventions that people are tied into or that they may be rejecting, and can reveal something of speakers' emotions, attitudes and values' (Cameron 2010b, p. 7).

Perspectival and Methodological Foci

The chapter begins with a focus on the participants' perspective and involves an examination of metaphors occurring in the interviews with students and tutors as they discuss the nature of creative activity in the contemporary university studio context. This initial phase draws upon Cameron's (2010a) discourse dynamics approach, which is concerned with identifying and evaluating the deployment of what she refers to as *systematic metaphors* in the discourses of those engaged in either social interaction, or in lengthy structured participant interviews. A systematic metaphor classifies a set of metaphor vehicles, including phrases and individual words, which are all connected to the same topic. Systematic metaphors are usually identified in the following way. Firstly, linguistic metaphors appearing in the data are grouped according to the basic meanings of their vehicle terms; for instance, those relating to the general theme of exploration.[1] This more general grouping is then further examined to find smaller subsets of semantically connected vehicles, each of which is provided with a classifying label. An example is the systematic metaphor *THE BRIEF IS A GUIDE MAP FOR THE STUDENTS' JOURNEY OF EXPLORATION*. This component of the analysis follows the convention of using italicised small caps when referring to systematic metaphors. Metaphor vehicles relevant to the discussion will also be underlined in extracts.

Taking into consideration Cameron's (2007) view that conventionalised metaphors can be accounted for as stabilised forms emerging from prior language use, the second phase of the analysis focuses on the interdiscursive relations between the semiotic resource and socio-historical perspectives to examine how the discourses, values, and beliefs revealed through the metaphorical analysis have their foundations in the social, institutional, and linguistic practices of the past (see also Layder 1993). The principal focus of this analytical phase involves a metaphor analysis of the textual resources of the Bauhaus, a pioneering German school of art and design established in 1919, whose curriculum and teaching methods are widely recognised as transforming the teaching of visual arts and design education throughout the West. Furthermore, and as support, the metaphors found in the published writings and personal correspondence of two early twentieth-century artists will also be examined. In the final analytical phase for Chap. 6, the historical source of the exploration metaphor will be further investigated by identifying salient themes in secondary data discussing the great nineteenth-century journeys of exploration. These great explorations are viewed as shaping the scientific, aesthetic, literary, economic, religious, and political life of early modernism. Informed by a discourse-historical approach (Wodak 2001), issues of intertextuality and interdiscursivity will play a central role in the second and third phases of the analysis in this chapter (see also Fairclough 1992; Candlin 2006). Finally, in places, the unfolding analysis will seek support through the corpus analysis of reference corpora. The reference corpora provide comparative information about the wider historical and contemporary use of certain words found to be of interest in the context of this study. Table 6.1 indicates the methodological resources used in this chapter with respect to the data collected from the different perspectives.

Table 6.1 The data analysed and methodological focus for each of the perspectives

Perspective	Data	Methodological Orientation	Tools
Semiotic resource perspective	The text of the Binary Opposites brief. The Corpus of Historical American English (COHA) The Corpus of Contemporary American English (COCA) The British National Corpus (BNC)	Metaphor analysis Corpus analysis	Observation of metaphor vehicles Collocation analysis Frequency analysis
Social action perspective	N/A	N/A	N/A
Participants' perspective	Semi-structured interviews with tutors and students.	Metaphor analysis	Observation and categorisation of metaphor vehicles into systematic metaphors
Socio-historical perspective	Published texts containing interviews with artists/designers, and personal accounts of their practices. Published documents from the Bauhaus school of art and design. Secondary data/ published literature on the great nineteenth-century explorations of Africa.	Metaphor analysis Discourse-historical analysis	Observation of emergent metaphor vehicles. An account of wider socio-political and historical contexts to identify how these have shaped the phenomena and context under analysis Thematic analysis Interdiscursivity

Systematic Metaphors in Accounts of Tutors and Students

An analysis of the interview data revealed that three systematic metaphors within the *EXPLORATION* grouping were frequently deployed by the tutors and students to describe creative activity in the studio context. These are:

THE STUDENTS' CREATIVE ACTIVITIES INVOLVE A JOURNEY OF EXPLORATION
THE BRIEF IS A GUIDE MAP FOR THE STUDENTS' JOURNEY OF EXPLORATION
THE TUTORS ARE GUIDES IN THE STUDENTS' JOURNEY OF EXPLORATION.

Another systematic metaphor, *THE STUDENTS' CREATIVE ACTIVITIES ARE AN EXPERIMENT*, was also added to this group. This is because not only are the concepts of exploration and experimentation closely linked in the interactions and accounts of both the students and tutors (see Chap. 5), but also because they are closely associated in discourses of both science and nineteenth-century exploration. Each of these systematic metaphors will be discussed in turn, first, by demonstrating how they are deployed by the participants, and then by examining what they reveal about the participants' attitudes and values towards student creative activity. It is important to reiterate that the focus on systematic metaphors simply provides a convenient way to describe larger sets of linguistic metaphors.

This systematic metaphor *THE STUDENTS' CREATIVE ACTIVITIES INVOLVE A JOURNEY OF EXPLORATION* is the most prominent in the interview data, and is realised by each of the tutors in different ways.

Extracts 6.7–6.12: Interview with the Tutor Anna

Ex. 6.7: … if they have <u>explored</u> lots of <u>different ways</u> of making art lots of strategies I think particularly in graphic design all <u>areas</u> um then, then that <u>puts</u> them in a <u>better position</u> for next year. This is a good year for <u>exploring</u> those kinds of things, yeah.

Ex. 6.8: … I think that how we teach and certainly with product design <u>next door</u> where they, they have really interesting briefs, they <u>get</u> students to <u>go to new environments.</u>

Ex. 6.9: ... and then of course um that comes into the end point which would be um an assessment requirement as well ...

Ex. 6.10: ... for some of those people just exploring and experimenting is giving them a chance to be creative.

Ex. 6.11: ... often the starting point can be quite hard for students they actually sort of need to um I guess also find their own way.

Ex. 6.12: ...it's been quite an interesting thing to explore because it actually sort of goes beyond just, um, putting things into kind of categories ...

The tutor, Anna, deploys *THE STUDENTS' CREATIVE ACTIVITIES INVOLVE A JOURNEY OF EXPLORATION* metaphors to characterise the creative activity of the students as something that involves *exploring different ways* or *areas*, so that the student might reach a *better position* (Extract 6.7), *new environments* (Extract 6.8), or *end point* (Extract 6.9). In Extract 6.10, Anna clearly views exploration and experimentation as leading to creativity; however, she makes the point that there is only a *chance* it might be reached, perhaps evoking a belief that not all metaphorical journeys of exploration will guarantee a creative outcome. In extract 6.11, Anna characterises the *starting point* of the metaphorical journey as a difficult one from which students need to *find their own way*, implying firstly that the students are responsible for their own creative practices, and secondly that the focus of their individual creative activities is established as the semester progresses. This latter view is supported by Anna's comment that the journey might involve the exploration of less familiar areas (*goes beyond*, extract 6.12).

Extracts 6.13–6.15: Interview with the Tutor Claire

Ex. 6.13: I suppose as tutors we think about, um, what we would like the students to be exploring.

Ex. 6.14: ... and particularly with the assessment requirements and make sure that they're on track.

Ex. 6.15: ...because they haven't really found what is that they want to do ...

The tutor Claire deploys *THE STUDENTS' CREATIVE ACTIVITIES INVOLVE A JOURNEY OF EXPLORATION* metaphors to show that, in contrast to Anna, she constitutes the direction of the students' explorations as fundamentally established by the tutors. This can be seen in her comments *what we would like the students to be exploring* (Extract 6.13) and *make sure that they're on track* (Extract 6.14). Claire implies that providing directions is necessary because students are often unaware of what they are attempting to find in the journey (Extract 6.15), perhaps supporting Anna's comments in Extract 6.11 above.

Extracts 6.16–6.18: Interview with the Tutor Mike

Ex. 6.16: But in the second one we decided, because it went sort of nowhere, and what we felt was students were narrowing too quickly, you know, they were exploring too narrow in the first brief.

Ex. 6.17: Well, as, as I said before, I think it's nice if there are, if the student has the possibility to go wider and not be too diagnostically tied-down.

Ex. 6.18: I think that where, more, more dictates this end, as opposed to this end. Like this end can be very, you know ah, the universe, but this end ((*Mike is referring to a C- grade here*)) has to be you know, Springdale, or Point Avon.

Like Anna, the tutor Mike deploys *THE STUDENTS' CREATIVE ACTIVITIES INVOLVE A JOURNEY OF EXPLORATION* metaphors to characterise the students' creative process as involving a number of different possible paths, including those that fail to lead the students to a potential destination (*it went sort of nowhere,* Extract 6.16). Mike describes these less creatively productive paths or destinations as *narrow* (Extract 6.16), because they limit exploratory activity, and describes those that are potentially more creatively productive as *wider* (Extract 6.17), because they perhaps maximise exploratory activity and the possibility of a suitable destination being found. For Mike, the most appropriate destination is one that is metaphorically located some distance away from the students' starting point. This view can be seen in Extract 6.18, where he positively characterises the student's journey of exploration as having the potential to *end* anywhere in *the universe,* or less positively to end in areas local to the context of the study. Mike is most likely using the metaphor of a long explorative journey to conceptualise a positive creative outcome as one that does not occur immediately, and is the result of a sustained process of development. Reinforcing the discussion in Chap. 4, Mike is also concerned that a student should not be overly constrained or *tied down* (Extracts 6.17) as this could prevent the potential for wider exploration.

Extract 6.19–6.20: Interview with Student 3

Ex. 6.19: … we were given the brief which tells us to explore different avenues …

Ex. 6.20: … when I read a brief, I like to have instructions of what we should explore.

The' students also regularly deploy *THE STUDENTS' CREATIVE ACTIVITIES INVOLVE A JOURNEY OF EXPLORATION* metaphors. In Extract 6.19, for example, student 3 characterises the scope of the journey of exploration as simply involving different *avenues.* This characterisation of student creativity sits in contrast to Mike's focus on the *universe* (Extract 6.18), or Anna's area *beyond* (Extract 6.12), perhaps implying that the student has less challenging expectations of the creative process than the tutors. Student 3's deployment of the metaphor vehicles, *tells* (Extract 6.19) and *instructions* (Extract 6.20), as well as the modal *should* (Extract 6.20) suggests he views the journey of exploration as strongly directed by the brief.

Interestingly, the verb *explore* occurs 41 times in the student brief corpus, *exploration* occurs 23 times, and the gerund *exploring* occurs 10 times. A comparison of the relative frequencies of these words in the student brief corpus and in the interview data collected for this study with the British National Corpus (Davies 2004) and the Corpus of Contemporary American English (Davies 2008) can be seen in Table 6.2. If their frequencies are converted into a value per million words to make the comparison easier, it is clear that *explore, exploration,* and *exploring* occur significantly more often in the data collected for this study than they do in the two reference corpora. Of course, many of the uses of these cognates in the reference corpora are literal, rather than metaphoric.

Table 6.2 Comparison of word frequency

	Student brief corpus		Interview Data		COCA		BNC	
Metaphor	Freq.	Freq. per million words	Freq.	Freq. per million words	Freq.	Freq. per million words	Freq.	Freq. per million words
explore	41	1120.07	13	603.2	12,601	29.6	2227	22.27
exploration	23	628.33	1	46.4	7037	16.56	1528	15.28
exploring	10	273.19	5	232	6206	14.60	1022	10.22

The interview data also includes a number of linguistic metaphors that can be grouped as *THE TUTORS ARE GUIDES IN THE JOURNEY OF EXPLORATION*.

Extracts 6.21–6.23: Interview with the Tutor Claire

Ex. 6.21: ... we're there hopefully just to harness something for them and help guide them in an interesting direction.

Ex 6.22: ... we would like the students to be exploring and hopefully can provide, um, a provocation which is going to, um, guide them in the direction we want them to go in.

Ex. 6.23: ... we're trying to encourage students to think and work independently, and so we, rather than, I mean I suppose we're just there to sort of guide and support and hopefully we get to follow their lead a bit.

In her deployment of *THE TUTORS ARE GUIDES IN THE JOURNEY OF EXPLORATION* metaphors, Claire identifies the responsibilities of the tutors as guides. These include guiding the students *in an interesting direction* (Extract 6.21), which she reveals is the direction that the tutors *want them to go in* (Extract 6.22). To achieve this, she believes the tutors need to *harness something* (Extract 6.21) for the students, although the nature of this harnessed phenomenon is never explained. There is also something of an ideological dilemma in the contradiction between Claire's belief that the students should work *independently* (Extract

6.23) or Anna's belief that they *find their own way* (Extracts 6.11) and the role of the tutors as guides. Perhaps, in an acknowledgment of this dilemma, Claire adds that she hopes the students take on a guiding role (*hopefully we get to follow their lead a bit,* Extract 6.23), albeit occasionally.

Extract 6.24: Interview with the Tutor Mike

Mike: … to me it's always, to me, my guiding forces has always been to try and open them up. More than focus them, and, and hopefully give them, you know, okay I could maybe do that, or, or I could explore that.

Mike's deployment of *THE STUDENTS' CREATIVE ACTIVITIES INVOLVE A JOURNEY OF EXPLORATION* metaphors is not unlike that expressed by Claire. In Extract 6.24, Mike views his guiding role as one where he is *opening* students *up,* rather than trying to *focus them.* Here, he is briefly combining a *LENS* metaphor with the *JOURNEY* metaphor, characterising the student as a camera lens that can be adjusted by the tutor to delimit or increase their view of the directions available to explore. He presents his position of power over the students as particularly strong through his suggestion that he has the capacity to *give* students the choices available to them, and through his earlier use of the noun *forces.*

Interviews with the students extend the metaphorisation of the tutors as guides, through the use of linguistic metaphors that characterise the brief as something resembling a guide map. These can be grouped as the systematic metaphor, *THE BRIEF IS A GUIDE MAP FOR THE STUDENTS' JOURNEY OF EXPLORATION.*

Extracts 6.25–6.26: Interview with Student 1

Ex. 6.25: …the brief, I think is really, it's real- it's like a safety guide sort of thing.

Ex. 6.26: [the brief] … sort of guides you back in to it again, rather than you just shooting off in some random direction.

Extract 6.27: Interview with Student 2

Student 2: I think this brief is not really umm guiding on towards our finish, it's kind of just giving us a start point.

Student 1 views the student brief as *safety guide* (Extract 6.25) which ensures that they avoid *shooting off in some random direction* (Extract 6.26), while student 2 characterises the brief as a guide map which is useful for commencing the journey, but which lacks details regarding the destination (Extract 6.27). There is conceivably a metaphoric connection here between this characterisation of the student brief and the explorer's map, as the latter would be unlikely to contain information about the final unknown stages of the explorer's route. The tutors deploy a similar metaphorisation of the brief as guide map, which is restricted to providing initial directions for the journey of exploration.

Extract 6.28: Interview with the Tutor Claire

Claire: ...we use the brief as a means to get them started.

Extract 6.29: Interview with the Tutor Mike

Mike: Well, it gives them, it gives, well the provocation's a starting point,
it gives them ah, I don't know, what would you call it,
it gives them ah, something from which to begin ...

Extract 6.30: Interview with the Tutor Anna

Anna: ... we're going to give you a brief that lets you explore new ideas.

In these extracts, the brief is described as enabling the students to start their journey (*get them started*, Extract 6.28; *starting point,... from which to begin*, Extract 6.29). However, rather than serving as a simple guide map, the tutors' extracts appear to characterise the brief as an authorisation or official license to explore. This characterisation is evidenced in use of metaphor vehicles *gives* (Extract 6.29) and *lets* (Extract 6.30). This metaphorical description of the brief resembles the exploration manuals provided by the Royal Geographical Society for prospective explorers during the nineteenth century, some correspondingly referred to as '"*brief* instructions" for travellers' (Driver 2001, p. 48, citing the Journal of the Royal Geographical Society 1, 1831, p. vi, italics added). A discussion on the connection between the nineteenth-century culture of exploration and the metaphoric conceptualisation of art and design education in the twentieth century will take place later in this chapter.

Finally, a number of linguistic metaphors in the data can be grouped as the systematic metaphor *THE STUDENTS' CREATIVE ACTIVITIES ARE AN EXPERIMENT*.

Extracts 6.31–6.33: Interview with the Tutor Anna

Ex. 6.31: I think in the criteria we <u>talk about,</u> um, <u>exploring</u>, and <u>experimentation</u>.

Ex. 6.32: ...You know, if you look at the criteria, it could be yes, they've done lots of work, and um done some <u>experimentation</u> for that person.

Ex. 6.33: ... I think it's, I think it's possible to teach it or uh, maybe it's possible to <u>set up</u> a <u>situation</u> where creativity can happen, almost like a <u>laboratory</u>.

These are largely deployed by Anna to characterise the students' creative practice as a process of *experimentation* (Extract 6.31–6.32), which can take place in a scientific *laboratory* (Extract 6.33). In the previous chapter, we also saw how Anna attempted to facilitate the creative activities of the students through her demand that the students *do some experimental things* (Chap. 5, Extract 5.8).

This metaphoric conceptualisation of art and design practice as an experiment frequently occurs in the literature. Webster (2003), for example, suggests the conceptualisation of the art and design studio as a laboratory has its basis in the design educational writing of Schön (1985), who developed the laboratory as a paradigm for professional education.

Yeomans (2005), however, states that it has its roots in the foundation or Basic Design courses initiated by art educationalist Harry Thubron (1915–1985) who developed 'an experimental approach to art teaching' (p. 196) in the early 1950s. According to Yeomans (2005), Thubron's Basic Design framework was developed further by Victor Pasmore (1908–1998) and Richard Hamilton (1922–2011) at Newcastle University in 1954. Hamilton, in particular, was interested in developing a foundation design pedagogy that enhanced students' rational and intellectual (rather than emotional) faculties, embraced modern science and technology, but most importantly, eradicated preconception and the propagation of other design styles. Yeomans states that Hamilton's pedagogical approach was 'analytical, looking at various internal processes and procedures in an open-ended and experimental manner which precluded any predetermined outcome' (p. 198). He also suggests that the emphasis on the experimental, rather than on technique, was due to the fact that Pasmore and Hamilton were both practicing artists, as well as educators:

> This drive towards *experimentation* was spearheaded by artists, like Victor Pasmore, who regarded their teaching as a natural extension of their studio researches. The studios were *laboratories* and the spirit in which the teaching was carried out was more important than the content. (Yeomans 2005, p. 209, italics added)

It could be argued, however, that Yeoman overlooks the influence of the wider socio-cultural environment in shaping the increasing scientificity of art and design education. Efland (1990), for example, charts the ways in which science began to shape arts education at the beginning of the twentieth century. Such an influence could be felt, for example, in the values of abstraction and scientific reductionism championed by Victor Pasmore, and the values of rationalism and observation that Hamilton introduced into his teaching.

The following sections examine the emergence of JOURNEY OF EXPLORATION metaphors in the context of art and design education. Of course, it is acknowledged that journey metaphors are highly conventionalised and frequently occur in English (Cameron 2010a), particularly within a range of different educational contexts (e.g. Turner 1998; Cortazzi and Jin

1999; Goatly 2002). Nevertheless, it will be suggested below that a significant discursive shift took place in the early twentieth century, which metaphorically reconceptualised the nature of art and design practice and had a powerful influence on the way in which creative activity is discursively facilitated within the context of the university art and design studio.

The Emergence of the *JOURNEY OF EXPLORATION* Metaphor in Art Education

As indicated in Chap. 2, the discourse-historical approach, with its emphasis on intertextuality and interdiscursivity, provides a conceptual framework for understanding how prior discourses can shape the structures, values, ideological positions, and discursive resources of existing social and institutional practices, such as those found in the university art and design studio. It also aligns with the discourse-dynamics approach to metaphor, which holds the view that speech communities, over what are often long periods of time, develop, share, modify, and eventually conventionalise metaphors through the ongoing spoken and written interactions concerning their particular areas of interest. Taking these views into consideration, the following section seeks to trace the historical emergence of the *JOURNEY OF EXPLORATION* metaphor in art and design education in order to develop additional insights about the values and perspectives expressed in the interview extracts presented above.

Since the time of Athenian culture (450BC), and prior to the early twentieth century, most art education and art practice was limited to three primary functions. The first involved capturing the beauty of nature through accurate observation and the use of technical skill, the second involved developing moral or spiritual character through exposure to the classical works of the past, and the third involved developing drawing skills necessary for vocations in industry (Efland 1990). As a result, art education has historically not been viewed as a process of exploration or discovery, but one where students focused on learning a series of techniques and skills, which allowed them to imitate nature or copy models, objects, and the work of past Masters. At times, there has been some emphasis on creative self-expression, as in nineteenth-century romanticism; however, this was still strongly constrained by the skills, techniques, and stylistic preferences of the educational theorist—for example, Ruskin's famous advocacy of the Gothic style during this period. For Efland (1990), the first noticeable evidence of any shift away from this focus on technique and skill was the foundation programme of the innovative Bauhaus art school in Germany, where an emphasis on exploration was introduced. This was largely the result of applying design-based approaches, developed for working with the many new industrial materials, to a visual arts context. According to Efland, the convergence of design theory and academic art theory, which paved the way for the Bauhaus curriculum, was initially introduced into art educative practices by the art educationalist Arthur Wesley Dow in the early 1900s due to 'an increasing hostility to academic approaches to art that based the study of art in the skills of representational drawing' (Efland 1990, p. 177). However, unlike the later Bauhaus tutors, Dow still had as his central focus the representation of beauty. Efland states that:

> For Dow the purpose of the study of design was to enable the student of art to understand the basis for beauty. From the Bauhaus perspective, Dow's view of beauty would have been regarded as a sentimentalized version of nineteenth-century romanticism. Instead, they saw design as *exploration* to *discover* the basis for vision. The elements of design were fundamental *discoveries* one made through the *investigation* of materials. (Efland 1990, p. 218, italics added)

Due to the relatively similar socio-cultural context experienced across Europe, it is unlikely that the conceptualisation of creativity as discovery and exploration had its genesis solely at the Bauhaus, as Efland states in the previous quote. The private art school of German painter, printer, and photographer Edmund Kesting (1892–1970), for example, was named 'Der Weg' (The way/path), a title that could be argued is a significant entailment of the JOURNEY metaphors discussed earlier. Kesting's school, which was established in Dresden in the same year as the Bauhaus, used the programmatic subtitle, 'Neue Schule für Kunst' (New School for Art), and had a similar educational emphasis to the Bauhaus (Wick 2000). Extracts from a 1926 pamphlet clearly indicate the use of JOURNEY OF EXPLORATION metaphor vehicles:

Extract 6.34: 1926 Pamphlet from Der Weg

1 Every human being travels a different path
2 But all of them should find a single goal.
(…)
3 We summon all who want to explore the experience of creative laws.
(…)
4 Because we walk the path to the human being.
5 Because we walk the path to art.
(cited in Wick 2000, p. 307)

However, due to the important legacy of the Bauhaus, an extensive collection of Bauhaus-related documents remains available for examination. These documents include official Bauhaus correspondence, pamphlets, course descriptors, and the accounts of Bauhaus students and teachers. Together, these provide consistent evidence that JOURNEY OF EXPLORATION metaphors were being increasingly deployed in context of Bauhaus art and design education to constitute a shift from the traditional emphasis on the representation, creation, study, or appreciation of beauty.

As an example, in one of his earliest addresses to students (Extract 6.35), at the 1919 exhibition of student work, Walter Gropius (1883–1969), the director and creator of the Bauhaus, repeatedly deploys JOURNEY OF EXPLORATION metaphor vehicles to convey his future vision for the creative practices of the school.

Extract 6.35: Address to Students of the Staatliche Bauhaus

1 I suggest, that for the time being, we refrain from public
2 exhibitions and work from a new point of departure …
3 for what we need is the courage to accept inner
4 experience, then suddenly a new path will open
5 for the artist. … Some day you will break free of your

own limitations and will know where you have to go. We will encounter surprises, some will make decisions to start anew …
(Gropius 1919, cited in Stein 1980, p. 36)

Among the more commonplace *JOURNEY OF EXPLORATION* metaphor vehicles, such as *point of departure* (line 2) or *path* (line 4), Gropius extends the metaphor to include the entailment of freedom (line 5), which is often equated with the act of leaving on a journey of exploration, and makes reference to the view of the journey as involving an encounter of the unexpected or surprising (line 7). He also refers to the *courage* (line 3) required to commence a journey of exploration, as well as the requirement for a strong self-belief (*accept inner experience*, lines 3–4).

Extract 6.36: Breviary for Bauhaus Members

Art and technology, a new unity! Technology does not need art, but art very much needs technology—example: architecture! They differ in nature; therefore their addition is not possible, but their common creative source must be explored and rediscovered by those who are endeavouring to establish the 'new "idea of building."
(Gropius 1924, cited in Stein 1980, p. 76)

Gropius' 1924 draft of a 'Breviary for Bauhaus Members' (Extract 6.36) is also dominated by *JOURNEY OF EXPLORATION* metaphors (*explored*, line 6; *rediscovered*, line 7), where they are deployed to suggest that the search for a metaphorical creative *source* (line 6, c.f. an explorer's search for the source of a river) will facilitate some new knowledge (*the new idea*, line 8). He positions the context for these explorations *in nature* (line 4).

Other Bauhaus masters' deployed *JOURNEY OF EXPLORATION* metaphors in their descriptions of Bauhaus pedagogy, including those published after the Bauhaus was closed. For example, Johnannes Itten (1888–1967), writing about Bauhaus assignments on colour and textural studies in his book

Design and Form: The Basic Course at the Bauhaus, states, 'A whole new world was discovered ... Manual abilities were discovered and new textures invented. They started a mad tinkering, and their awakened instincts discovered the inexhaustible wealth of textures and their combinations' (Itten 1964, p. 147). In a discussion on the technical aspects of art, Paul Klee's collection of writings, titled *The Thinking Eye*, also makes use vivid and repeated use of the *JOURNEY OF EXPLORATION* metaphor (Extract 6.37):

Extract 6.37: The Thinking Eye

II. Let us develop: let us draw up a typographical plan and take a little journey to the land of better understanding. The first act of movement (line) takes us far beyond the dead point. After a short while we stop to get our breath (interrupted line or, if we stop several times, an articulated line) And now a glance back to see how far we have come. (Klee 1961, p. 76)

As in the extracts provided above, Klee metaphorically identifies the main outcome of the journey of exploration as the development of knowledge (*journey to the land of better understanding*, line 2). However, this initial pedagogical deployment of the metaphor is extended by Klee to simultaneously refer to the process of drawing. For example, *movement* (line 3) metaphorically refers to the physical process of drawing of a line, while a *stop to get our breath* (line 5) refers to a literal gap in the line. Klee's vivid use of *JOURNEY OF EXPLORATION* metaphors to simultaneously constitute two different conceptual domains shows a conscious and strategic use of the metaphor.

Finally, where Bauhaus students reproduced or reformulated the school's pedagogies in their post-Bauhaus teachings positions, *JOURNEY OF EXPLORATION* metaphors are also evident. For example, extracts from a text outlining the teaching method at the Cooper Union Art School where Bauhaus Master Hannes Beckman worked at the time, state: 'experimental exploration of the arts' is 'one of the many methods by which the processes of learning become in reality an exciting adventure and exploration' (cited in Grawe 2000, p. 341). It would also appear that more recently written texts discussing the Bauhaus pedagogical approach deploy a higher incidence of *JOURNEY OF EXPLORATION* metaphors. This increase could indicate some degree of stabilisation of the metaphor in this context, and is perhaps why it is now commonplace for the discourses of exploration and discovery to be associated with the creative activities of the Bauhaus, as seen in the earlier quote by the art historian Efland (1990).

Interestingly, however, there is a noticeable absence of *JOURNEY OF EXPLORATION* metaphors in the official description of the Bauhaus teaching programme in a pamphlet distributed by the school in January 1921 titled 'The statutes of the Staatliche Bauhaus' (Extract 6.38).

Extract 6.38: The Statutes of the Staatliche Bauhaus

2. Form instruction:
a) <u>study</u> of elementary materials;
b) nature <u>study</u>;
c) <u>instruction</u> in design (drawing, painting, modelling, building), <u>study</u> of elementary forms, design of surface, body and space, <u>instruction</u> in composition;
d) technical drawing (<u>instruction</u> in projection and construction drawing) and building of models of all three-dimensional structures (objects of daily use, furniture, rooms, buildings).
3. Supplementary subjects of instruction:
a) <u>study</u> of materials and tools;
b) physical and chemical theory of colour (in connection with rationalized methods of painting);
c) basic elements of bookkeeping, contract making, price calculating;
d) lectures of all areas of art and science of the past and present.
(cited in Stein 1980, p. 45)

What is immediately noticeable in this extract is that the prominent linguistic metaphors are those of *instruction* and *study.* A possible reason for this is that, as a formal descriptor of the Bauhaus teaching programme, the document needed to satisfy the requirements of the educational authorities of the Weimar republic, and as a result, education metaphors typical of such documents at the time were given prominence. However, it could also be argued that before the 1920s, metaphors of instruction and study, rather than exploration, were those most commonly deployed to conceptualise the experience of creative activity, especially when referring to the act of painting or drawing. It is this point which will now be developed further in the next section, by examining the personal accounts of two modernist artists, Vincent van Gogh (1853–1890) and Henri Matisse (1869–1954). These artists have been selected for a number of reasons. Firstly they both produced a comprehensive amount of accessible documents about their creative work, Van Gogh through his letters and Matisse through his published writings and interviews. Secondly, they are both widely perceived as innovative facilitators of change in the arts, and thirdly, the respective periods during which they were practising will provide some clarification into what I believe is a shift from creativity as an educational pursuit, to creativity as a *JOURNEY OF EXPLORATION*.

Metaphors of Study: Prior Conceptualisations of Creativity

In an interview with Léon Degand, Henri Matisse made the often-cited comment that 'an artist is an explorer' (reproduced in Flam 1994, p. 162). The interview took place in 1945, by which time *JOURNEY OF EXPLORATION* metaphors would have sedimented into the discourses of contemporary art and design contexts, as demonstrated in the quotations provided in the introductory section of this chapter. Hence, it is perhaps not surprising that the metaphor was used by the artist at this time. However, Matisse's conceptualisation of art practice was shaped well before the conventionalisation of the metaphor in the art and design context, and an examination of the publication *Matisse on Art* (Flam 1994), which contains a comprehensive collection of the major writings and transcripts of important interviews, shows that the word *explore* is only used twice by Matisse, once in 1945 and once in 1956. Instead, the prevalent metaphor in Matisse's accounts of his creative processes is that *ART IS A STUDY*, a metaphor which is absent from the data collected from the context of the university art and design studio. The word *study* occurs 66 times in Flam's collection of Matisse's writings, interviews, and broadcasts given throughout his career. 10 uses are literal, 18 are used to refer to the study of another artists work, and may or may not be literal, while 38 uses involve the word *study* to metaphorically describe the creative act. For example:

Extracts 6.38–6.41: Metaphoric Uses of *Study* by Matisse (Flam 1994, Italics Added)

Ex. 6.38: One would do a first *study* after the model on the first floor. (p. 56)
Ex. 6.39: A *study* in depth permits my mind to take possession of the subject of my contemplation and to identify myself with it in the ultimate execution of the canvas. (p. 92)
Ex. 6.40: I believe *study* by means of drawing to be essential. (p. 121)
Ex. 6.41: These rebellions led me to *study* separately each element of construction: drawing, colour, values, composition; … (p. 128)

Furthermore, in a preamble to Matisse's essay 'Observations on Painting', Flam suggests that the essay reiterates Matisse's previously stated view 'that great painting is a product of the synthesis between *study* of the past and *study* of nature' (p. 101, italics added).

Like Matisse, the modernist painter Vincent van Gogh is widely viewed by art historians as a ground-breaking artist who played an important role in influencing the early artistic developments of the twentieth century. Van Gogh also left a large collection of correspondence about his evolving art practice, mostly in the form of personal letters to friends and family members, and these provide a further opportunity for examining the historical emergence of the *JOURNEY OF EXPLORATION* metaphor. As Van Gogh's letters were written prior to the period when I believe the emergence of the metaphor in the art and design context took place, one would expect the metaphor to be absent, or at least extremely rare, in his letters.

In the English translations of the 902 letters made freely available through the website of the Van Gogh museum (Jansen et al. 2009), there are only two instances of the verb *explore*. The first occurs in letter 535 (*na sporen*—Dutch) and the second in letter 638 (*exploré*—French). Similarly, there are only two instances of the gerund *exploring*, in letter 353 (*zoeken*—Dutch, to seek out) and in letter 153; the latter referring to something other than Van Gogh's art practice. The past participle *explored* occurs twice in letters 544 and 638, but only in its literal sense, and the noun *exploration* doesn't occur at all. Instead, Van Gogh also prefers to make use of the *STUDY* metaphor when referring to his creative activity of painting or drawing. The word *study* (*etude*—French, or *studie*—Dutch) occurs in 323 letters; although in his early letters this is often used literally in the context of education. Examples of the metaphoric use of study can be seen in letter 805 (written on Friday 20 September 1889), where Van Gogh refers to his 1989 painting of an Olive Grove as a *study* (Extract 6.42). In this letter, the word *study* is also closely collocated with the verbs *teaches* (Extract 6.43) and *learn* (Extract 6.44), which are both semantically related to education.

Extracts 6.42–6.44: Letter 805 by Van Gogh

Ex. 6.42: The olive trees are more in character, just as in the other *study* and I've tried to express the time of day when one sees the green beetles and the cicadas flying in the heat.

Ex. 6.43: … for really I must do more figure work. It's the *study* of the figure that *teaches* one to grasp the essential and to simplify.

Ex. 6.44: I would like to have all of this, at least the etchings and the wood engravings. It's a *study* I need, for I want to *learn*.

A historical corpus analysis can support the view that the use of *JOURNEY OF EXPLORATION* metaphors to conceptualise creative activity is a relatively new phenomenon, by showing that the metaphoric use of *explore* was, in fact, quite rare at the beginning of the twentieth century. To carry out this analysis, the 15 most frequent collocations with *explore* between 1810 and 1920 were identified using the Corpus of Historical American English (Davies 2010). These were compared with the 15 most frequent collocations of the word *explore* from the Corpus of Contemporary American English (Davies 2008) between 1990 and 2011. The Corpus of Historical American English was used for the historical search because it is one of the most accessible historical corpora of English. While it could be argued that it is not representative of European language use, most of the texts of the great European explorers were translated into English and were popular with readers in the United States. Furthermore, journeys of exploration by North Americans were extremely popular during the nineteenth century, many of which were influenced by the values emanating from the British and German explorers. As a result, it could be concluded that the semantic association of the word *explore* would be similar across Western Europe and North America.

A comparison between the most frequent historical collocations on the left hand side of Table 6.3, with the most frequent contemporary collocations on the right hand side of the table, shows that the discourse semantics of *explore* has shifted dramatically between the 1920s and its more recent usage.[2] Between 1810 and 1920, *explore* is mostly used literally and is semantically connected to the exploration of the geographic (*country, interior, island, river, mountains, coast,* etc.). Desiderative process

Table 6.3 A comparison of collocations with *explore*

Corpus of Historical American English Using texts between the years 1810–1920 (total words unknown)			Corpus of Contemporary American English Using texts between the years 1990–2010 (410 million words)		
Rank	Word	Freq.	Rank	Word	Freq.
1	country	46	1	ways	257
2	sent	29	2	further	214
3	interior	17	3	issues	214
4	island	17	4	opportunity	187
5	determined	17	5	options	161
6	river	17	6	possibilities	155
7	expedition	16	7	opportunities	143
8	unknown	16	8	relationship	135
9	recesses	15	9	article	126
10	region	15	10	differences	116
11	desire	14	11	possibility	114
12	regions	12	12	potential	106
13	mountains	12	13	ideas	101
14	eager	11	14	relationships	89
15	coast	11	15	fully	82

verbs (Halliday and Matthiessen 2004) including *determined*, *eager*, and *desire* are also frequent collocations. However, this semantic relationship with geography is absent in more contemporary usage, seen on the right hand side of Table 6.3, and has been replaced with a connection to abstract nouns such as *issues*, *possibilities*, *relationships*, *potential*, *ideas*, and so on. The only possible exception is the item *ways*. However, in contemporary usage *ways* is more likely to be used metaphorically, than in a literal sense.

Interestingly, a number of the 15 most frequent abstract nouns that collocate with *explore* in the contemporary corpus are also found in the texts of the student brief corpus (Extracts 6.45–6.48). These represent the types of themes that inform many contemporary art and design works (i.e. the exploration of ideas, issues, options, possibilities).

Extracts 6.45–6.48: Extracts from the Student Brief Corpus (Italics Added)

Ex. 6.45: Uses a variety of media and processes appropriate to the work produced and uses 2D and 3D media to ***explore***, develop and communicate *ideas/issues* being addressed. (Brief 5)

Ex. 6.46: ***Explore*** visual *possibilities*/concepts (do not jump to one solution immediately ***explore***!) (Brief 34)

Ex. 6.47: What is important is how you ***explore*** various *options* for translating your on site material. (Brief 12)

Ex. 6.48: It is important to ***explore*** the various *ways* in which physical connections can be made between the parts (Brief 15)

I would argue, therefore, that in the 1920s the metaphoric schema shaping the emerging processes of creative exploration at the Bauhaus was most likely motivated by notions of geographic exploration, because, as we see in Table 6.3, exploration was semantically *primed* (Hoey 2005) for geographic association, rather than—as it is now—for the types of abstract nouns listed on the right hand side of Table 6.3. If correct, then it is also likely that certain characteristic values and practices of nineteenth-century journey of exploration discourses would have been recontextualised in the construction of early twentieth-century art and design practice. To examine this proposition further, the following section provides a cursory examination of some of the characteristic values and practices associated with the nineteenth-century journey of exploration.

The Nineteenth-Century Journey of Exploration

It is well documented that a 'culture of exploration' (Driver 2004, p. 73) was prominent throughout Europe in the nineteenth century and became a primary focus of scientific, aesthetic, literary, economic, religious, and political life (e.g. Cruz 2011; Cusack 2008; Driver 2001, 2004; Koivunen 2009; Sachs 2007). A defining characteristic of this culture were the great nineteenth-century explorations of Africa, Australasia, South America, the Arctic, and the Antarctic, which were still very much in the consciousness of the general European public in the early twentieth century. This is largely due to the regular presence of information about the expeditionary ventures of the explorers in the wider media, which according to Henderson (2007), created a celebrity status for many of the explorers. Furthermore, exploration narratives, which mythologised the persona of the explorer and their exploits, were a popular theme of the romantic literature of the time (Cusack 2008; Fulford et al. 2004), and similarly, the travel guide, which had only emerged as a genre during the mid-nineteenth century, developed a wide readership by the early twentieth century (Gasson 2005). The influence of these publications, the emerging technological advances of the late nineteenth and twentieth centuries, as well as the improved knowledge of the world resulting from geographic mapping (Driver 2001), meant that there was a proliferation of travel to exotic destinations.[3] Driver states that by the end of the nineteenth century, a 'modern cult of exploration' (p. 1), had emerged, in which 'the business of the scientific explorer was not always, or easily, distinguished from that of the literary *flâneur*, the missionary, the trader or the imperial pioneer' (p. 2, original italics). It is almost certain, then, that the artists and designers of the time—including those involved with the Bauhaus—would not have escaped the Western obsession with travel and exploration. German travel literature, written by authors such as Gustav Frenssen and Frieda von Bülow, describing their travels to the many German colonies in Africa and the Pacific, was extremely popular and widely read throughout Germany in the nineteenth century (Conrad 2012).[4] The physical and psychological descriptions of these journeys of exploration would have provided a relevant and opportune vocabulary to conceptualise the emerging creative practices responding to the political shifts and industrial advances taking place in Europe in the early twentieth century. Hence, it is not unexpected that Gropius conceptualised the Bauhaus as being '*preoccupied with exploring the territory* that is common to the formal and technical spheres' (Gropius 1965, p. 90, italics added), or that Bauhaus supporter Heinrich König (1889–1966) described the creative products of the Bauhaus workshops as '*attempts to conquer new territory* with new shapes and colors' (König cited in Neumann 1993, p. 128, italics added). The central characteristic values and practices of the nineteenth century of exploration, which I believe are relevant to the metaphorisation of art and design as a journey of exploration, are described in the following four categories.

A Belief in Exploration as a Scientific Pursuit

The concept of scientific discovery was a central tenet of exploration and the role of the explorer. According to Koivunen (2009), 'various scientific objectives' (p. 26) were usually provided as the primary justification for the expeditions of late-nineteenth-century explorers. While the scientific inquiry was often of a geographic or mapping nature, she states that travellers also routinely promised 'to make contributions to many other branches of science, such as zoology, botany, meteorology, linguistics and ethnology' (p. 26). Koivunen cites the notable historian of exploration Roy Bridges, who points out that 'scientific information '… was the most convenient touchstone by which contemporary Europeans could measure an explorer's achievement' (p. 27), and more importantly, 'the pressure to conduct scientific observations was also closely connected with the ways in which journeys of exploration were financed' (p. 28).

In his work on the wanderer in nineteenth-century German literature, Cusack (2008) also identifies a strong connection between science and the notion of the journey of exploration, suggesting that the link has much to do with the romantic ideals prevalent during the period, where science was seen as a complimentary practice to aesthetics. In late nineteenth-century German literature, the wanderer or explorer motif was used 'as a vehicle for the theme of scientific curiosity' (p. 94), where the hero would travel the world 'in restless scientific investigation' (p. 93). Cusack, like others (e.g. Pratt 2008; Reidy et al. 2007; Sachs 2007), suggests that the celebrated Prussian explorer-scientist Alexander von Humbolt was a seminal influence in the nineteenth-century conceptualisation of exploration as inherently related to a belief in the progressive nature of scientific work, and points to von Humbolt's important book *Kosmos*, where his investigative travels are described as 'a contribution to the perfection of human knowledge' (Cusack 2008, p. 86).[5] The metaphoric conceptualisation of art and design education as experimentation, including the use of metaphors alluding to the laboratory, rationalism, objectivity, observation, curiosity, and the creation of new knowledge, is pervasive throughout the data collected for this study.

The Desire to be First

In his discussion of the psychology of the great nineteenth-century explorers, McLynn (1993) argues that that a desire to be the first to reach unchartered territory was 'clearly a powerful conscious motive' (p. 342) for their explorations. He suggests that the celebrated missionary and explorer David Livingstone had a 'pathological determination to be "first" in his explorations' (p. 355), and a 'refusal to share glory with other Europeans' (p. 356). McLynn cites Cornwallis Harris, an early traveller in the Transvaal, as saying 'there was something God-like about being the first white man in an area' (p. 342). Furthermore, the explorers' celebrity and likelihood of securing finances for further travel was often determined by their ability to return to Europe with the new knowledge, scientific observations, and discoveries resulting from their expeditions (Driver 2001; Koivunen 2009; McLynn 1993). According to Driver

(2001), this new information was often presented at scientific societies, such as the Royal Geographical Society in Britain, where its members had a 'craving for sensation' (p. 48) of new scientific information. Throughout this study, the students' creative actions are metaphorically conceptualised as a journey to discover new knowledge, create individual outcomes, find new ways, and be the first to bring this information back into the studio environment.

The Centrality of Observation, Sketching, and Note-taking

Koivunen (2009) argues that the seventeenth-century belief that the world could be mastered by collecting and representation 'strengthened the connection between travelling and picture-making' (p. 33). She states that scientific societies of the time instructed seamen to include sketches of coastlines and islands with their reports, and drawing schools were established for sailors. As a result, visual documentation was a firmly established practice in nineteenth-century journeys of exploration. Even in 1880, when the camera was included as standard equipment on many journeys of exploration, Koivunen (2009) states that the practices of sketching, drawing, or painting were still preferred due their perceived scientific reliability as they allowed for the use of colour, were more reliable than the photographic apparatus of the time, and were regarded as 'a more suitable means than photography to characterize new countries in a vivid and comprehensive manner' (p. 37). Furthermore, instructions regarding the requirements for visual documentation would often be formally stated in the documents from the scientific society or the British Foreign Office funding an expedition. Consequently, explorers routinely carried a range of sketchbooks and notebooks.

> A selection of pens, pencils, inks and papers for writing and mapping served as standard equipment for every expedition. These basic materials also enabled sketches to be made. In addition, many explorers were equipped with a wide selection of materials specially intended for painting and sketching: brushes, paints, water-colours, sketchbooks, canvases and special painting paper. (Koivunen 2009, p. 49)

The use of notes, in the form of annotations, was also a central feature of the explorers' sketchbooks:

> ... pictures were deemed to be the most effective method of representing scenes or phenomena, but travellers also resorted to language in order to convey various messages. The margins of sketchbooks were often crammed with annotations and important landscapes and other subjects were likely to be described in great detail in journals. (Koivunen 2009, p. 58)

The Explorer's Gaze

In his work on travel, tourism and the gaze, Urry (2002) identifies an increased privileging of the visual as reshaping the journey of exploration.

> During the eighteenth century a more specialized visual sense developed based upon the *camera obscura*, the Claude glass, the use of guidebooks, the widespread knowledge of routes, the art of sketching and the availability of sketchbooks ... This can be seen in the case of Sweden, between Linnaeus' scientific expeditions in the 1730s to collect flowers and minerals, to Linnerhielm's travels in the 1780s to collect views and moods. The latter expresses this shift in the nature of travel: 'I travel to see, not to study'. (Urry 2002, p. 147, original italics)

Urry argues that this increased visual sense was transforming the traveller/explorer's perception of the natural wilderness from something terrifying and inhospitable into an object for visual consumption, and in doing so introduced a discourse of 'scenery, landscape, image, fresh air' (Williams 1972, p. 160). The result was an increasing aesthetisation of foreign landscapes throughout the nineteenth century in which they were perceived and described as though they were paintings (Koivunen 2009; Pratt 2008; Urry 2002). Citing the influence of new technologies such as postcards, guidebooks, photographs, dioramas, along with the origin of the package tour in 1851, Urry (2002) uses Foucault's expression the 'unimpeded empire of the gaze' (Foucault 1973, p. 39) to describe nineteenth-century culture and its influence on the increasingly popular practices of tourism and travelling. The discourse of the gaze is firmly entrenched in the educative context of this study, where looking, viewing seeing, observing, and noticing are central to the students' creative activities.

The final extract in this section (Extract 6.49) comes from an interview with student 4, and it demonstrates how the *JOURNEY OF EXPLORATION* metaphors embodies the creative processes of the students, and recontextualises the discourses described in the four sections above. The student is being asked about a page in his sketchbook. The page contains a mind map showing the student's attempt to explore notions of 'black and white' for the Binary Opposites brief.

Extract 6.49: Interview with Student 4

Int: You've got words like night and morning, black and white in the centre, and there's positive and negative.

S4: Yeah. Like what I can like first think of for black and white and then from that, I pick something that interests me most, and then I do another, like little brainstorm about it. And then I like, jot down some notes about it, and things like that. And then I just move on, so then, yeah, so I write down or sketch down, kind of like the ideas I see from the work. I try to make it my own, and give it like meanings and something. You know, so. Mmm from that, yeah so then, I was looking at some, you know, painters' work then I thought of ideas of mask and how it was like two [unintelligible] things. But then, when I came back, like, so many people was doing that and I didn't want to like, repeat it and umm it was kind of repetitive, and um yep.

Int: How does that go back to the brief?

S4: Umm, so it's kind of like follows the binary opposites, and umm, like from one of my binary

opposites I like, go on from that idea and
then it's kind of the same, but I just try doing
it in a different way.

Structured by *JOURNEY OF EXPLORATION* metaphors, and reproducing nineteenth-century discourses of exploration and travel, the student's creative process *moves on* (line 9) *from* (lines 5 and 13) one selected (*pick*, line 5) point of interest (*something that interests me*, line 6) to the next. Like the nineteenth-century explorer or traveller, he attempts to *sketch down* (line 10) or *jot down some notes* (lines 7–8) about the things that he can *see* (line 10) or finds himself *looking at* (line 13). When he returns (*came back*, line 16), he realises that others have already journeyed to the same destination (*so many people was doing that*, lines 16–17), and as a result he rejects these initial discoveries (*I didn't want to like repeat it*, line 17). Responding to the question regarding the connection that his description of the creative process has to the brief, the student states that it gave him something to initially follow (line 20); however, he decided to *go on from* (line 22) this and try a different *way* (line 24). This final comment metaphorically captures the nineteenth-century practice whereby explorers, travellers, missionaries, or colonists were only provided with details about the first stage of their journey, the remainder of which they went on to discover.

Concluding Comments

This chapter has examined how the creative activities of the contemporary university art and design studio are discursively conceptualised and facilitated through *JOURNEY OF EXPLORATION* metaphors. However, art and design education has not always been conceptualised in this way. The art historian Efland (1990), for example, first mentions the concepts of exploration and discovery in the context of the German Bauhaus, established in 1919, and further investigation of Bauhaus documents and accounts of Bauhaus educators and students would suggest that this is the case. Furthermore, a comparison between a historical and contemporary corpus, provides evidence that the term *explore* had very little metaphorical use prior to 1920, while today, its metaphorical use is habitual and widespread. An examination of the accounts of two pioneering artists from the modern period supports the view that metaphors of exploration were not used to describe creative action prior to 1920, finding instead that the educative metaphor *study* was prominent. As a result, the chapter posits that the Bauhaus tutors, and other art educators of the time, are likely to have recontextualised the still ubiquitous modernist discourses of exploration, discovery (and science) in their attempts to describe and facilitate the emergent creative processes they believe were required to embrace the challenges of a rapidly changing modern world. The subsequent emigration of many central Bauhaus figures to North American universities and colleges (due to the school's closure by the Nazis in 1932), and the subsequent worldwide dissemination of the Bauhaus' curriculum and teaching methods (Efland 1990; Grawe 2000; White 2004), has also resulted in the eventual spread of the *JOURNEY OF EXPLORATION* metaphors across the wider context of art and design education. The chapter concludes by describing some of the prominent discourses of nineteenth-century exploration and discovery, and then returns to the participants' perspective to briefly reiterate how these are metaphorically recontextualised in the context of the university art and design studio.

Notes

1. Cameron and Maslen (2010) uses the term *linguistic metaphor* to describe a word or phrase 'that can be justified as somehow anomalous, incongruent or "alien" in the on-going discourse, but that can be made sense of through a transfer of meaning in context' (p. 102). A linguistic metaphor is viewed as involving the *metaphor vehicle*, that is, the actual word or phrase used in the discourse and its explicit or implied referent or topic.
2. The analysis calculates words occurring four places to the right or left of the search word *explore*. It also uses a Mutual Informal criterion of 3.0 to avoid high frequency grammatical and function words.
3. The travel agency Thomas Cook & Son, formed in 1872, contributed to the proliferation of mass tourism to 'exotic' destinations in the late nineteenth century, primarily by making foreign travel accessible to the working and middle classes.

4. Following the influence of the pioneering British travel agency Thomas Cook & Son, a large number of travel agencies successfully opened throughout Germany during the nineteenth century, including Rominger (Stuttgart), Schenker & Co. (Munich), and Stangen Brothers (Breslau). These agencies all organised travel to exotic locations throughout the world (Gry 2010).
5. I would perhaps add that the alignment of science with exploration has its foundation in Francis Bacon's support for the scientific method, whereby the production of scientific knowledge was seen as grounded in personal observation and experiment. According to Reidy et al. (2007), Bacon believed the method would advance the knowledge required for voyages of oceanic discovery and assist in colonial expansion.

References

Burke, K. (1969). *A grammar of motives*. Berkeley, LA: University of California Press.

Cameron, L. (2007). Patterns of metaphor use in reconciliation talk. *Discourse & Society, 18*(2), 197–222.

Cameron, L. (2010a). The discourse dynamics framework for metaphor. In L. Cameron & R. Maslen (Eds.), *Metaphor analysis: Research practice in applied linguistics, social sciences and the humanities* (pp. 77–94). London, UK: Equinox.

Cameron, L. (2010b). What is metaphor and why does it matter? In L. Cameron & R. Maslen (Eds.), *Metaphor analysis: Research practice in applied linguistics, social sciences and the humanities* (pp. 3–25). London, UK: Equinox.

Cameron, L., & Maslen, R. (2010). Identifying metaphors in discourse data. In L. Cameron & R. Maslen (Eds.), *Metaphor analysis: Research practice in applied linguistics, social sciences and the humanities* (pp. 97–115). London, UK: Equinox.

Candlin, C. N. (2006). Accounting for interdiscursivity: Challenges to professional expertise. In M. Gotti & D. S. Giannoni (Eds.), *New trends in specialized discourse* (pp. 21–45). Bern, Switzerland: Peter Lang.

Charteris-Black, J. (2004). *Corpus approaches to critical metaphor analysis*. Basingstoke, UK: Palgrave Macmillan.

Conrad, S. (2012). *German colonialism: A short history*. Cambridge, UK: Cambridge University Press.

Cortazzi, M., & Jin, L. (1999). Bridges to learning: Metaphors of teaching, learning and language. In L. Cameron & G. Low (Eds.), *Researching and applying metaphor* (pp. 149–176). Cambridge, UK: Cambridge University Press.

Cruz, J. (2011). *The rise of middle-class culture in nineteenth-century Spain*. Baton Rouge, LA: Louisiana State University Press.

Cusack, A. (2008). *The wanderer in 19th-century German literature: Intellectual history and cultural criticism*. Rochester, NY: Camden House.

Davies, M. (2004). *BYU-BNC. (Based on the British National Corpus from Oxford University Press)*. Retrieved from http://corpus.byu.edu/bnc/

Davies, M. (2008). *The Corpus of Contemporary American English: 425 million words, 1990-present*. Retrieved from http://corpus.byu.edu/coca/

Davies, M. (2010). *The Corpus of Historical American English: 400 million words, 1810–2009*. Retrieved from http://corpus.byu.edu/coha/

Deignan, A. (2005). *Metaphor and corpus linguistics*. Amsterdam, Netherlands: John Benjamins.

Driver, F. (2001). *Geography militant: Cultures of exploration and empire*. Oxford and England: Blackwell.

Driver, F. (2004). Distance and disturbance: Travel, exploration and knowledge in the nineteenth century. *Transactions of the Royal Historical Society: Sixth series, 14*, 73–92.

Efland, A. (1990). *A history of art education: Intellectual and social currents in teaching the visual arts*. New York, NY: Teachers College Press.

Fairclough, N. (1992). *Discourse and social change*. Cambridge, UK: Polity Press.

Flam, J. D. (1994). *Matisse on art*. Berkeley, CA: University of California Press.

Foucault, M. (1973). *The birth of the clinic*. London, UK: Tavistock Publications.

Fulford, T., Lee, D., & Kitson, P. (2004). *Literature, science and exploration in the romantic era: Bodies of knowledge*. Cambride, UK: Cambridge University Press.

Gasson, R. (2005). The first American tourist guidebooks: Authorship and print culture of the 1820s. *Book History, 8*(1), 51–74.

Goatly, A. (2002). Conflicting metaphors in the Hong Kong Special administrative region educational reform proposals. *Metaphor and Symbol, 17*(4), 263–294.

Grawe, G. D. (2000). Continuity and transformation: Bauhaus pedagogy in North America. In R. K. Wick (Ed.), *Teaching at the Bauhaus* (pp. 338–365). Ostfildern-Ruit, Germany: Hatje Cantz Verlag.

Gropius, W. (1965). *The new architecture and the Bauhaus*. Cambridge, MA: MIT Press.

Gry, U. (2010). The history of tourism: Structures on the path to modernity. *Europäische Geschichte Online*. Retrieved from http://www.ieg-ego.eu/gyru-2010-en

Halliday, M. A. K., & Matthiessen, C. M. I. M. (2004). *An introduction to functional grammar* (3rd ed.). London, UK: Arnold.

Henderson, L. (2007). *John Murray and the publications of David Livingstone's missionary travels*. Retrieved April 26, 2012, from http://www.livingstoneonline.ucl.ac.uk/companion.php?id=HIST2

Hoey, M. (2005). *Lexical priming: A new theory of words and language*. London, UK: Routledge.

Itten, J. (1964). *Design and form: The basic course at the Bauhaus*. London, UK: Thames and Hudson.

Jansen, L., Luijten, H., & Bakker, N. (Eds.). (2009). *Vincent van Gogh: The letters. Version: December 2010*. Amsterdam & The Hague: Van Gogh Museum & Huygens ING. Retrieved from http://vangoghletters.org

Klee, P. (1961). *The thinking eye*. London, UK: Lund Humphries.

Koivunen, L. (2009). *Visualizing Africa in nineteenth-century British travel accounts*. New York, NY: Routledge.

Lakoff, G., & Johnson, M. (1980). *Metaphors we live by*. Chicago, IL: University of Chicago Press.

Layder, D. (1993). *New strategies in social research*. Cambridge, UK: Polity Press.

McLynn, F. (1993). *Hearts of darkness: The European exploration of Africa*. London, UK: Pimlico.

Neumann, E. (1993). *Bauhaus and Bauhaus people*. (E. Richter & A. Lorman, Trans.). New York, NY: Van Nostrand Reinhold.

Pratt, M. L. (2008). *Imperial eyes: Travel writing and transculturation*. New York, NY: Routledge.

Reidy, M. S., Kroll, G. R., & Conway, E. M. (2007). *Exploration and science: Social impact and interaction*. Santa Barbara, CA: ABC-CLIO.

Sachs, A. (2007). *The Humboldt current: A European explorer and his American disciples*. Oxford, UK: Oxford University Press.

Schön, D. (1985). *The design studio: An exploration of its traditions and potential*. London, UK: RIBA.

Stein, J. (Ed.). (1980). *The Bauhaus: Weimar, Dessau, Berlin, Chicago*. (W. Jabs & B. Gilbert, Trans.). Cambridge, MA: Massachusetts Institute of Technology.

Turner, J. (1998). Turns of phrase and routes to learning: The journey metaphor in educational culture. *Intercultural Communication Studies, 11*(2), 23–36.

Urry, J. (2002). *The tourist gaze*. London, UK: Sage Publications.

Webster, H. (2003). Facilitating critically reflective learning: Excavating the role of the design tutor in architectural education. *Art, Design & Communication in Higher Education, 2*(3), 101–111.

White, J. H. (2004). 20th-century art education: A historical perspective. In E. W. Eisner & M. D. Day (Eds.), *Handbook of research and policy in art education* (pp. 55–84). Mahwah, NJ: Lawrence Erlbaum Associates.

Wick, R. K. (2000). *Teaching at the Bauhaus.* (S. Mason & S. Lébe, Trans.). Ostfildern-Ruit, Germany: Hatje Cantz Verlag.

Williams, R. (1972). Ideas of nature. In J. Benthall (Ed.), *Ecology: The shaping enquiry.* London, UK: Longman.

Wodak, R. (2001). The discourse-historical approach. In R. Wodak & M. Meyer (Eds.), *Methods of critical discourse analysis* (pp. 63–94). London, UK: Sage.

Yeomans, R. (2005). Basic design and the pedagogy of Richard Hamilton. In M. Romans (Ed.), *Histories of art and design education: Collected essays* (pp. 195–210). Bristol, UK: Intellect Books.

7

Ideas

Introduction

Chapter 6 examined how journey of exploration metaphors contribute to the facilitation of student creative activity in the context of the university art and design studio. It was also suggested that the deployment of exploration metaphors in this context is a historically recent phenomenon, one likely to have originated in the art and design schools of the early twentieth century where nineteenth-century discourses of exploration were used to conceptualise new and emerging creative practices. The current chapter shifts from this focus on the metaphorical process of exploration to what is often metaphorically perceived as the object or goal of exploration, that is, the *idea*. This is evident in Anna's comment in Extract 7.1.

Extract 7.1: Interview with the Tutor Anna

Anna: …we're going to give you a brief that lets you explore new ideas.

The chapter traces the discursive conceptualisation of the creative artifact as an idea, from the tutors' interactions in the brief writing meeting

D. Hocking, *Communicating Creativity*, Communicating in Professions and Organizations, https://doi.org/10.1057/978-1-137-55804-6_7

through to the production of the students' work. As the analysis unfolds, it becomes evident that this conceptualisation is crucial to the participants' reflexive understanding and ongoing practical accomplishment of their creative practice.

Perspectival and Methodological Foci

The chapter's analytical focus begins at the participants' perspective with a preliminary examination of student accounts discussing the purpose of the brief. According to Dörnyei (2007), the gathering of preliminary impressions is a crucial move for qualitative research and can help lead the analyst towards more significant findings. In order to corroborate the initial observations from the interviews regarding the facilitative role of *ideas* for the students' creative practice, the analysis moves to the semiotic resource perspective, where a keyword and frequency analysis is carried out on the corpus of student brief texts. As Baker (2006) has stated, a keyword analysis can identify the 'presence of discourses' in a collection of texts and provide information to assist a further investigation into the data. Next, and in response to Sarangi and Candlin's (2010, 2011) recommendation that descriptions of discursive practice should be grounded in ethnographic analysis, results from the corpus analysis (the significance of the concept ideas in the data) are extended to both the social action and participants' perspectives using the qualitative analysis software NVivo and ethnographic procedures of coding and categorising. The result suggests that student creativity in the university art and design is conceptualised by the tutors and students through a CONDUIT[1] metaphor which involves the transference of ideas from the brief, to the student's mind, to the student's creative work. Drawing from ethnography, linguistic ethnography, and corpus analysis, these perspectives are explored to further corroborate and extend the analysis. As a concluding level of validation and explanation, an examination of the socio-historical perspective, broadly informed by the discourse-historical approach of Wodak (2001), is carried out. The discourse-historical approach recommends that the researcher integrate the analysis and interpretation of linguistic data with accounts of related socio-political and historical contexts.

Accordingly, the concept of ideas is examined across a number of twentieth-century art historical texts, interviews with artists, their personal correspondence to family members, and manifestos of art and design movements. An ethnomethodological slant (Garfinkel 1967) underpins the analysis in this chapter. Pollner and Emerson (2007) suggest that ethnomethodology can often draw attention to what ethnography may often overlook as the taken-for-granted, orderly activities or experiences of participants, and will instead treat these as practical and local accomplishments and phenomena of inquiry. Table 7.1 indicates the methodological resources used in this chapter with respect to the data collected from the different perspectives.

Ideas and the Conduit Model

An initial examination of responses elicited from students to an interview question asking about the purpose[2] of the student brief suggested a key role attributed to the concept of ideas. In Extract 7.2, for example, student 4 sees the brief as facilitating the exploration of ideas which are subsequently transformed into, or expressed in, a creative work, while student 2 (Extract 7.3) views the brief primarily as an initial stimulus (*a start point*), which will enable the students to *think* about *a lot of ideas*, again viewed as a stage in the development of their creative works.

Extract 7.2: Interview with Student 4

Interviewer: What do you think the purpose is of a studio brief?
Student 4: Um, to explore like *ideas*, of like, the *idea* that we have and to make it into work and express that through work.

Extract 7.3: Interview with Student 2

Student 2: Umm, I think this brief is not really umm guiding on towards our finish, it's kind of just giving us a start point and we can think a lot of *ideas* and then we can create a (*unintelligible*), our own um work.

Table 7.1 The data analysed and methodological foci for each of the perspectives

Perspective	Data	Methodological Orientation	Tools
Semiotic resource perspective	A 36,605 word corpus of 33 student briefs and a 109,809 word corpus of 60 professional briefs	Corpus analysis Ethnographic analysis	Frequency, keyword and concordance analysis The use of NVivo software to search for patterns in the data
	The British National Corpus (Davis 2004)	Corpus analysis	Collocation and frequency analysis
Social action perspective	Audio recordings of the second brief writing meeting, the brief launch, studio tutorials, and casual studio interaction (279,201 words in total)	Corpus analysis Ethnographic analysis Linguistic ethnography	Concordance and collocation analysis The use of NVivo software to search for patterns in the data Observation of salient themes in the participants' interactions Micro analysis of the participants' unfolding interactions
Participants' perspective	Semi-structured interviews with tutors and students	Ethnographic analysis Corpus analysis	The use of NVivo software to search for patterns in the data Observation of salient themes in the participants' interactions Concordance and collocation analysis
Socio-historical perspective	Published texts containing interviews with artists/designers, and personal accounts of their practices Art historical texts The letters of Van Gogh	Discourse-historical analysis	An account of wider socio-political and historical contexts to identify how these have shaped the phenomena and context under analysis Thematic analysis Interdiscursivity

Extract 7.4: Interview with Student 1

Interviewer:	What do you think the purpose of the brief is?
Student 1:	Just to, I thought, I thought it was just to show your understanding of like, the work that you produce, so when we were told to produce binary opposites, it was, I thought it was just to, like, use it as an *idea*, chose one, use it as an *idea* and then expand on that …

In Extract 7.4, Student 1 echoes the views of the other students, but adds that the idea is contained in the brief. In this case, he points to the Binary Opposites brief, which directs students to *generate ideas* using *notions of binary opposition*. This directive appears in the final paragraph of a section of the brief, which is referred to by tutors as the *provocation* section (see Chap. 5 for a discussion on the provocation section).

To further validate the salience of ideas in the context of the university art and design studio, a frequency and keyword analysis was subsequently carried out on the student brief corpus. The results identify *ideas* as the fifteenth most frequent lexical (non-grammatical) word in the corpus, having a frequency of 80 and appearing in 32 of the 33 brief texts in the corpus. It is also the seventeenth highest keyword in the student brief corpus when the corpus is referenced with the Wellington Corpus of Written English (Table 7.2). Furthermore, and following Baker's (2006) suggestion that the particular significance of the keywords of a corpus representing a specific genre or context (e.g. the student briefs in this study) can also be evaluated by comparing them with a similar sized corpus of related, yet contextually different, texts or genres, the student brief corpus was compared with the two professional brief corpora. It was found that *ideas* did not appear as a keyword in either the professional brief corpora (design briefs or creative briefs). Finally, a frequency analysis of words occurring in the ethnographic data (participant interactions and interviews) was also carried out. This analysis revealed that *ideas* occurs 132 times in the ethnographic data and was the twelfth most frequent lexical word. Taken together, these corpus-based statistics suggest that the word *ideas* is 'primed' (Hoey 2005) for use in the context of the university art and design studio.

Table 7.2 Student brief 25 top keywords using the Wellington Corpus of Written English as a reference corpus

Rank	Keyword	Frequency	Number of Texts (T = 33)	Frequency of reference corpus	Keyness
1	your	499	32	894	1784.22
2	studio	186	21	32	1141.83
3	work	334	29	1025	918.46
4	brief	141	25	58	765.06
5	design	157	23	131	726.32
6	drawing	106	21	48	564.77
7	you	419	32	3358	541.61
8	research	133	23	186	522.41
9	etc	72	21	0	511.46
10	start	127	19	192	484.60
11	art	131	15	324	403.34
12	week	130	25	322	399.96
13	materials	83	25	60	398.58
14	assessment	82	16	65	384.48
15	project	90	20	126	353.28
16	visual	71	21	45	352.04
17	**ideas**	**80**	**24**	**93**	**334.86**
18	will	257	28	2093	325.71
19	presentation	57	20	19	320.51
20	working	96	22	282	270.00
21	critique	41	11	9	244.60
22	possibilities	47	13	29	234.47
23	semester	31	17	0	220.18
24	space	65	16	113	218.81
25	media	61	24	111	216.06

In order to further examine the notion of ideas in the data, and the way that they facilitate student creative activity, NVivo qualitative analysis software was used to code and categorise how participants talk about and characterise ideas in the ethnographic data (interviews and interactions), as well as in the textual data of the student brief corpus. The intention was that the dominant themes to emerge would provide a useful starting point for a richer and more systematic analysis of the data, and signal a methodological way forward for the analysis. This process first involved searching for the words *idea* or *ideas* and coding the participants' use of these words as they occurred in the expanded excerpts that emerged from the NVivo search queries. Patterns or similarities were then identified among the large list of initial codes so that they could be regrouped into broader thematic sets of second-level codes. After a further categorisation of these second-level codes, it became clear that the words *idea* and *ideas* were associated with four central parent themes or topics: the brief, the students' minds, the creative work, and transformation. An NVivo-generated model of the final coding is reproduced in Fig. 7.1.

If the parent themes in Fig. 7.1 are aligned with the responses of the students in Extracts 7.2–7.4, there is an implication that the facilitation of art and design creativity is conceptualised as a process of transference, whereby an idea which is entextualised (Sung-Yul Park and Bucholtz 2009) in the student brief by the tutors, metaphorically passes through the students' minds and eventually emerges in the form of a creative work. There is also evidence that within this process of idea transference, some process of transformation or development occurs, perhaps constituted through the metaphors of exploration and experimentation as discussed in Chap. 7. This process of 'idea transference' appears to draw upon the CONDUIT metaphor (Prior 1998; Reddy 1979). According to Prior, the CONDUIT metaphor is an underlying structuralist trope that 'implicates particular views of knowledge, learning, communities and the person' (p. 17). He describes how communicative interaction is understood through the CONDUIT metaphor:

> The conduit metaphor depicts speech as a three-step process. The speaker puts thoughts into word-containers. These word-thought objects are then transferred from the speaker's mind through a conduit (the air) to the mind of the listener. Finally, the listener extracts the thoughts from the words. (Prior 1998, p. 17)

Given these preliminary observations, the following sections will now examine in detail the following three focal areas; (i) the student brief, (ii) the students' minds, and (iii) the students' creative works. Taking into consideration the CONDUIT metaphor conceptualisation of creative activity in the university art and design environment, metaphor analysis will be employed to further evaluate the extent to which the CONDUIT metaphor interacts with a discourse of ideas to facilitate creative practice. Following this, the role of idea transformation will also be considered in relation to

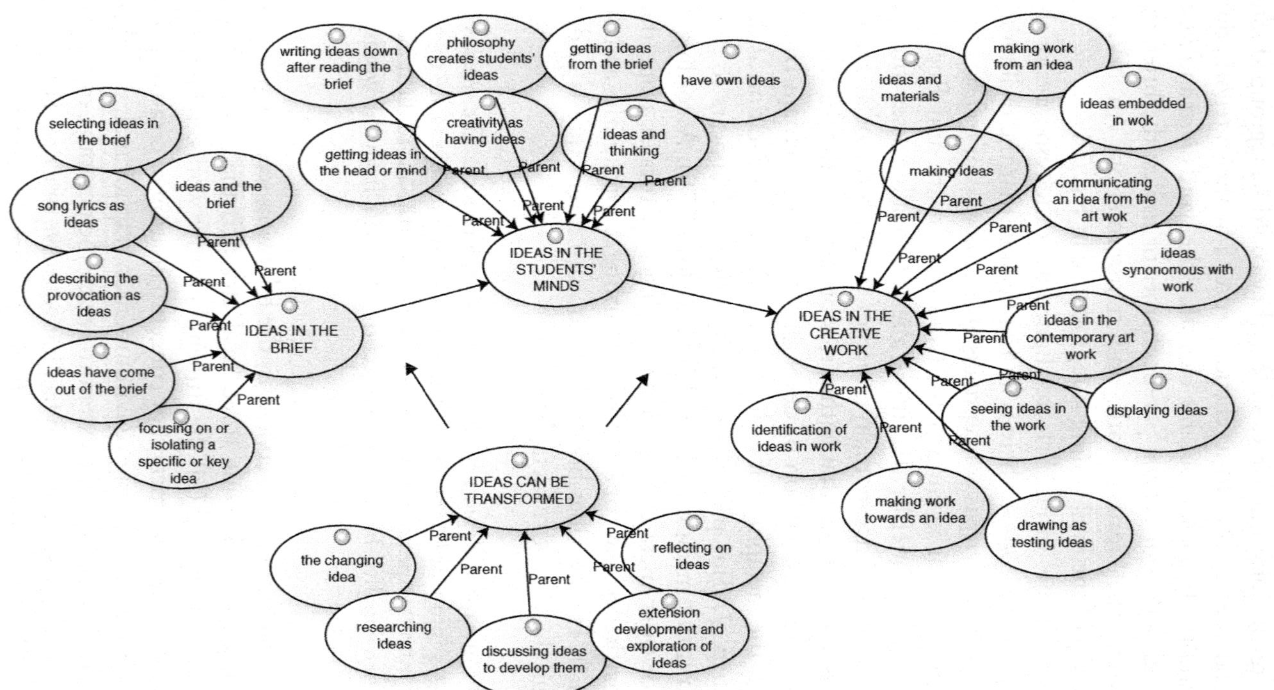

Fig. 7.1 An NVivo-generated model (NVivo qualitative data analysis software; QSR International Pty Ltd. Version 9, 2010) of the thematic coding of the words *idea* and *ideas* found in the student brief corpus and ethnographic data (participant interviews and interactions)

the CONDUIT models' property of transference. Finally the discourse of ideas will be examined in published historical texts containing interviews with artists/designers, and the personal accounts of their practices.

Ideas in the Student Brief

In Extract 7.5, the tutor Claire makes reference to contrary conceptual categories. Here she is discussing the Binary Opposites brief, in particular the *provocation* section. The Binary Opposites provocation section includes three direct quotations, each describing the way in which binary oppositions are manifest in a different culture. In the brief, these three paragraphs are preceded by a statement that defines the notion of binary oppositions, and, as discussed in Chap. 5, are followed by excerpts of song lyrics from two well-known popular songs, both of which have employed binary oppositions for poetic effect (e.g. brave/chickenshit, hot air/cool breeze). Of note is that Claire conceptualises the provocation section as an *idea* that is presented to students, and that this *idea* comprises the *contrary conceptual categories.*

Extract 7.5: Interview with the Tutor Claire

Interviewer: What are the typical characteristics of a brief?
Claire: The typical characteristics of the brief are the provocation, which is the *idea* that we present them with, so in this case it's the *idea* of um contrary conceptual categories …

In interview Extracts 7.6 and 7.7, the tutor Anna states that ideas *come out of* the brief, a metaphor which she uses again in Extract 7.8 in response to a student question during the launch of the student brief. This latter extract is particularly significant, as Anna's response reconceptualises the student's perception of their work as being *based on the songs* (the extracts contained in the brief), to one whereby the work is based on *ideas that come out of* the brief. In Extract 7.9, Anna characterises the tutors as metaphorically being able to increase the *depth* of the brief through an increase in the readings (e.g. binary opposites). In 7.10, the final extract in this group, Anna metaphorically describes a desired future outcome (cf. come out) of the brief as one where students *take* the ideas and transform these into *work*.

Extract 7.6: Interview with the Tutor Anna

Anna: ... that some of the kind of the philosophical *ideas*, um, that actually *come out of* the briefs and I think that that's been quite useful.

Extract 7.7: Interview with the Tutor Anna

Anna: ... a lot of those kind of *ideas* actually *came out of* that [the brief]

Extract 7.8: Brief Launch

Student: Is our work based on the songs, on one of the songs?
Anna: Or it can be *ideas* that *come, come out of* it ...

Extract 7.9: Interview with the Tutor Anna

Anna: ... we've been looking at quite a bit actually, giving students a little bit more, a bit more sort of text, a little bit of reading to give it [the brief] a bit more *depth.*

Extract 7.10: Interview with the Tutor Anna

Anna: ... these are the *outcomes* that we want, so then please go ahead and, you know, will you *take* those *ideas* and *make work*

It could be argued that in these extracts, the tutors are characterising the brief as an idea-container, an important entailment of the CONDUIT metaphor (Prior 1998). This characterisation is widespread throughout the ethnographic data and is also evidenced in the way that the brief is routinely metaphorised as something that can be opened or closed. An example of this can be seen Extract 7.11 where the tutor Anna recounts a student's experience at an application interview for a subsequent course.

Extract 7.11: Interview with the Tutor Anna

Anna: Um, one student sort of said well she quite liked the fact that some of our briefs were quite *open* and gave, gave them more freedom what to do …

Extract 7.12 reproduces part of the interaction which occurred in the brief writing meeting for the Binary Opposites Brief. Lines 3 (*I'm just wondering whether this should come here*), 9 (*maybe the definition should come first*), and 13 (*then we put the um the lyrics from the songs last*) of the interaction focus on establishing how the different source texts selected will be structured and juxtaposed with one another to eventually become the Binary Opposites brief provocation section.

Extract 7.12: Second Brief Writing Meeting

1	→	Anna:	they they they they all are
2	→	Claire:	hmmm
3	→	Sam:	yeah but I'm just wondering whether this should come here further
4			cause these are kind of
5	→		whether if these statements here
6	→	Anna:	mmm
7	→	Sam:	cause they kind of [get are distinct
8	→	Anna:	[yep
9	→	Anna:	yep maybe the definition should come first
10			I was thinking about that too
11			so maybe in western culture
12			the Chinese philosophy and the Māori one
13	→		and then we put the um the lyrics from the songs last
14	→	Sam:	mm
15	→	Anna:	because those do introduce the ideas further

[don't they
→ Sam: [because I think they'll they'll see these and go
ah that's like our assignment ah
→ Claire: that's what I thought [as well
→ Anna: [yeah yeah yeah
→ Sam: the one that they're doing at the moment
→ Claire: you know
→ Sam: pick one of these
→ Claire: yeah pick a line or you know
→ Anna: yeah yeah
→ Claire: pick one of these ideas

It is within the talk-in-interaction of the brief writing meeting that the tutors begin to reconstitute the texts as ideas. In Extract 7.12 the different source texts are in the first instance respectively referred to as *statements* (line 5), a *definition* (line 9), and *lyrics* (line 13). As they are combined to establish the structure of the provocation, they are subsequently referred to as *ideas* (lines 15 and 26), which the students can *pick* (lines 24 and 26) for eventual transformation into creative work.

This re-categorisation of the source text as ideas, eventually to be transferred to a creative work, would appear to be of critical importance to the ensuing process of creativity in the university art and design studio. Before the source texts of philosophical statements and song lyrics are re-categorised as ideas, they are simply philosophical statements or song lyrics, not ideas to be transferred into creative works. The next section examines the students' mind as a stage in this metaphorical process of transference.

Ideas in the Students' Minds

In Extract 7.13, student 1 metaphorically characterises the brief, and the tutor's discussion of the contents of the brief as motivating the acquisition of ideas in his mind (*get some ideas in my head*, lines 5–6; *ideas come to mind*, lines 7–8). This extract also identifies the way in which the ideas constituted in the brief as written text undergo what appears as a natural or taken-for-granted transformation into the student's mind to become ideas as *images* (line 3); images which can subsequently be transferred to paper (*stuff that I can put on paper*, line 3).

Extract 7.13: Interview with Student 1

1 → S1: … as soon as I receive the brief I immediately like start thinking,
2 like even when the teacher is going over it with us, like start trying
3 → to get images in my head, stuff that I can put on paper, like
4 (*unintelligible*) ideas that I don't usually research right away,
5 → I do, I do, pretty soon, but the first thing I do is just to get some ideas
6 → in my head, is usually sketch on a piece of paper, and usually, um,
7 → produce a certain amount of sketches and if no ideas come to
8 → mind yet, sort of just expand on the sketches I like …

In Extract 7.14, student 2, influenced by the utterances of the tutor Claire, views the idea already in his head as needing to be drawn out (*I just don't know how to draw it out*), and by implication transferred to the next object-container in the creativity process.

Extract 7.14: Studio Tutorial between the Tutor Claire and Student 2

Claire: [*laughs*] No, I'm saying that could be a good thing.
Student 2: Oh, you know. Well, I did it in my head, as things pretty good.
Claire: What's the idea in your head?
Student 2: But I just don't know how to draw it out.

In the same way that the brief is conceptualised as an object-container, which can be opened and closed at the direction of the tutors, so is the object-container of the student's mind. This is evidenced in Extracts 7.15 and 7.16, where the tutors Anna and Mike both equate thinking and learning with *opening* the students *up*. The metaphorical implication here is perhaps that it is preferable that the object-container of the students' minds are open, so that it is easy to deposit ideas (originating from the brief).

Extract 7.15: Interview with the Tutor Anna

Anna: … and, sometimes they haven't ever thought about those before. Um, so it's kind of *opening, opening* them [the students] *up*.

Extract 7.16: Interview with the Tutor Mike

Mike: … what are you wanting the students to learn? What are you wanting them to, to do, or to get? You know, um, and to me at this level, to me it's always, to me, my guiding forces has always been to try and *open them up*.

Once the ideas, (initially generated by the tutors from prior texts) *come out of* the briefs and are transferred to the students' minds, it would appear that they are subsequently constructed by tutors as belonging to the students, strategically evoking a creative discourse of originality. Extract 7.17 shows the tutor Claire repeatedly using the collocation *your ideas* to frame the initial interactional stages of the studio tutorial.

Extract 7.17: Studio Tutorial between Claire and Student 2

Claire: Shall we have a talk about
how *your ideas* are developing?
(…)
So what do you want to do this time round,
with *your ideas*?

Table 7.3 An example of ten concordances from the student brief corpus involving the collocation *your ideas*

1	clarify and consolidate **your**	**ideas**	in relation to the objects and images that
2	can be used to convey **your**	**ideas**	and thoughts efficiently and effectively
3	a sounding board for critiquing **your**	**ideas.**	4) Talk to me . . . but only when you have
4	your taste and discussing **your**	**ideas**	which relate to the language and visual
5	Explore and experiment with **your**	**ideas**	and methods as you produce a series of
6	media to discuss and enhance **your**	**ideas.**	Work on synthesising and refining your
7	are shaped and formed by **your** own	**ideas,**	concerns and interests surrounding the
8	will be applied to this work, **your**	**ideas**	and interest over the following four weeks
9	to collect Research: Evidence **your**	**ideas**	through: Visual, written, related material
10	essential tool for communicating **your**	**ideas**	to the general public. In later courses

On further examination, the process of constituting ideas as belonging to the student occurs much earlier in the brief itself. In the corpus of student briefs, *ideas* has a frequency of 80 and collocates 23 times with *your*, the second most frequent collocate of *ideas* after the grammatical word *and*. An example of ten concordances involving the collocation *your ideas* can be seen in Table 7.3.

This projected discourse of ownership/originality is subsequently reproduced by the students, as can be seen in Extract 7.18, where the collocation *my idea* is used twice in the short utterance. Again, in this utterance we also see a clear example of the CONDUIT model conceptualisation of creative practice in action, whereby the student's idea is characterised as being transferred into the installation work.

Extract 7.18: Interview with Student 4

Student 1: So then, from the idea of black and white, I developed *my idea*. So *my idea* now is kind of like an installation piece.

Table 7.4 An example of ten concordances from the combined interview and interactional data involving the collocation *my ideas*

1	Yeah that's **my**	**idea.**	It would be like a ghost studio.
2	I want to. I uh based on **my**	**idea**	of making lamps and then could be ...
3	... to see through and interactive. **My**	**idea**	is to put this in between the space ...
4	... of based, I just kind of changed **my**	**idea,**	like base it on interactive umm, and people
5	... thinking of this which related to **my**	**idea,**	umm, I was just thinking of making ...
6	... thing that I can incorporate into **my**	**idea.**	I take a photo and come back to Uni the ...
7	... of black and white I developed **my**	**idea.**	So now my idea is kind of like an ...
8	... the world, so I like to quickly jot **my**	**ideas**	down and then um, kind of brainstorm a ...
9	... for the binary thing, like maybe **my**	**ideas**	um man and women, I did the, I did the ...
10	... because I think I have **my** own	**ideas**	about, yeah, but this has got nothing for ...

My collocates 16 times with *ideas* in this data. All utterances of the collocation *my ideas* were made by students

In order to further explore the significance of the collocations denoting ownership in Tables 7.3 and 7.4, a comparative examination was carried out of these collocations (*your ideas* and *my ideas*), along with *the ideas* (due to its possessive neutrality), as found in: (i) the student brief corpus, (ii) the combined data collected for this study (student brief and transcribed ethnographic data), and (iii) the British National Corpus (BNC) (Davies 2004). The latter was used to help identify significant findings in the analysis of student brief or combined data. Furthermore, to take into account the possibility of adjectives occurring before the node word *ideas*, for example, *my own ideas* or *my stupid fussy frilly ideas* (an actual example from the BNC), collocations where *my*, *your*, or *the* was up to four places to the left of the node word *ideas* were included in the analysis. The results can be seen in Table 7.5.

The results in Table 7.5 also identify the percentage that each collocation represents of the total collocations with the node word *ideas* (for each corpus set). It could be suggested that the personal pronoun *your* is

Table 7.5 A comparative analysis of collocations involving the node word *ideas*, found in (i) the student brief corpus, (ii) the combined data collected for this study (student brief and ethnographic data), and (iii) the British National Corpus (Davies 2004)

	Student brief corpus		Combined student brief and ethnographic data		British National Corpus (BNC)	
Collocation with *ideas*	Freq. left	% collocation with node	Freq. left	% collocation with node	Freq. left	% collocation with node
my	0	0	4	1.89	99	0.92
your	24	28.75	32	15.09	205	1.92
the	7	8.75	30	14.15	2219	20.73

more likely to collocate with the node word *ideas* in the studio context than it might do in general speech and writing. Furthermore, the determiner *the*, which is more likely to be used to construe an ideas as not belonging to a participant, occurs more frequently in general writing and speech than it does in the student brief corpus. It is possible, then, that the personal attribution of the idea or ideas to the participant is a characteristic of the studio environment and that the pronoun *your* is especially primed to occur with *ideas* in this context.

Ideas in the Students' Work

Extract 7.19 exemplifies both the CONDUIT metaphor process of transference, as well as the conceptualisation of ideas as existing in the object-container of the students' creative work. In line 1, the student, describing his work on the studio wall, uses the mental process *thought* to construe the idea of *leaking and spreading* as something he initially experienced in his mind. Towards the end of the extract, these ideas are constituted as being present in his work (*that's supposed to be an idea of it there*, line 5).

Extract 7.19: Interview with Student 1

S1: I *thought* of *leaking and spreading* and maybe, absorbing or like,
again or you could also relate it to rising and to climbing. (...)

Just a further advancement on that *spreading* and umm so just instead of the word *leak*, I just decided to use the word *spread* and see how that works. That's supposed to be an idea of it there, spreading across, almost like a plague.

Extracts 7.20, from a studio tutorial where Anna and student 3 discuss the student's creative work in progress, reinforces the argument that the work is primarily conceptualised as a container for ideas. In the extract, Anna, who is looking at the work as she speaks, suggests to the student that *you've got some really great ideas*. She goes on to mention that these ideas, and not the creative work itself, need to be further refined.

Extract 7.20: Studio Tutorial between Anna and Student 3

Anna: I'd say just, just work a little bit more with it, because what you've got, is you've got some really great ideas, but this is your opportunity to refine those ideas.

One result of the metaphorical conceptualisation of the students' creative work as an idea-container is that the semiotic distinction between the referents *ideas* and *work* can at times collapse, with each used interchangeably in the data. In the earlier Extract 7.18, student 4 clearly categorises her installation work as an idea; furthermore, in Extract 7.21 below, it is not the completed creative work itself that student 8 rejects, but the idea itself.

Extract 7.21: Casual Studio Interaction

Student 8: I don't like my idea any more.
Student 9: Why not?
Student 8: It turned out crap.

The collapse of the distinction between the idea and the creative work also routinely occurs in the brief writing meeting. In Extract 7.22, for example, Anna describes other tutors as wanting the students to *make … ideas* (line 4), rather than 'make work'. The use of the collocation *make ideas*

Table 7.6 Collocations with *idea/s* as evidenced in: (i) the combined student brief corpus and ethnographic data collected for this study, (ii) the BNC (Davis 2004), and (iii) the combined Wellington corpora of spoken and written New Zealand English

	Combined student brief corpus and ethnographic data		British National Corpus		Combined Wellington Corpora of Written and Spoken NZ English	
idea/s	L1	L1-4	L1	L1-4	L1	L1-4
made	0	0	0	29	0	0
make	0	6	0	33	0	2
makes	0	0	0	11	0	0
making	1	2	2	13	0	0
Total	1	8	2	86	0	2
Total per million words	11.77	94.13	0.02	0.86	0	1

In the L1 columns, the lemmas of *make* occur one place prior to the node word *idea*, while in the L1-4 columns the lemmas of *make* occurs up to place four places prior to the node word

is significant in this context due to its relative absence in conventional usage. This can be seen in Table 7.6, which compares the frequencies of collocations containing lemmas of *make* and the words *idea/s* from the combined ethnographic and student brief data collected for this study with the combined Wellington corpora of spoken and written New Zealand English and the BNC. It should also be noted that Anna chooses the collocation *final ideas* (line 7), rather than the expected *final work,* later in her turn.

Extract 7.22: First Brief Writing Meeting

1 → Anna: the feedback that I've been getting from Karen and Paul
3 is that they actually do want us to get students
4 → to *make* more refined *ideas*
5 that they're feeling that
6 maybe the short briefs
7 → the students get to get to the *final ideas* too quickly
8 and they're a little bit unresolved
9 so they're actually quite keen for us to
10 maybe somehow in the briefs...

Transformation

It is important to emphasise that the metaphorical process of transferring an idea from one medium to another (brief, to mind, to creative object) also involves some form of *transformation*—of both the idea itself, as well as the 'container' in which the idea is transferred. Without some degree of transformation, creative works motivated by the same brief would hypothetically be indistinguishable from one another. Of course, the brief necessarily places constraints on the students' work—for example, the 2D version of the Binary Opposites brief requires the use of both image and text—and therefore some degree of resemblance is always likely. However, given that students from each discipline area in the studio are provided with the same brief, it is interesting to consider what facilitates the transformations that take place as the idea metaphorically transfers along the trajectory of container objects to produce different creative outcomes. The data from this study suggest that three important phenomena contribute to the transformation of ideas as they pass from one container object to the next. These are: (i) the deployment of ambiguity in the brief, (ii) the collocation of the word *idea* with a range of material verb processes, and (iii) the habitus of individual students. They are discussed in turn below.

Ambiguity in the Brief

Brief-related research routinely states that the generation of multiple different responses (Dineen and Collins 2005; Parker et al. 2006) or distinctly individual solutions (Oak 2000) is the desired outcome of the student brief in the educative context. It also suggests that as a strategy for facilitating multiple interpretations and a variety of creative responses, the student brief is intentionally 'unspecific', 'ambiguous', 'imperfectly formed' or 'ill-defined' (Garner and McDonagh-Philp 2001, p. 60), 'vague' (Parker et al. 2006, p. 91), or 'open-ended' (Dineen and Collins 2005, p. 48). There are six types of ambiguity in the student brief corpora: *antonymic ambiguity*, *semantic ambiguity*, *ambiguity of choice*, *paradoxical ambiguity*, *subjective ambiguity*, and *ambiguity of process*. Of course a single brief will often employ more than one type of ambiguity.

Antonymic ambiguity is usually constructed by positioning the design issue or provocation within a theoretical context that involves oppositional themes—for example, 'Real and Unreal' (student brief 4), 'Public and Private' (student brief 11), 'Singles and Plurals' (student brief 25). Such antonymically ambiguous briefs generally require students to develop works that investigate the 'relationship' or 'play' 'between' these oppositional concepts (Extract 7.23).

Extract 7.23: Student Brief 4

> Create a body of work that plays with notions of 'real' and 'unreal';
> -works that play on the imagined moments between objects, images and materials.

The Binary Opposites brief, and its requirement that students 'explore visual interpretations of contrary conceptual categories', is explicit in its use of antonymic ambiguity.

Semantic ambiguity describes the use of expressions, phrases, or statements in the brief, which, because they are devoid of context, could be interpreted by the student in a multiplicity of ways. In the student brief corpus, semantically ambiguous statements are frequently found in lists (Extract 7.24).

Extract 7.24: Student Brief 6

1. 'My last purchase'
2. 'No direction home'
3. This way and that'
4. 'I walk the line'
5. 'Take it from the top'
6. 'Round the outside'
7. 'On the edge'
8. 'Off the wall'
9. 'Bringing it all back home'

> Choose ONE of the phrases above.
> Take your chosen phrase as a starting point and begin to generate ideas:
> Research and make work about those ideas.

Ambiguity of choice refers to the provision of multiple options (at a verb or noun phrase level), characteristically presented in the brief as an embedded list. (Extract 7.25).

Extract 7.25: Student Brief 4

> What we are asking you to do is research a culturally significant topic and then creatively distill, communicate, transform, re-present, and make visually interesting this cultural knowledge/memory/issue, thereby contributing/communicating to a wider audience ...

Paradoxical ambiguity occurs when the brief sets up a paradox as the central provocation. This mode of ambiguity is predominantly found in student briefs of a design nature (Extract 7.26).

Extract 7.26: Student Brief 2

> You are required to select a product or service that has little or 'no use value' or conceivable appeal.

Subjective ambiguity occurs when the brief requires the student to develop an individual, subjective or personal response to a particular location, object, or concept. (Extract 7.27).

Extract 7.27: Student Brief 12

> The way in which the site is interpreted is up to you. Whether the work be representational or not is based on your relationship to the environment.

Ambiguity of process appears in brief statements that encourage students not to consciously rationalise the creative processes of making and exploring (Extracts 7.28 and 7.29).

Extract 7.28: Student Brief 10

> You will be asked to make rather than attempting to make conscious representations. 'Stop making sense', and start making.

Extract 7.29: Student Brief 1

> Try not to think too much about what you are doing; what it might mean and whether or not it makes sense in relation to "post-modern pedagogy".

Paradoxically, brief 10 (Extract 7.28 above), in particular, draws attention to the taken-for-granted metaphor of idea transference as a facilitating concept for creative action by requiring students to disregard it. The brief asks students to *'Stop making sense', and start making*, thus constituting the absence of an idea as the idea.

Verb Collocations with Idea

Another way in which the transformation of ideas (as they transfer from one medium to the next) is discursively facilitated involves the semantic association of the concept *ideas* with an array of largely material verb processes, in order that some transformational action on the idea might occur. Table 7.7, provides a list of the most frequent collocations of verbs (root and gerund) with the node word *idea* in the student brief corpus. Interestingly, the table has some resemblance to the sculptor Richard Serra's famous work *Verb List* (1967–1968), which lists the infinitives of 84 verbs (for example, to roll, to crease, to fold, to store, and the like) that Serra viewed as guiding his creative practice.

Habitus

The unique habitus[3] of the individual student will inevitably result in divergent interpretations of the idea as contained in the brief, a point partly indicated by student 3 in Extract 7.30.

Table 7.7 Lemmas of verbs collocating with *ideals* in the student brief corpus

	Collocations with node word *ideals*	Texts (T = 33)	Frequency
1	explore	8	9
2	develop	7	9
3	research	5	7
4	communicate	5	6
5	relate	4	4
6	generate	4	4
7	make	4	5
8	clarify	3	3
9	synthesise	2	2
10	extend	2	2
11	do	2	2
12	resource	2	2
13	select	2	2
14	draw	2	2
15	begin	2	2
16	experiment	2	2
17	inform	1	2
18	have	1	2
19	trace	1	2
20	combine	1	2
21	display	1	2

Extract 7.30: Interview with Student 3

Student 3: … like people interpret it [the brief provocation] in different ways, whichever they feel like, um but I mean, usually, I know that I said that they were quite constrained and stuff, but to an extent, they are quite broad. You can interpret them in whatever way you feel.

Similarly, the way in which an individual student carries out any of the different verb processes identified in Table 7.7 will also inevitably be shaped by their habitus. At the same time, however, the relatively similar socio-economic and cultural backgrounds of many of the students in this study account for some similarity of habitus, so that while the students are able to interpret the provocations in whatever way they *feel* (Extract 7.30), their interpretations are inevitably '"regulated" and "regular" without being in any way the product of obedience to the rules' (Bourdieu

1990, p. 53). Furthermore, the experiences of the past practices, as well as the present conditions of its production within a particular practice, can constrain the generating capacity of the individual habitus (Bourdieu 1990, 1993). The next section will now examine how the discourse of ideas and its facilitation of creative practice is located within a wider socio-historical context.

The Socio-historical Conceptualisation of Ideas

In the context of art and design creativity, the concept of ideas is a somewhat vague term. Historical works on art education, such as Efland (1990), often use the term *ideas* to refer to the socio-cultural values that frame a particular art and design movement, for example:

> The *ideas* of the humanists were reflected in a new architecture based upon the study of monuments from classical antiquity. The centrality of man is abundantly evident in such paintings as Raphael's *School of Athens* ... (Efland 1990, p. 28, italics added to the word ideas, other italics are original)

Alternatively, such texts use the term to refer to the more specific beliefs about the creative practice of an individual artist or designer, for example:

> Fortunately, Edward T. Cook, his biographer and anthologist, prepared a concise, sympathetic digest of his [Ruskin's] leading *ideas* in *Studies in Ruskin* (Cook 1890). In its opening chapter, Cook describes Ruskin's view of art as "the expression of man's rational and disciplined delight in the forms and laws of creation of which he is part". (Efland 1990, p. 134, italics added to the word ideas, other italics are original)

At times, art historical texts conceptualise ideas themselves as the ultimate objective of artists and designers:

> What defines art, then, is not any difference in materials or techniques from the applied arts. Rather, art is defined by the artists' willingness to

take risks in the quest for bold, new *ideas*. (Janson and Janson 2004, p. 31, italics added)

Evidence from interviews with artists or from their published writings also indicates a broad semantic usage of the term *ideas*. In the translated letters of Van Gogh (Jansen et al. 2009), for example, the painter frequently uses the term to refer to a future course of creative action, often denoting his recognition of a previously unconsidered subject (Extract 7.31).

Extract 7.31: Letter 666 by Van Gogh (Italics Added)

I have a whole heap of *ideas* [French-idées] for new canvases. Today I saw that same coal-boat again, with workers unloading it, that I've already told you about; in the same place as the sand-boats, of which I've sent you a drawing. It would be a grand subject.

Perhaps representing a CONDUIT metaphor, Van Gogh metaphorically constitutes *ideas* as arriving from some other place and materialising in his mind. This can be seen in his frequent collocation of the metaphor vehicle *come* (*venir*—French) with *ideas* (Extracts 7.32–7.34).

Extracts 7.32–7.34: Letters by Van Gogh

Ex. 7.32: You'll see how the *ideas* will *come* [French-viendront] to you. (letter 693)

Ex. 7.33: ... the more *ideas* will *come* [French-viendront] to him [Gaugin] ... (letter 694)

Ex. 7.34: *Ideas* for work are *coming* [French-viennent] to me in abundance (letter 680)

Van Gogh also uses *ideas* to refer to the values which frame a particular movement, not unlike Efland's (1990) usage identified above. However, Van Gogh's emphasis is almost always on aesthetic or technical properties (Extract 7.35).

Extract 7.35: Letter 626 by Van Gogh (Italics Added)

> I say this to get you to understand what sort of tie binds me to the French painters whom people call the Impressionists—that I know many of them personally and like them. And furthermore that in my own technique I have the same *ideas* [Dutch- idees] concerning colour ...

While *ideas* appear to be strongly tied to the aesthetic or technical for the modernist artists of the late eighteenth and early twentieth century, in the conceptual art that emerged in the mid-twentieth century, ideas were given prominence over, and separated from, traditional aesthetic or material concerns (Godfrey 1998). This shift is clearly evident in the oft-cited manifesto of conceptual artist Sol Le Witt (Extract 7.36):

Extract 7.36: Paragraphs on Conceptual Art

> The *ideas* need not be complex. Most *ideas* that are successful are ludicrously simple. Successful ideas generally have the appearance of simplicity because they seem inevitable. In terms of ideas the artist is free to even surprise himself. Ideas are discovered by intuition. What the work of art looks like isn't too important. It has to look like something if it has physical form. No matter what form it may finally have it must begin with an *idea.* (...) If the artist carries through his *idea* and makes it into visible form, then all the steps in the process are of importance. The *idea* itself, even if not made visual is as much a work of art as any finished product. (Le Witt 1967, cited in Stiles and Selz 1996, pp. 822–824, italics added)

For Le Witt, the creative object is simply an object utilised for the visualisation of an initial idea. However, in actuality, the ideas of conceptual art were still essentially tied to the materiality of the art object, even if 'not made visual', because they were typically motivated by a challenge to the traditional status of art as unique, collectable, and saleable (Godfrey 1998).

Providing further insights into the emergent discourse of the idea in twentieth-century art is American art patron and critic Seth Siegelaub, who was instrumental in promoting the work of the conceptual artists (Alberro 2003). Siegelaub would curate group exhibitions which involved no exhibition site and instead consisted solely of a catalogue detailing the artists' works. Alberro cites Siegelaub as stating that 'people who have galleries can show their objects only in one place at a time. I'm not limited. I can have my *ideas* in twenty different places at once. *Ideas* are faster than tedious objects' (p. 155, italics added). For Alberro, this new exhibition method 'shifted the emphasis from objects to *ideas*' (p. 155, italics added).

Bourdieu (1993, 1996) argued that conceptual art's emphasis on the idea is the result of a struggle that continually takes place between dominant figures of the art world and newcomers as they compete for positions in the cultural field.

> The field of cultural production is the area par excellence of clashes between the dominant fractions of the dominant class, who fight there sometimes in person but more often through producers oriented towards defending their 'ideas' and satisfying their 'tastes', and the dominated fractions who are totally involved in this struggle. (Bourdieu 1993, p. 102)

As an example, he makes reference to the early twentieth-century painter Marcel Duchamp. Bourdieu (1996) argues that Duchamp, a newcomer to the field with a desire for recognition, consciously set out to rupture the history of painting 'by getting rid of the "physical aspect"' and the 'strictly retinal' (p. 246) values of existing art. He primarily achieved his aim through the concept of the readymade, a manufactured object (that is, a bicycle wheel, bottle rack, urinal) to which the artist conferred the symbolic status of an art object.

Often drawing upon the work of Duchamp, the influential British art of the 1990s was similarly motivated to challenge traditional assumptions about art. However, unlike the conceptual art movement, interviews with the leading Young Brit artists provide evidence of ideas as fully autonomous from the eventual creative production of the work. This can be seen in an extract from Stuart Morgan's 1995 interview with the artist Damian Hirst (Extract 7.37a).

Extract 7.37a: Interview with Damian Hirst

Morgan: How did you plan the present show?

Hirst: I based it on the idea of corruption and tried to see that as positive.
Morgan Corruption of flesh or moral?
Hirst: I'm trying to see them as the same or connected. You can say it's corrupt to sell cigarettes because they corrupt the flesh. One piece is called 'Loving in a World of Desire'. It's about how love becomes problematic when faced with the corruption of the flesh and the idea of creating a world of desire that you meet in advertising—which makes things difficult.
(Morgan 1995)

Hirst describes the exhibition as being 'based on the idea of corruption' and states that the work itself is 'about how love becomes problematic', along with the 'idea of creating a world of desire'. It could be argued that these utterances all refer to ideas which exist independently of the work itself, rather than ideas that, as in the examples discussed above reference: (a) socio-cultural values that frame a particular art and design movement, (b) an individual artist or designer's specific beliefs about their art and design practice, (c) a technical or aesthetic realisation for a future work, (d) a literal subject for a work, or (e) the concept of art itself. Instead, Hirst's usage of ideas refers to an autonomous 'aboutness' of the work, an emphasis with is repeated throughout the interview (Extract 7.37b).

Extract 7.37b: Interview with Damian Hirst (Italics Added)

Morgan: What was 'Pharmacy' (1992) *about*?
Hirst: Confidence that drugs will cure everything.
(Morgan 1995)

The significance of the idea is not restricted to the contemporary visual arts and is also viewed as fundamental to design practice in both the professional and educative setting. Cuff's (1991) interviews with architects repeatedly convey the centrality of the idea in their design thinking, with one architect describing a project as 'once again show[ing] us the power of architecture as an *idea* and that you can convey *ideas* regardless of the size or the scope of a project' (p. 203, italics added). Similarly, Akin (2002) holds the view that:

> Most successful designs, at least ones that are recognized in the field as notable, have explicable *ideas* underlying these dimensions; for instance, the core and open-plan layout of the Farnsworth house by Mies van der Rohe, the served and servant spaces of the Salk Institute by Louis Kahn, the exploded box of Fallingwater by Frank Lloyd Wright. (Akin 2002, p. 410, italics added)

He goes on to argue that 'how these *abstract* concepts in fact give rise to and later are used to justify and explain explicit physical descriptions of designs is a particular skill that the architectural student must learn in school' (p. 410, original italics). Casakin (2004) holds the view that 'the design studio is the place where students are expected to grasp, present, and defend design *ideas*' (p. 2, italics added), while Goldschmidt and Sever (2011) argue that 'design products of the tangible kind such as objects or buildings are said to be designed on the basis of a "design concept", which is an *idea* that drives many of the major preliminary design decisions' (p. 139, italics added). They make the point that 'mature designers make frequent use of "stock ideas" accumulated over time and stored in memory and personal archives' (p. 139); a resource that they suggest novice designers often tend to lack. They carry out a controlled experiment to show how the reading of textual stimuli containing ideas (either related or unrelated to the design problem) before embarking on a design project 'can be inspiring and enhances originality and creativity of designs produced by students in short-term design exercises' (pp. 150–151).

Concluding Comments

It could be concluded that the findings generated from multi-perspectival analysis presented in this chapter are broadly ethnomethodological in nature, in that they describe the locally produced, organisational procedures or 'methods' (Garfinkel 1967, p. 33) of the tutors and their students as they concertedly accomplish, and reflexively make sense of their actions as creative practice, through a discourse of ideas. In other words, the metaphoric procedure of 'idea transference' from one 'object-container' to the next is conceptualised as a taken-for-granted process which provides a sense of order or intelligibility in the studio environment, and as a result structures much of the verbal content of the written and interactional genres in the studio.

It was also suggested that as the idea metaphorically transfers from one object container to the next, it undergoes a process of transformation. Interestingly, the transformation of phenomena, as they are transitioned from one mode of representation to the next, has been the subject of a number of ethnomethodologically influenced studies. Latour (1999), for example, conceives of the concept 'chain of transformation' (p. 71), to show how soil from the Amazon forest is transformed through a number of stages (measurements, notebook annotations, graphs) into a scientific report. Brown (2001), using Latour's notion of the chain of transformations, examines the way that the time spent by oil company employees working on various projects for different organisations is transformed, firstly into financial codes on a timesheet, then into the database of a computer system, and finally into money transfers for work rendered. Iedema (2003) uses the term *resemiotisation*, rather than transformation, to emphasise the multi-semiotic complexity of the transformative process and the practices in which they occur. He shows how the verbal interactions of face-to-face meetings to discuss the building of a health facility project are resemiotised as a written summary in the form of the planners report, and again as an architect-planner's design proposal.

Finally, Latour's (1999) point that the chain of transformation has 'no limit at either end' (p. 70) is relevant to this chapter. Prior to the interaction of the brief writing meeting (which was transformed into the provocating ideas of the brief), the tutors would have referred to web pages containing the lyrics of songs or the definitions of binary opposites. Similarly, each student's creative work was eventually transformed into a series of evaluative written comments provided in their formative feedback. These comments are ultimately transformed into final grades, certificate of qualifications, and so on.

Notes

1. Following the conventions of cognitive linguistics, small caps without italics, are used here to denote reference to a structural metaphor. Structural metaphors, unlike the systematic metaphors discussion in Chap. 6, do not necessarily occur directly in the language, but instead describe the conceptual framework of language.
2. Swales (1990) identifies the communicative purpose or rationale of a genre as the 'principal criterial feature that turns a collection of communicative events into a genre' (p. 46).
3. Habitus (Bourdieu 1993) can be glossed as the unique dispositions of an individual developed over time through a combination of the social conditions of their upbringing, as well as their education. The effects of the individual habitus are the reactions or responses, actions or activities, ways of behaving or thinking of an individual in a specific context that occur as a result of their unique dispositions.

References

Akin, Ö. (2002). Case-based instruction strategies in architecture. *Design Studies, 23*(4), 407–431.

Alberro, A. (2003). *Conceptual art and the politics of publicity*. Cambridge, MA: MIT Press.

Baker, P. (2006). *Using corpora in discourse analysis*. London, UK: Continuum.

Bourdieu, P. (1990). *The logic of practice*. Stanford, CA: Stanford University Press.

Bourdieu, P. (1993). *The field of cultural production: Essays on art and literature*. New York, NY: Columbia University Press.

Bourdieu, P. (1996). *The rules of art: Genesis and structure of the literary field*. Stanford, CA: Stanford University Press.

Brown, B. (2001). Representing time: The humble timesheet as a representation and some details of its completion and use. *Ethnographic Studies, 6*, 45–59.

Casakin, H. (2004). Metaphors in the design studio: Implications for education. In P. Lloyd, N. Roozenburg, C. McMahon, & L. Brodhurst (Chair), Symposium conducted at the meeting of the 2nd *International Engineering and Product Design Education Conference: The Changing Face of Design Education*, Delft.

Cuff, D. (1991). *Architecture: The story of practice.* Cambridge, MA: Massachusetts Institute of Technology.

Davies, M. (2004). *BYU-BNC (Based on the British National Corpus from Oxford University Press).* Retrieved from http://corpus.byu.edu/bnc/

Dineen, R., & Collins, E. (2005). Killing the goose: Conflicts between pedagogy and politics in the delivery of a creative education. *Journal of Art and Design Education, 24*(1), 43–52.

Dörnyei, Z. (2007). *Research methods in applied linguistics.* Oxford, UK: Oxford University Press.

Efland, A. (1990). *A history of art education: Intellectual and social currents in teaching the visual arts.* New York, NY: Teachers College Press.

Garfinkel, H. (1967). *Studies in ethnomethodology.* Cambridge, UK: Polity Press.

Garner, S., & McDonagh-Philp, D. (2001). Problem interpretation and resolution via visual stimuli: The use of 'mood boards' in design education. *Journal of Art and Design Education, 20*(1), 57–64.

Godfrey, T. (1998). *Conceptual art.* London, UK: Phaidon Press.

Goldschmidt, G., & Sever, A. L. (2011). Inspiring design ideas with texts. *Design Studies, 32*(2), 139–155.

Hoey, M. (2005). *Lexical priming: A new theory of words and language.* London, UK: Routledge.

Iedema, R. (2003). Multimodality, resemiotisation: Extending the analysis of discourse as multi-semiotic practice. *Visual communication, 2*(1), 29–57.

Jansen, L., Luijten, H., & Bakker, N. (Eds.). (2009). *Vincent van Gogh: The letters. Version: December 2010.* Amsterdam & The Hague: Van Gogh Museum & Huygens ING. Retrieved from http://vangoghletters.org

Janson, H. W., & Janson, A. F. (2004). *History of art: The Western tradition.* Upper Saddle River, NJ: Pearson Education.

Latour, B. (1999). *Pandora's hope: Essays on the reality of science studies.* Cambridge, MA: Harvard University Press.

Morgan, S. (1995). *An interview with Damien Hirst.* Retrieved from http://www.damienhirst.com/texts/1996/jan--stuart-morgan

Oak, A. (2000). It's a nice idea, but it's not actually real: Assessing the objects and activities of design. *Journal of Art and Design Education, 19*(1), 86–95.

Parker, T., Hiett, S., & Marley, D. (2006). Moving minds. *International Journal of Art & Design Education, 25*(1), 86–85.

Pollner, M., & Emerson, R. M. (2007). Ethnomethodology and ethnography. In P. Atkinson, A. Coffey, S. Delamont, J. Lofland, & L. Lofland (Eds.), *Handbook of ethnography* (pp. 118–135). London, UK: Sage.

Prior, P. A. (1998). *Writing/disciplinarity: A sociohistoric account of literate activity in the academy*. Mahwah, NJ: Laurence Erlbaum Associates.

Reddy, M. (1979). The conduit metaphor: A case of frame conflict in our language about language. In A. Orotony (Ed.), *Metaphor and thought* (pp. 284–324). Cambridge, UK: Cambridge University Press.

Sarangi, S., & Candlin, C. N. (2010). Applied linguistics and professional practice: Mapping a future agenda. *Journal of Applied Linguistics and Professional Practice, 7*(1), 1–9.

Sarangi, S., & Candlin, C. N. (2011). Professional and organisational practice: A discourse/communication perspective. In C. N. Candlin & S. Sarangi (Eds.), *Handbook of communication in organisations and professions*. Berlin, Germany: Mouton de Gruyter.

Stiles, K., & Selz, P. (Eds.). (1996). *Theories and documents of contemporary art: A sourcebook of artists' writings*. Berkeley, CA: University of California Press.

Sung-Yul Park, J., & Bucholtz, M. (2009). Introduction. Public transcripts: Entextualization and linguistic representation in institutional contexts. *Text and Talk, 29*(5), 485–502.

Swales, J. M. (1990). *Genre analysis: English in academic and research settings*. Cambridge, UK: Cambridge University Press.

Wodak, R. (2001). The discourse-historical approach. In R. Wodak & M. Meyer (Eds.), *Methods of critical discourse analysis* (pp. 63–94). London, UK: Sage.

8

Identity

Introduction

In Chap. 5, it was shown how the tutors categorised the art and design students as creatively unmotivated, thus constituting the need for a strategy to motivate the students into creative action. The development of the motivating strategy took place through the interaction of the brief writing meeting and emerged as the decision to implement a critique session early into the 5-week assessment event. To support their strategy, the tutors decided to include the details and requirements of the critique session in the Binary Opposites brief. This chapter examines other categorisation work routinely accomplished in the texts and talk of the university art and design studio. An example can be seen in Extract 8.1, the final part of the provocation section from the Binary Opposites brief, which through the imperative mood and the emboldening of text obligates students to orient their creative work towards one of a number of listed art and design disciplines.

D. Hocking, *Communicating Creativity*, Communicating in Professions and Organizations, https://doi.org/10.1057/978-1-137-55804-6_8

Extract 8.1: The Binary Opposites brief (Original Bold)

Develop work within the parameters and requirements of your elective studies choice; i.e. 2 Dimensional Design (Graphic and Digital Design), 3 Dimensional Design (Fashion, Product and Spatial Design) and Visual Arts.

The chapter will examine how the categorisation of students' work into these different disciplinary activities inevitably orients the students' towards a particular creative identity, for example, graphic designer, spatial designer, visual artist, etc., along with the values and practices typically associated with that identity. The chapter will also show that, although constrained by wider institutional structures, much of the categorisation work in the university art and design studio is accomplished according to 'the locally situated conditions of relevance, activity and context' (Housley and Fitzgerald 2002, p. 66), including the collective and contingent common-sense assumptions and interests of the tutors.

Perspectival and Methodological Foci

In order to examine the discursive construction of student identity in the art and design studio, this chapter draws upon the concepts of Membership Categorisation Analysis (MCA), originating in the work of Sacks (1992) and subsequently developed by others, including Antaki and Widdicombe (1998), Eglin and Hester (2003), Hester and Hester (2012), Housley and Fitzgerald (2002), and Stokoe (2012). MCA views a group or individual's identity as their orientation to the membership of some feature-rich category or categories. The nature of the categories and process of categorisation is accomplished by the interactants (rather than assigned by the analyst) through the local, situated, and emergent properties of their interaction, where they inevitably draw upon the resources of their normative assumptions or common-sense knowledge. Of interest to the analyst is not simply the categories displayed by the interactants, but the actions (category-bound activities) and characteristics (category-based predicates) ascribed to the categories, how these are made relevant in the interaction, and the consequences that follow (Antaki and Widdicombe 1998). Furthermore, categorisation work also defines the actions and characteristics which are seen as not belonging to a particular category, thus identifying those to be excluded from a particular group or community (Nilan 1994).

Two important developments in MCA are taken into account in this chapter, the first of which involves the issue of context. In general, MCA does not view social interaction as the simple reflection of existing macro social structures, and therefore, like Conversation Analysis, it has tended to concentrate on what is observable within the locally produced constraints of everyday interaction while disregarding its wider social contexts (Benwell and Stokoe 2006; Housley and Fitzgerald 2002). However, in institutional and organisational settings, where specialised vocabularies and labels are associated with specific professional groups, and where in situ categorisation work is inevitably tied to the institution and its particular function, MCA researchers recommend a greater sensitivity to the socio-institutional context of the interaction (Antaki 2011; Hester and Eglin 1997; Housley and Fitzgerald 2002). As a result, this chapter views the socio-institutional context as a resource that shapes, and is shaped by, the participants' interactional accomplishments, particularly with respect to the categorisation of the art and design disciplines. The second development relevant to this chapter is MCA's extension into the territory of non-personalised categories (Housley and Fitzgerald 2002; McHoul and Watson 1984). For example, while visual arts, graphic design or spatial design, and so on might simply be viewed as the category-bound activities of the personalised categories 'painter', 'designer', or 'architect', it is clear from the data in this study that these art and design disciplines are constituted by the participants as independent and powerful categories in their own right, and as such, they are routinely utilised as resources for the constitution of student identity. Furthermore, like personalised categories, non-personalised categories are perceived as variable and sensitive to the situated and locally achievements of the participants and exhibit their own category-based predicates.

The categorisation analysis in this chapter initially focuses on the interactions of the students and the tutors and is therefore representative of the social action perspective; however, interviews, which represent the participants' perspective, are also used to corroborate and further extend the key points that emerge from the categorisation analysis of the interactional data. These accounts provide insights into the socio-institutional contexts of the participants, as well as their individual and collective common-sense beliefs, personal values and interests, and how these are utilised as resources in the situated and occasioned category work occurring in the interactional data.

Intersecting the semiotic and interactional perspectives, the analytical tools of multimodal (inter)action analysis (Norris 2004, 2007, 2011) are also used in this chapter. Norris (2007) identifies her views on identity construction as being built 'very much' (p. 655) upon the categorisation theories of Sacks (1992); however, she includes a range of other modes, including gesture, gaze, posture, body movement, and layout as central to the construction of identity.[1] Table 8.1 indicates the methodological resources used in this chapter with respect to the data collected from the different perspectives.

Disciplinary Categorisation and Identity in the Art and Design Studio

This section begins with an interaction between the tutor Claire and student 3. The extract presents a noticeable example of the way that disciplinary categorisation is a fundamental feature of interaction in the university art and design studio context, and how the students and tutors routinely orient themselves, and others, to particular art and design institutional and disciplinary identities in order to carry out and make sense of their creative activities.

Table 8.1 The data analysed and methodological foci for each of the perspectives

Perspective	Data	Methodological Orientation	Tools
Semiotic resource perspective	Video of the students' creative activities in the studio	Multimodal (inter)action analysis	Gaze Posture Layout Head Movement
Social action perspective	Audio recording of the first brief writing meeting, where the tutors co-establish the text of the Binary Opposites brief. The tutors Anna and Mike are participants in this meeting. Audio recording of a student brief launch Audio recording of the studio tutorials where students discuss their visual work with tutors Video of the students' interaction in the studio	Linguistic ethnography Membership Categorisation Analysis (MCA) Multimodal (inter)action analysis	Micro analysis of the participants' unfolding interactions. Categories (personalised and non-personalised) Category-bound activities Category-based predicates Relevance Consequentiality Gaze Posture Layout Head Movement
Participants' perspective	Semi-structured interviews with tutors	Ethnographic approach to discourse analysis	Observation of salient themes in the participants' accounts Analysis of lexico-grammatical features, for example, lexical repetition, pronominal use
Socio-historical perspective	N/A	N/A	N/A

Extract 8.2: Studio Tutorial between the Tutor Claire and Student 3

→ Claire: shall we have a talk about
→ how your . ideas are developing
→ isn't it amazing
→ the amount of dust that comes in here.
→ S3: I know.
→ Claire: someone should do a piece of work
→ which is just about collecting dust
→ why don't you stick a piece of paper on the ground
→ and see how much dust you can get in four weeks
→ and turn it into a fabulous piece of artwork. ((*laughs*))
→ S3: I'm not a visual artist. ((*laughs*))
→ Claire: I know but you could make it into a kind of
→ really edgy piece of design then

Claire's initial turns in Extract 8.2 clearly show that she is controlling the flow of the interaction. Firstly, she specifies the topic using an initial modulated interrogative (lines 1–2), then, without any pause, which in usual circumstances would enable student 3 to respond to the interrogative in the expected way (Atkinson and Heritage 1984; Schegloff and Sacks 1973), she immediately changes the topic using a negative interrogative (lines 3–4). Negative interrogatives are syntactical constructions that are typically used when the response is expected to be in the affirmative, and moreover, they are often used by tutors in educational contexts to establish a sense of authority over their students (Fairclough 1989). Interestingly, the topic of this second utterance is a seemingly offhand observation, unrelated to her previous question, about the amount of dust in the studio. However, after a brief agreement (*I know*, line 5) by student 3, this topic is further developed by Claire through a declarative statement which positions the collection of dust as potential idea for an artwork (lines 6–7); one that she subsequently suggests—again using a negative interrogative—should be used by student 3 to develop a creative work (lines 8–10). It would appear from Claire's two initial turns, which together consist of three interrogatives and one declarative, that Claire is categorising herself as someone who has the ability to, and is simultaneously empowered to, identify ideas for art works. The laughter at the end of the turn (line 10) potentially signals that the idea identified is not necessarily to be taken too seriously; nevertheless a degree of initial categorisation work, relevant to the occasion of the studio tutorial, has been accomplished by Claire.

The procedural consequences of Claire's opening remarks (lines 1–10) in Extract 8.2 draw attention to a recurring aspect in the interactional data, which in the context of this chapter merits further examination. This is Student 3's response; *I'm not a visual artist* (line 11), which might initially be viewed as a straightforward resistance to Claire's recommendation. However, in making this utterance, student 3 accounts for Claire's 'dust' idea as belonging to the discipline of visual arts and at the same time orients his own work and creative identity as belonging outside this particular disciplinary category. Through this response, student 3 also establishes the particular disciplinary frame (Goffman 1974) through which he would like the remainder of his interaction with Claire to be carried out. Student 3's categorising work and its interactional implications are acknowledged by Claire in her next turn, *I know but you could make it into a kind of really edgy piece of design then* (lines 12–13). This response could be seen as a redressive face-saving action (Brown and Levinson 1987), as Claire, cognisant of her earlier mis-categorisation, reorients towards her recognition of student 3's self-categorisation as a designer, rather than a visual artist.

Extract 8.3 provides further evidence of studio-based categorisation work which concerns disciplinary identities.

Extract 8.3: Studio Tutorial between the Tutor Anna and Student 7

1	→	Anna:	… we're going to look at the <u>work</u>
2			that you've got up on the wa:ll
3			um to <u>start off</u> with
4			and I'm just going to ask you a couple of questions about your um
5	→		about what you think is the <u>strongest work</u>
6			and um . yeah
7	→		which <u>direction</u> you want to <u>go with</u> this=
8	→		=is it is it visual↑
9	→		or is it graphic desi:gn
10	→	S7:	graphic de[si:gn.

Anna: [graphic okay.
oka:y.

The tutor Anna begins the extract by signalling the topics of the ensuing interaction, that is, questions about the student's *strongest work* (lines 5) and its future *direction* (line 7). However, before Anna moves the interaction to these topics, she immediately—and without pausing, so as to prevent a response to her first question—asks the student whether her work is visual or graphic design (lines 8–9). The question is made relevant by Anna for two reasons. Firstly, the student's response enables Anna to select the appropriate frame for the interaction of the tutorial. This is because the activity of doing graphic design, and being a graphic designer, is constituted as involving certain category-based predicates which are different from the discipline of visual art. Secondly, it is likely that Anna is unable to establish directly from the work itself, which disciplinary category student 7 has attributed to her work, and therefore finds it necessary to ask. Had this clarification not been carried out, and had Anna selected an inappropriate frame for the tutorial (e.g. categorised the work as visual art and framed the tutorial as a visual arts tutorial), the sequential flow of the interaction may have been ruptured as the interpretative mismatch was amended, perhaps even resulting in a loss of face to one or both of the participants.

The categories/identities that are evoked in the extracts above are inevitably informed by the institutions' separation of the undergraduate area into six different autonomous departments: Graphic Design, Digital Design, Fashion, Product Design, Spatial Design, and Visual Arts. Student 3, for example, makes reference to the category visual artist, rather than that of painter or sculptor, which is used by a neighbouring institution. However, it is within the local interactional context of the studio that the connection between disciplinary category and the students' creative identities are produced. Extract 8.4, reproduced from the brief launch of the Binary Opposites brief, provides an example of such categorisation work taking place.

Extract 8.4: Student Brief Launch

→ Anna: … visual artists are going to . produce work
that's more i- in the visual art area

3 → the um . . uh graphic designers and digital designers are going →
4 → to be working ah making 2D work
5 → and they're going to be working mostly with image and text
6 → and the spatial people can make models
7 → they can make objects
8 → they can make clothes
9 → anything in that kind of spatial form.

At the commencement of the brief launch, the students are provided with a copy of the Binary Opposites brief. The brief contains the directive reproduced earlier in Extract 8.1 above, which requires the students to *work within the parameters and requirements* of a particular disciplinary focus. In Extract 8.4, Anna explains these parameters and requirements to the students and does so by evoking the personalised categories associated with each disciplinary area (*visual artists*, line 1; *graphic designers*, line 3; *digital designers*, line 3; *spatial people*, line 6). In naming the students as such, she confers them with their respective identities, and simultaneously constitutes these identities with their associated category-bound activities. For example, *graphic designers and digital designers are going to be … making 2D work … working with image and text* (lines 3–5); *spatial people can make models … objects … clothes anything in that kind of spatial form* (lines 6–9). Furthermore, the students' ownership of these identities (as seen earlier in Extract 8.2) is, in part, legitimated by Anna's authority as a tutor and representative of the wider art and design institution.

During this brief launch, students are provided with an additional brief document that contains information relevant to their choice of disciplinary focus. The respective documents are printed on paper of a different colour to signal the particular disciplinary category represented. Similarly, following the brief launch, students are assigned to separate studios relative to their respective disciplinary area. As Wodak (1996) has pointed out, 'the construction of identity is a process of differentiation, a description of one's own group and simultaneously a separation from the "others"' (p. 126). Differentiation and separation will be the focus of the next section, which focuses on a multimodal (inter)action analysis of the different ways that the visual art and design students carry out their creative practices in their respective studio environments. For Norris (2011), the term *(inter)action* with parenthesis refers to 'each and every action that an individual produces with tools, the environment and other individuals' (p. 1). She views these actions, which include gaze, gesture, body position, verbal interaction, as well as the objects and layout of an environment—themselves infused with prior actions—as mediating and being mediated by identity:

> Actions and identity are so closely interconnected in interaction that they cannot be viewed as two completely different concepts. An action always is identity-telling and identity is always produced through action. One is not possible without the other. There is no action that does not speak of identity and there is no identity without action. (Norris 2011, p. 53)

Identity and Multimodal (Inter)Action in the Studio

Figure 8.1 shows a group of six graphic design students working in a designated studio. In the image, the six students (a–f) sit at long tables positioned side by side and placed lengthwise against a wall. The wall is a large moveable partition, situated to demarcate the studio space for the graphic design students and separate them from other disciplinary groups. While the partitioning wall was originally placed in this position by the tutors, the layout within the partitioned studio space itself is created by the students. As they sit at their tables in close proximity to each other,

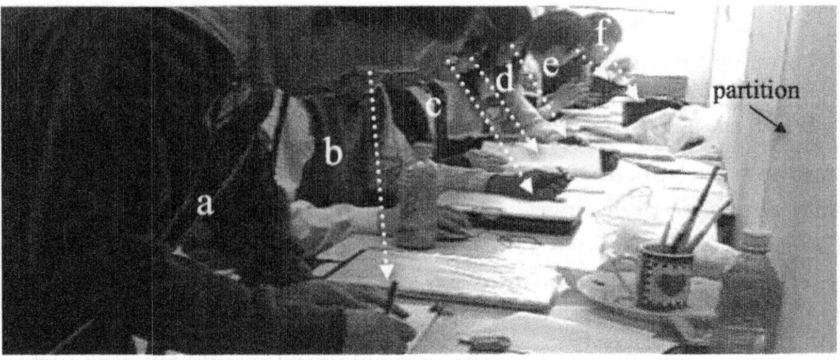

Fig. 8.1 Graphic design students in the studio

their other (inter)actional modes are structured by the layout of the studio and their positions within this layout. In Fig. 8.1 the students tilt their heads downwards towards the tables and focus their gaze on the objects (A4/A3 sheets of paper, notebooks, etc.) and activities immediately in front of them. Their (inter)actions have been constrained by the partitioned wall and by the placement of their resources flat on the narrow space in front of them. For example, verbal interaction is largely limited to adjacent pairs of students, as evidenced in Fig. 8.2 where students a and b, and students e and f, can be observed communicating with one another. To do this, they temporarily cease their creative activities, which generally require a focused gaze. In Fig. 8.2, student d has left the table, and student c continues to focus her gaze on the creative activity she is carrying out directly in front of her.

The objects spread out on the tables, which are the focus of the design students' creative activities, could be described as representative of the taken-for-granted resources of the category-bound activity of graphic design. The graphic students orient towards these taken-for-granted resources, for example, pencils, pens, A4/A3 paper dimensions, A4 sketchbooks, small brushes,[2] based in part on these objects' normative, common-sense associations with graphic design and, in part, on the requirements set out in the student briefs. Evidence of the latter can be seen in Extracts 8.5 and 8.6, both sourced from briefs in the student brief corpus. Of interest is the foregrounding of the size specifications in both examples, which works to maintain the small desk-sized dimensional constraints attributed to the practice of graphic design.

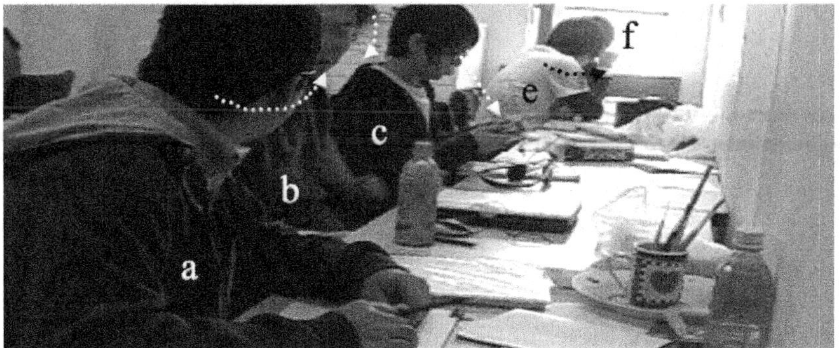

Fig. 8.2 Graphic design students in the studio

Extract 8.5: Extract from Graphic Design Brief 3 (Original Bold)

> There are no restrictions on medium(s) or scale, other than that it should, when closed, fit in, and be **presented in a NZ Post A4 Handibox** (outside dimensions 340 x 220 x 45mm).

Extract 8.6: Extract from Graphic/Digital Design Brief 7 (Original Bold and Underline)

> **Each cover is to be presented in dimensions no smaller than 25 x 35 cm or larger than 30 x 42 cm.** (…) Use stock (e.g. papers/boards) appropriate to your chosen media and illustration techniques

The layout (e.g. single table placed lengthwise against the wall) is, in part, structured by the taken-for-granted resources that the graphic design students are able to use. However, the layout also mediates the resources and creative activities of graphic design. Boden (1994), drawing upon Giddens' (1979) view that the (re)production of social institutions is accomplished through the 'essential recursiveness of social life as constituted in social practice' (p. 5), similarly argues that it is the recursive property of institutional life which enables social actors to make sense of and accomplish their shared activities. It could be argued then that the students' briefs, the studio layout, and their (inter)actional resources are part of a 'recognizable, repeatable and recursive' (Boden 1994, p. 13) process that produces and reproduces the institutional categories/identities ascribed to, and by, the students. Similarly, Hyland (2012) argues that the construction of disciplinary identity is accomplished through the reproduction of the specific symbolic systems of a discipline (i.e. discourses, genres, texts, lexico-grammar). He states that the emergence of these systems is 'often not a matter of conscious individual awareness, but of routine and habit, accumulated, acquired and changed through myriad repeated interactions' (p. 57).

In Fig. 8.3, which contains three still images from a brief video sequence, we see the same group at work on their creative activities (students e and f have temporarily left their table and d has returned). The creative activity of these students, which as stated above is mediated by

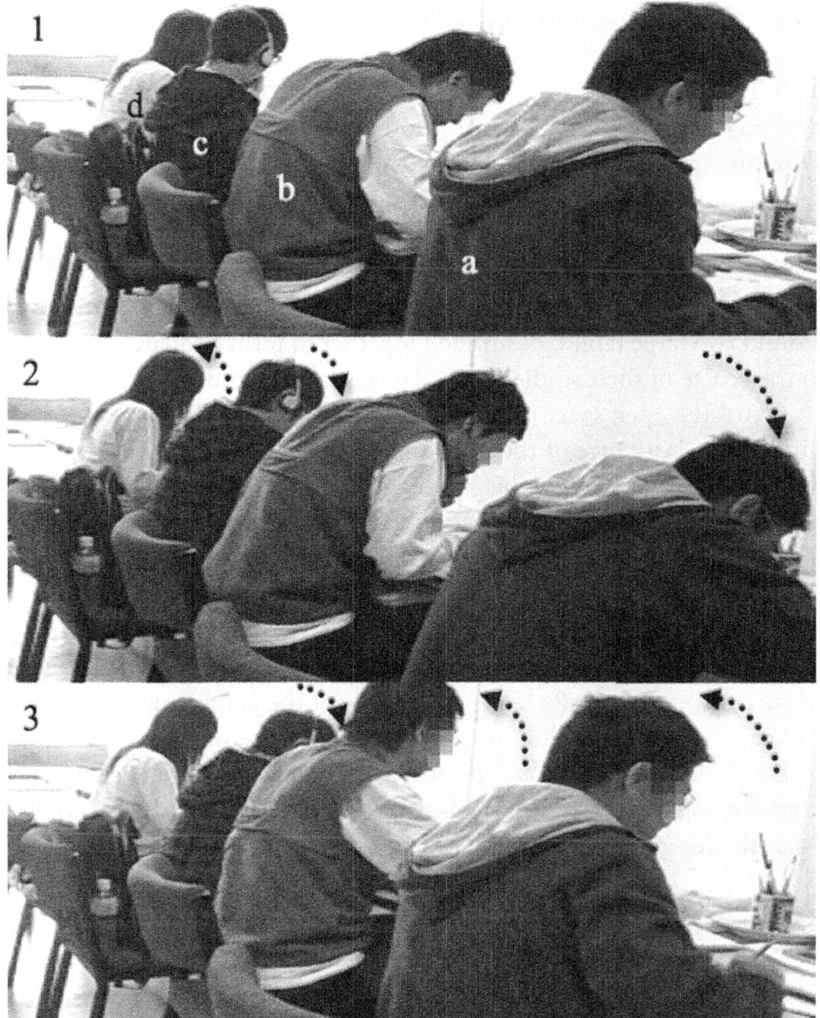

Fig. 8.3 Graphic design students in the studio

the layout, and the resources employed as a component of the layout, takes place on the surface of the table. As they carry out this activity, the students: (i) maintain a close proximal gaze in order to focus on a narrower component of their creative work, or (ii) pull back their heads and broaden their gaze in order to evaluate the specific component within the frame of the entire creative work. The students repeatedly alternate between these two actions, with each student creating a temporally distinct sagittal (nodding) rhythm (Norris 2004). The need to maintain a close proximal focus on the creative work at hand, the relative absence of verbal interaction, and the regularity of the sagittal rhythm creates an overall effect that work (Chap. 4) is being carried out.

Figure 8.4 illustrates the layout of a group of three visual arts students. In contrast to the graphic design students, the visual arts students sit around two large tables, positioned together to form a square and located in the centre of their studio space. The visual arts students verbally interact across the open space of the table (students 8 and 10), or gaze beyond the proximal distance of their creative activities (student 9) into the studio space beyond. Unlike the graphic design students, the visual arts students' creative activities are not limited to the surface of the table. Student 8's creative activities, for example, take place in her hands, which are raised above the table in front of her, while student 9's creative activities take place in a bucket, which is situated on her knees. The resources of the visual students (e.g. branches from a tree, plaster in a bucket, and a white cloth) are typically larger than those of the graphic design students and can easily be placed on the table or against the wall partitions in the spaces around the table. A number of student 8's large branches, for example, can be seen resting against the partition on the wall behind her. As with the graphic design studio, the layout of the visual arts studio

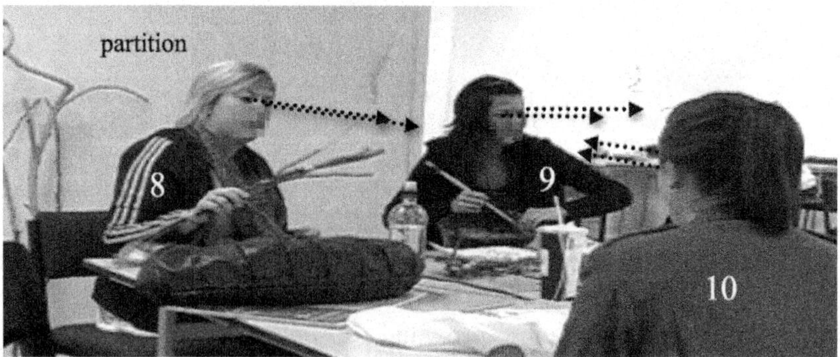

Fig. 8.4 Visual arts students in the studio

structures, and is at the same time structured by, the type of (inter)actions and resources employed by the visual arts students.

The relationship between the layout, (inter)actions, and creative activities of the visual arts students can also be seen in Fig. 8.5, which again contains three still images from a video sequence. Student 10 moves freely through the space around the table, her gaze shifting from student

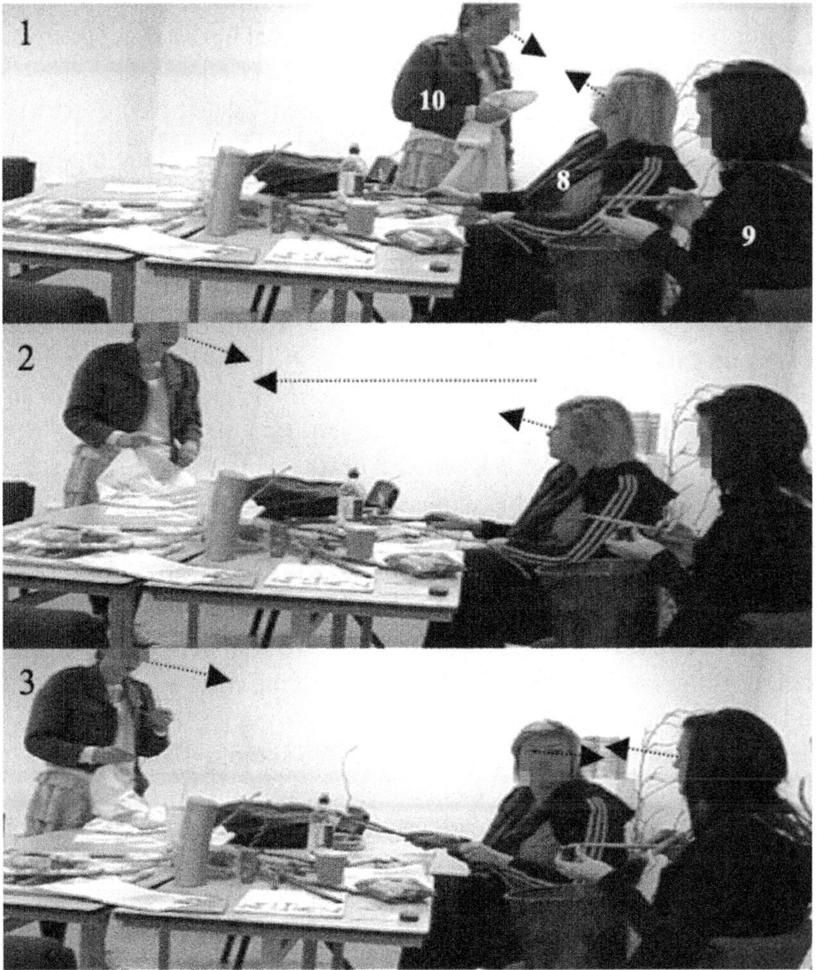

Fig. 8.5 Visual arts students in the studio

8 in frame 1 to student 9 in frame 3. Throughout this (inter)actional sequence, she continues her creative activity, which primarily involves stitching a piece of fabric. Student 8, also with her creative work in hand (which involves binding twigs), shifts her gaze from student 10 in frame 2 to student 9 in frame 3. Student 9's gaze is focused on her creative work in frames 1 and 2; however, she lifts her head to interact with student 10 in frame 3. Throughout this (inter)action, she continues her creative activity, which involves filling cups with plaster from a bucket. Although it is not possible to see from the still images, verbal interaction takes place continuously throughout the sequence.

A pattern of (inter)action is evident in the visual arts studio, which is distinct from the graphic design studio discussed earlier. Firstly, the relatively repetitive nature of the visual arts students' creative actions, for example, stitching fabric, binding twigs, etc., results in these actions being 'backgrounded' (Goffman 1974; Norris 2004, 2011) to the verbal interactional mode. In contrast, the creative (inter)actions of the graphic students, that is, drawing on A4/A4 paper, require a closer proximal focus and carry a higher 'modal intensity' (Norris 2004). Consequently, when (inter)acting using the spoken mode, the graphic design students discontinue their focus on these creative actions. Furthermore, while the gaze of the graphic students is focused on the work at hand, the gaze of the visual art students shifts in accordance with their verbal (inter) actional modes. Finally, the specific characteristics of the layout and creative resources of the visual arts students enables them to move around the room, sometimes carrying and continuing to work on their creative activities. In contrast, the layout and creative resources of the graphic design studio constrains the students' work to the creative action directly in front of them.

Like Sacks' work on membership categorisation, Norris' theory of multimodal (inter)action views identity as a continually negotiated and co-produced phenomenon made possible within the affordances and constraints of a particular social-time-place. However, and perhaps extending the theories of MCA, while Norris views these identities as always developing, she also argues that some, such as national identity, are relatively more stable than others, because they are deeply rooted in a social actor's habitus, while some may change or be discarded (e.g.

occupational identities). Others, particularly those selected actions which are routinely performed and accompanied by 'learned inferences and behaviors' (Norris 2011, p. 257), may become more stable overtime and sediment into the social actor's embodied habitus. I also contend that many of the multiple (inter)actional modes, inclusive of layout and spoken language, routinely produced by the students within the social-time-place of the university art and design studio will over time become learned in (inter)actions, embodied within the students habitus and therefore constitutive of their future disciplinary activities and identities.

Disciplinary Categorisation as Locally Situated and Emergent

As discussed earlier in the introduction, the data in the verbal and multimodal extracts and figures above are representative of the type of identity work which, although (inter)actionally accomplished, is partially constrained by the wider macro-structures of the university art and design institution. As mentioned earlier, the most prominent of these institutional constraints involves the separation of the students' creative activity into six different autonomous departments, Graphic Design, Digital Design, Fashion, Product Design, Spatial Design, and Visual Arts, along with requirement that students, once completing their preliminary year, normally select a single discipline represented by one of these departments for their subsequent programme of study. However, in many instances the interactional and ethnographic data collected for this particular study provides strong evidence of more local disciplinary categorisation work, which rather than simply reproducing these institutional structures, utilises them as resources to be invoked or transformed for the specific goals or tasks at hand.

In an especially manifest example of this tension between the institutional and interactional orders, the tutors, Anna and Mike, have re-categorised the six disciplinary areas of the institution as two-dimensional design (commonly referred to as 2D), three-dimensional design (commonly referred to as 3D), and visual arts, the result of which can be seen in the directive from the Binary Opposites brief (Extract 8.1) at the beginning of this chapter. Extract 8.7 shows one of a number of instances where this re-categorisation is locally produced and accounted for in the situated talk-in-interaction of the first brief writing meeting.

Extract 8.7: The First Brief Writing Meeting

1	→	Mike:	I just put it together for us
2			because . remember at an earlier meeting how we talked about
3			cos [now there's . there's six degrees . that the school offers.
4	→	Anna:	[yep
5	→	Mike:	[and they're six different degrees
6	→	Anna:	[yeah yeah
7	→	Mike:	you've got graphic design digital design fashion spatial product
8	→	Anna:	hmm
9	→	Mike:	and visual arts
10	→		and you know how w-
11	→		cos that's too many briefs to write=
12	→	Anna:	=exactly [so-
13	→	Mike:	[and it just gets too compli[cated
14	→	Anna:	[so I think-
15			I I agree I had that the same thing . . t- three
16	→		2D . . 2D 3D and visual work which you suggested there
17	→		yeah . that looks good
18	→		.hh so that the <u>2D</u> yeah graphics and digital
19	→		<u>3D</u> . can be very broad and the visual

Mike and Anna intersubjectively account for their re-categorisation by agreeing it reduces the number of different brief versions required for the ensuing 5-week assessment event (lines 10–12) and also agreeing that writing six different brief versions would be too complex a task to carry out (line 13). These emergent categories are subsequently reinforced through the development of a 2D, 3D, and visual version of the brief (lines 16–19), which as mentioned earlier are marked by being printed on a different colour of paper. A consequence of this situated re-categorisation of disciplinary identity can be seen in an extract from an interview with student 2 (Extract 8.8) where he orients to his creative work through the category 3D (lines 1 and 7), rather than through one of the dominant institutional categories, fashion, product, or spatial design.

Extract 8.8: Interview with Student 2

1 → S2: I'm doing 3D one, so I umm, the afternoon I get this brief I just,
2 I went to the second floor library and I just look through the
3 magazines and just think of like actually making an object which
4 relates to this brief . . .
(…)
5 Yeah, cause I mean, I'm actually making a lamp, and uhh, at
6 first I just put down some words ((*points to list of words in*
7 → *notebook*)), which is more likely to be a 3D work.

The view that the nature of disciplinary categories are often locally accomplished is further corroborated in the interview with Anna (Extract 8.9), where she discusses the attributes of the personalised categories, visual artist and designer. In the interview, Anna was asked about how the specific types of creative practices (category-bound activities and predicates) expected for each of the different art and design disciplines were established.

Extract 8.9: Interview with the Tutor Anna

1 → Int: And those expectations for the different disciplines how do you
2 determine those?
3 → Anna: Um, well, we've got this kind of philosophy, that with, that
4 → visual artists seem to be intuitive with the way that they work,

5 → and I guess we're also going on a bit of a model with how they
6 → teach on the degrees, so that, so that you keep on building um,
7 → on ideas, so that you wouldn't want to, sort of, necessarily, um,
8 → start a whole new project each time, that students might already
9 → be building ideas, and it would continue, so that this was, I think
10 → it was the first brief, so that these ideas are strong enough that
11 → they could actually be built on, we could change the
12 → specifications for the next couple of briefs, briefs with that they
13 → could actually sort of grow and develop those ideas, um for a
14 → whole semester. Um, when we look at graphic design we
15 → definitely want students to be broadening their making skills and
16 → abilities, but we generally sort of ask them to put some kind of
17 text in. With this one we weren't specific about what kind of
18 output we wanted. We didn't say that we wanted it to be a
19 poster, you know, what kind of form it was, we didn't want it to
20 → be a postcard or anything, we just wanted them to play with
21 → image and text …

In her response, Anna implies that the *intuitive with the way that they work* (line 4) and *building on ideas* (lines 6–7) attributes associated with the category of visual artist are partly a result of the local and collective philosophising (line 3) of the group of tutors at the centre of this study (Anna, Claire, Mike, and Sam),[3] and partly a result of a pedagogical model used on the degree programmes, which many of their students will eventually enter (lines 5–6). As a consequence, the visual arts students are presented with versions of the student briefs over the assessment period that require them to build on, grow, or develop their initial ideas, rather than having to *start a whole new project* (line 8) for each assessment event. In the interview Anna repeatedly emphasises her view that the metaphoric activity of building, or growing ideas, is perceived by the group of tutors as category-bound for visual artists:

(i) so that you keep on *building … on ideas* (lines 6–7)
(ii) the students might already be *building ideas* (lines 8–9)
(iii) these *ideas* are strong enough so that they could … be *built on* (lines 10–11)
(iv) they could … *grow* and *develop* those *ideas* (lines 12–13)

In contrast, Anna suggests that the category-bound activities of the graphic designers are conceptualised by the tutors as involving the *broadening* of *making skills and abilities* (lines 15–16), and they construct these activities as being concerned with text, as much as with image. Anna and her co-tutors have also determined that 'playing' with text and image (lines 20–21) is a category-bound activity of graphic designers, in contrast to the visual artists who, as we have seen, build on ideas. Throughout Extract 8.9, Anna repeatedly uses the personal pronoun *we* as she describes the student categories and their predicates. For example:

(i) *we*'ve got this kind of philosophy (line 3)
(ii) *we*'re going on a bit of a model (line 5)
(iii) when *we* look at graphic design *we* definitely want students broadening their making skills (lines 14–15)
(iv) *we* just wanted them to play with image and text (lines 20–21)

The use of the pronoun *we* is typically used to signal group membership, and to stress social distance from those viewed as belonging to other categories (Benwell and Stokoe 2006; Drew and Sorjonen 1997). Anna's repeated use of *we* in the interview extract would appear to perform this role, and in doing so, legitimise her categorisation work by making it explicit that it was collaboratively carried out by the group of tutors. Anna also chooses not to provide any generic or essentialist descriptions of the categories visual artist or graphic designer, as in the hypothetical example, 'graphic designers use both image and text', and instead chooses to more subjectively state that *we just wanted them to play with image and text* (lines 20–21). Here, she also emphasises the desiderative mental process *want*, which can be attributed to the collective desire of the group of tutors.

Tensions Between the Tutors' Individual and Jointly Constructed Categorisations

As discussed in Chap. 4, the interaction in the brief writing meeting and the drafting of the brief play a vital role by facilitating, at least for the present assessment event, the type of collective intersubjectivity described by Anna in Extract 8.9. However, there remains an underlying tension between the tutors' individual and jointly constructed categorisations of the different art and design disciplines. The interview and interactional data corroborates this tension. Claire, for example, who has previously worked as a professional designer, suggests that the requirements of the 3D brief (which as seen in Extract 8.1 encompasses fashion, product, and spatial design) and the visual arts brief are too similar and that the former lacks the problem-solving dimension which she views as occurring in the professional environment (Extract 8.10).

Extract 8.10: Interview with the Tutor Claire

1 → Claire: . . . the 3D brief is virtually the same as the visual arts brief,
2 → and I think for people that have a designer's brain, and a kind of
3 → designer's way of thinking, they need to be given the opportunity

4 to design and part of designing is, um, problem solving, um,
5 meeting set criterias, and kind of working within parameters and I
6 don't think that, um, the 3D brief as written, asks the student to
7 do that, we don't ask them to deal with specifics, unlike the
8 → graphic design brief, which asks the students some specifics,
9 → they have to deal with specific content, its specific amounts,
10 → specific styles, so they get all that kind of analytical and
11 problem-solving thinking happening. But the same, um, is not
12 true of the 3D design brief.

In Extract 8.10, Claire goes on to contrast this lack of direction in the 3D version of the Binary Opposites brief with that of the 2D version; the latter which she mistakenly refers to as the graphic design brief. For Claire, the 2D/graphic design brief appropriately provides more precise details about the creative activities of the students, for example, *specifics* (line 8), *specific content* (line 9), *specific amounts* (line 9), and *specific styles* (line 10). In other words, she believes that the 2D/graphic design version of the brief more comprehensively details the category attributes of 2D/graphic design, and thus those of the students' future creative practices.

In contrast to Claire, the tutor, Mike, repeatedly states that he prefers 'open' or 'generalised' briefs, rather than 'diagnostic' or 'pragmatic' briefs, which he associates with a 'sort of problem-solving sequence', and he frequently evokes the *JOURNEY OF EXPLORATION* metaphor (see Chap. 6) to convey his views. Mike states, for example, that the students at this level need 'to go wider and not be too diagnostically tied down', and he also mimics the voices of students as supportive of such creative freedom; 'I could maybe do that, or, or I could explore that'. Mike rationalises his preference for such 'generalised' briefs as simply a 'bias', which is determined by 'who I am and where I come from'. He also mentions that such 'open' briefs liberate the students from the constraints of the secondary school system where 'concrete … rote-learnt scenarios' result in 'everyone doing the same thing'.

The extracts above, then, point not only to a tension between the categorisation of the disciplines (and their category-based attributes) at the wider institutional level and the local realisation of these disciplinary categories in the art and design studio of this study, but to a palpable level of tension between the tutors' individual categorisations and those they jointly construct and entextualise in the student brief. In the earlier Extract 8.9, it was seen how Anna describes the collective philosophy of the studio tutors. In this view, the visual arts students work intuitively and do not require specific guidelines as to the ongoing development of their work, while the graphic design students need to focus on specific skills and abilities such as the integration of image and text, therefore requiring briefs, which explicitly direct the students towards these skills. In Extract 8.10, Claire expresses agreement that the graphic design students require problem-solving briefs focusing on specific skills; however, she disagrees with the particular content of the 3D version of the brief, which she describes as overly similar to the visual arts brief. Instead, Claire personally believes the 3D brief should resemble the graphic design brief in its specificity. Mike implies that his personal bias is towards open or generalised briefs, rather than what he refers to as the more specific 'diagnostic' or 'pragmatic' briefs, perhaps identified by Claire.

Concluding Comments

This chapter began by focusing on a particular section of the Binary Opposites brief regarding the students' elective choices (Extract 8.1), as the motivation for a wider analysis of the discursive events shaping identity in the university art and design studio. The chapter goes on to suggest that central to the context of the university art and design studio is the constitution of creative activity into a number of separate and distinct disciplinary categories, each distinguished by category-bound activities and category-based predicates. Although constrained, in part, by the existing structures and requirements of the institution, as well as individual values, the institutional categories and their attributes are non-essentialist, and as such are routinely being redefined, reshaped, invoked, and exploited for the local and situated business at hand, a process that primarily occurs within, and is subject to, the properties of interaction (itself informed in part by the interactants' habitus and surrounding discourses). A fundamental and institutionally crucial outcome of this process is that students orient to corresponding category identities, which as the multimodal data suggests, results in the performance of certain category-related behaviours. Of course, the orientation of the students to certain disciplinary categories may be seeded in the students' individual habitus (e.g. a family interest in the visual arts); however, this study suggests that the students' identification as members of a particular disciplinary category largely takes place in the local context of the university art and design studio. Interestingly, many of the disciplines that make up the departmental structures of the institution are not found in the students' prior secondary school education. For example, photography, a popular art and design discipline in many secondary schools, is typically reassigned as a potential activity of the visual arts in the institutional context of this study. A photographer re-categorised as a visual artist is likely to begin using other resources besides photography in their practice.

On a final methodological note, MCA traditionally views identity as 'an indexical, local and occasioned matter, shot through with speakers' interests' (Widdicombe 1998, p. 195), rather than an essential, internalised, and psychological reality. Hence, MCA is interested in the situated relevance of identity and its consequences for 'the local projects of speakers' (p. 195). Moreover, it sees identity as an appeal to normative or common-sense knowledge and is interested in how this knowledge is invoked, challenged, and transformed by interactants as a resource for identity work. Nevertheless, a speakers' interest (however situated) and their normative knowledge is necessarily an embodiment of their habitus, and furthermore, the situated and occasioned identity work constantly occurring throughout an individual's lives contributes to the ongoing reformation of the habitus. Such a view, which according to Blommaert

(2005) rejects an often-held view of the sedimented structures of the habitus as static, helps alleviate the theoretical conflict between subjectivity and situatedness.

Arguably, then, many of the effects of the local, situated, or occasioned categorisation/identity work that occurs in the type of art and design settings seen in this chapter become structured in the habitus of the participants and will inevitably be put to work in future (inter)actions in their local projects. The next chapter touches upon this issue by providing two case studies, one of a professional visual artist and the other of a professional graphic designer, both of whom studied on foundation courses similar to the one analysed in this book before moving on to undergraduate programmes. The chapter, among other things, will provide evidence regarding the degree to which their experiences, identities, and attributes ascribed to their particular professional disciplinary areas, while studying in these programmes, have been consequential for their professional lives.

Notes

1. Norris (2007, 2011) uses the terminology 'identity elements' rather than categories. This is because she correctly views an individual's personal identity as multiple in nature (i.e. gender, occupational, etc.) and thus finds useful the analogy of chemical elements, which combine in different ways and in different forms (some stable, some less stable) depending on situation. The term *categories* is preferred in this chapter, firstly because, as seen in the first extract from the data (Extract 8.1), the focus is on the predetermined category titles used by the institution/participants and secondly because the MCA literature involving categorisation and identity (e.g. Antaki and Widdicombe 1998) provides a useful framework from which to launch the analysis.
2. Computers are, of course, also viewed as a taken-for-granted tool of graphic designers, but within the situated context of this study, these resources were not provided by the institution for the studio environment.
3. Though it is not mentioned here, it is also clear that the tutors also draw upon their respective understandings of the history of the visual arts discipline.

References

Antaki, C. (Ed.). (2011). *Applied conversation analysis: Intervention and change in institutional talk.* Basingstoke, UK: Palgrave Macmillan.

Antaki, C., & Widdicombe, S. (1998). Identity as an achievement and as a tool. In C. Antaki & S. Widdicombe (Eds.), *Identities in talk* (pp. 1–14). London, UK: Sage Publications.

Atkinson, J. M., & Heritage, J. (Eds.). (1984). *Structures of social action: Studies in conversation analysis.* Cambridge, UK: Cambridge University Press.

Benwell, B., & Stokoe, E. (2006). *Discourse and identity.* Edinburgh, Scotland: Edinburgh University Press.

Blommaert, J. (2005). Bourdieu the ethnographer: The ethnographic grounding of habitus and voice. *The Translator, 11*(2), 219–236.

Boden, D. (1994). *The business of talk: Organizations in action.* London, UK: Polity Press.

Brown, P., & Levinson, S. C. (1987). *Politeness: Some universals in language usage.* Cambridge, UK: Cambridge University Press.

Drew, P., & Sorjonen, M. L. (1997). Institutional dialogue. In T. A. van Dijk (Ed.), *Discourse as social interaction: Discourse studies: A multidisciplinary introduction* (Vol. 2, pp. 92–118). London, UK: Sage.

Eglin, P., & Hester, S. (2003). *The Montreal massacre: A story of membership categorization analysis.* Waterloo, ON: Wilfrid Laurier University Press.

Fairclough, N. (1989). *Language and power.* London, UK: Longman.

Giddens, A. (1979). *Central problems in social theory: Action, structure and contradiction in social analysis.* London, UK: Macmillan.

Goffman, E. (1974). *Frame analysis: An essay on the organization of experience.* New York, NY: Harper & Row.

Hester, S., & Eglin, P. (1997). The reflexive constitution of category, predicate and context in two settings. In S. Hester & P. Eglin (Eds.), *Culture in action: Studies in membership categorization analysis* (pp. 25–48). Washington, DC: University Press of America.

Hester, S., & Hester, S. (2012). Categorical occasionality and transformation: Analysing culture in action. *Human Studies, 35*(4), 563–581.

Housley, W., & Fitzgerald, R. (2002). The reconsidered model of membership categorization analysis. *Qualitative Research, 2*(1), 59–83.

Hyland, K. (2012). *Disciplinary identities: Individuality and community in academic discourse.* Cambridge, UK: Cambridge University Press.

McHoul, A., & Watson, D. R. (1984). Two axes for the analysis of 'common sense' and 'formal' geographical knowledge in classroom talk. *British Journal of Sociology of Education, 5*(3), 281–302.

Nilan, P. (1994). Gender as positioned identity maintenance in everyday discourse. *Social Semiotics, 4*(1–2), 139–163.

Norris, S. (2004). *Analyzing multimodal interaction: A methodological framework.* New York, NY: Routledge.

Norris, S. (2007). The micropolitics of personal national and ethnicity identity. *Discourse & Society, 18*(5), 653–674.

Norris, S. (2011). *Identity in (inter)action: Introducing multimodal (inter)action analysis.* New York, NY: De Gruyter Mouton.

Sacks, H. (1992). *Lectures on conversation: volumes I and II.* Oxford and London: Blackwell.

Schegloff, E. A., & Sacks, H. (1973). Opening up closings. *Semiotica, 7*(4), 289–327.

Stokoe, E. (2012). Moving forward with membership categorization analysis: Methods for systematic analysis. *Discourse Studies, 14*(3), 277–303.

Widdicombe, S. (1998). Identity as an analysts' and a participants' resource. In C. Antaki & S. Widdicombe (Eds.), *Identities in talk* (pp. 191–206). London, UK: Sage Publications.

Wodak, R. (1996). The genesis of racist discourse in Austria since 1989. In C. R. Caldas-Coulthard & M. Coulthard (Eds.), *Texts and practices: Readings in critical discourse analysis* (pp. 107–128). London, UK: Routledge.

9

Professional Practice

Introduction

According to Candlin et al. (2002), the practices of the academy, including the interactions between and among tutors and students, are strongly influenced and constrained by the requirements of their related professional practices. As a result, they suggest that the analysis of academic discourse should be accompanied and supported by research into the discursive practices and contexts of the professions. Taking these views into consideration, Chap. 9 aims to establish an understanding of the interdiscursive relationship between the world of the academy and the professional world by examining how the discourses discussed in the preceding chapters are manifest in the practices of two different creative individuals: a painter with an international profile and a designer who runs a small and successful design business.

To achieve this, the chapter takes the form of two case studies. The use of case studies for comparative research in the social and human sciences has a precedent in the literature. Scheff (1997), for example, states that 'the intensive study of single cases, when accompanied by comparative study of cases, enables the researcher to understand human behaviour in

D. Hocking, *Communicating Creativity*, Communicating in Professions and Organizations, https://doi.org/10.1057/978-1-137-55804-6_9

all its complexity' (p. 4), while Sarangi and Candlin (2006, 2010) identify the case study as providing ideal opportunities for comparative accounts of professional practice. The use of cases in mixed methodological investigations, which analyse data collected from multiple sources, is also well supported in the literature (e.g. Schnell 1992; Yin 1981).

The selection of the professional visual artist and designer for the two case studies reflects the primary creative division found in the education context studied. As Robinson (2002) has pointed out, while artists and designers share an interest in creativity, work with similar visual and aesthetic ideas, and receive their professional training from departments of art *and* design, their intentions and purposes, however, are quite different, which is why 'practitioners in the field are usually very clear about whether they perceive themselves as artists or designers' (p. 125). From an analytical perspective, the selection of cases that are dimensionally quite distinct can also help to offer more meaningful findings regarding circumstances that are common to the cases (Flyvbjerg 2006). Taking this into account, the two case studies in this chapter are systematically structured around an examination of the salient discourses emerging as focal themes for analysis in the preceding chapters (i.e. work, agency, motivation, exploration, ideas, and identity). To provide a preliminary context for the case studies, each will commence with an outline of the participant's educational background and practice, followed by their particular conceptualisation of creativity.

The Case of the Professional Visual Artist

The data for the first case study was collected from the following sources:

1. An ethnographic examination of the artist working in his studio
2. A gallery visit to an exhibition of the artist
3. An interview with the artist
4. A public lecture by the artist about his work
5. A public lecture by the artist's dealer

Luke, who categorises himself as a painter, has an emerging international profile. He is represented by an international dealer, and like many professional artists he has also worked on occasion as a lecturer in a number of different art and design institutions. At the time this study was carried out, Luke was also considering re-entering the academy to complete an unfinished master's degree. In terms of his educational history, Luke attended a technical institute for a year and a half and, then after a break of 7 years, undertook a Foundation Certificate in Art and Design—a programme not unlike the one studied in the preceding chapters. Following this, he completed a 4-year bachelor's degree with honours at a leading art institute in the United Kingdom. While undertaking this degree, he was accepted for a 1-year scholarship to an American university to study art. The American university was undergoing a re-emergence of figurative art, and unfortunately Luke was 'not good at working with narrative'. He disliked the experience of studying art at this university and instead attended lectures on film politics and theory at the university's film school. He identified these lectures as his 'biggest influence to date' as they reinforced his interest in the process of painting. On his return to the art institute in the United Kingdom, a lecturer, who was also an internationally recognised artist, liked the emergent developments in Luke's work. He became a friend and motivated Luke to complete his undergraduate degree. Luke enrolled in the master's degree programme at the art institute, but only completed the first year.

Perceptions of Creativity

Luke states that he continually has *trouble with the word* creativity (Extract 9.1, line 1), a comment which is supported by the increase in his use of qualifying language (*I think*, lines 2, 5, and 6; *um to me*, line 2; *it's just, I don't know*, line 2; and *I suppose*, line 4) as he attempts to describe his understanding of the term.

Extract 9.1: Interview with Luke

1	→	Luke	I always have trouble with the word (*laughs*).
			(…)
2	→		I, I think, I think it's actually, um to me, it's just, I don't know, it's too

3 easy to put it so it's a kind of binary situation of having that somebody
4 → that's creative and that somebody that's not. And I suppose it's also too
5 → that I think about what it means to be creative. I think that everybody is
6 → creative. I think that anything we do to an extent is creative.

His belief that *everybody is creative* (lines 5 and 6) and that *anything we do to an extent is creative* (line 6) suggests an opposition to discourses of creativity as the innate ability of gifted individuals. Instead, Luke conceptualises creativity as simply 'doing'. This point is expanded in Extract 9.2 below, where he defines creativity as bringing a material object, or a thought, into existence (lines 1–4). However, evoking the socio-cognitive discourse of creativity as novelty (e.g. Amabile 1996; Sternberg 1999), he again struggles to determine (*it's very difficult to say*, line 5) whether the creative object or thought might also necessarily be *innovative* (line 6), or *something other than what we know, or* (…) *experience* (lines 6–7).

Extract 9.2: Interview with Luke

1 → Luke: I think there is something when we create something or we make
2 → something, or we produce something, or we think something, about
3 → something which doesn't exist, or we work with something in the (aim)
4 → to make something exist, but I think the thing is for me, that really
5 → difficulty about creativity is that it's very difficult to say whether it
6 → actually has to be innovative, whether it's creating something other than
7 → what we know, or something other than what we experience.

Luke's struggle to describe creativity could be the result of a tension between the various competing discourses of creativity (see Chap. 1), both in the educational environment and beyond. However, as the interview unfolds, he reaffirms his position that creativity is 'really just the act of making'. He also strongly criticises the perception that creativity is intentional or goal-oriented (Extracts 9.3 and 9.4).

Extract 9.3: Interview with Luke

1 → Luke: One of the worse things that I don't like about the notion of creativity is
2 that it often implies that somebody has an aim or an objective.

Extract 9.4: Interview with Luke

1 → Luke: I don't go in there and go I'm going to create. I don't, there's too many
2 other issues, about what I'm trying to do, I'm experiencing, I'm
3 researching, I'm developing, but it's not necessarily that it's going to
4 be-, I don't perceive that it's a creative act …

Luke's dealer also suggests an opposition to the conventional socio-cognitive definition of creativity with its emphasis on novelty. At a public discussion about his gallery, he stated that he is 'not religious about finding new stuff' and that he is 'not interested in newness' or 'contemporary relevance'. Consequently, he does not direct his artists to be 'new and relevant'. When I question Luke on this point, he agrees that his dealer is less interested in what he describes as the 'fashionable' and instead is more 'interested in content', the 'impetus for the work', and 'how the artist expresses or strategises around trying to create certain kinds of experiences for their viewers or even for themselves'. The following section will now elaborate on many of the points introduced above, through a focus on the discourse-based themes of the preceding chapters.

Work

In Extract 9.5 below, Luke corroborates the key points to emerge from Chap. 3 through his claim that creative practice *can just feel like a job* (line 4), and that as a result he is often *just going through the motions* (lines 4–5). Interestingly, in her interview, the tutor Claire similarly described the students as 'going through the motions'.

Extract 9.5: Interview with Luke

1	→	Luke:	I mean, I think that in order to create, it puts the (instance) that you're
2			going into a particular space, where it kind of implies that the intention is
3			to be creative. I don't often feel that way, when I go into it, in fact
4	→		sometimes it can just feel like a job, you know, I'm just going through
5	→		the motions.

Furthermore, during my visits to Luke's studio, he routinely made reference to the financial aspect of his creative practice. Being an artist is Luke's profession and the sale of his paintings, which takes place through his dealer, is his primary source of income. Luke mentions that the experience of needing to make a living from one's art work 'knocks the romance out of it straight away' and that it has a major impact on his practice. For instance, events such as the 2007 financial crisis strongly affected his income and livelihood. One result of this crisis was that the number of his works sold by his dealer at the time significantly decreased. This resulted not only in a reduction in income, but it also meant that his dealer was unable to reduce the number of completed paintings in stock, thus limiting the necessity and motivation for Luke to create further works. He argues that many university art students would leave their degree and intended profession if they knew the financial challenges of being a professional artist.

Luke's description of his practice often reproduces entailments of the work discourse discussed in Chap. 3. These include the reconstitution of the artist as worker, whereby the skills of art are replaced with the activities of work (Molesworth 2003) and the shift of artistic culture from its traditional associations as a pleasurable leisure activity to that centred around the practical and economic (Steinberg 1972). For instance, Luke produced his recent larger works in an automobile spray booth, immersed in a protective suit and helmet, and his other smaller works are rarely produced using the conventional tools of painters, such as the artist's paintbrush.

However, in contrast to the rigorous timetabled work schedule of the university art and design studio and the related requirement to produce large numbers of works, Luke's visits to his studio and the actual hours spent working on his paintings are relatively varied. This is because, as mentioned above, the market dictates the required output of creative works. During the economic downturn, when Luke's dealer has numerous works in stock, there is less pressure for Luke to produce new works. However, even in a buoyant market, professional artists need to avoid overproducing, as an excessive quantity of works on the market may result in their devaluation. Many buyers of Luke's paintings are concerned with their economic value and investment potential, as much as they are with their symbolic value. Crucially, both are inevitably enhanced by the symbolic power, that is, the prestige and artistic celebrity, of Luke himself. An important way in which Luke's symbolic power is sustained is through the representation of his dealer, an agent who is respected to exhibit works of a certain level of quality and economic value. Nevertheless, the economic value of the works is sustained by the dealer's restriction of the number of works produced. Luke also makes the point that even through the economic downturn, his dealer refused to reduce the purchase price of his paintings (Extract 9.6).

Extract 9.6: Interview with Luke

1 Luke: … lots of galleries are under-selling what they're doing. My dealer
2 said I don't do that, we just sit it out and we wait, there's no point in,
3 you know, having created a career and then trashing it, in the short term.

Agency

According to Luke (Extract 9.7), the study he undertook at an art institute in the United Kingdom has, for the most part, determined the subsequent constraints of his creative professional practice.

Extract 9.7: Interview with Luke

1 → Luke: Um, well actually, in many respects when I think back to the very first
2 time when I started studying as a painter, at (the art institute in the UK),
3 → um it's basically has set up the whole premise of my work right up to
4 → this day.

This point is supported in Extract 9.8 below, where Luke states that these constraints have limited his creative activities to *a specific specialised area* (line 1), and to working *in a particular way* (lines 1–2). He implies that the *following* (line 5), or *audience* (line 5), which has emerged around his work is tied to these constraints, and as a result his creative agency is mediated by the expectations of his audience, dealer, and critics that he will continue to produce a particular type of creative work.

Extract 9.8: Interview with Luke

1 → Luke: I've come through a specific specialised area, only work in a particular
2 → way, so for me, that thinking ahead is really important because I have to
3 think, okay how is my audience going to respond to this, will they just
4 find the shift too hard, or too difficult, um, because you do get a kind of a
5 → following, you do get a kind of an audience, how will my dealer respond

6 to that, um, how will the people that write, or who, um, write about my
7 → work respond to that, it's a really difficult fine line, it's a really fine line
8 → there, because it's a fine line between actually having to do it and
9 → needing to do it, and also not sort of, you know, it's- you're also fearful
10 too. There is an element of thinking, well how will other people respond
11 to this, and will I be trashed because of it.

In order to meet these expectations, Luke maintains a connection between the successive bodies of work that he produces (Extracts 9.9 and 9.10).

Extracts 9.9–9.10: Interview with Luke

Ex: 9.9 I suppose to me when I think about a brief for my work it's generally
based on the body of work that comes before.

Ex: 9.10 I'm one of those people that tends to like to make work where there's a kind of clear connection between one body of work and the next.

Luke is also interested in trying to 'break that up' and produce work that is 'much more varied' to avoid becoming 'a bit staid and a bit boring'. However, as stated in Extract 9.8 above, he believes that there would be a *fine line* (lines 7–8) between audience acceptance and rejection of a shift of focus in his future creative work, and consequently, he is *fearful* (line 9) of making such a shift, a point reiterated in Extract 9.11 below.

Extract 9.11: Interview with Luke

1 → Luke: ... it could actually mean the end of anybody even taking an interest, a

2 curator showing an interest, or whatever. They could just go to people,
3 this person's flip-flopping.

The notion of 'dialogue' is a theme that pervades Luke's interview, particularly in relation to the ongoing interaction he has with his dealer and his audience. I would argue that in these contexts Luke utilises dialogue as a strategy to avoid the potential issues associated with new developments in his creative work by establishing in advance how an audience might respond to his work in progress (Extract 9.12).

Extract 9.12: Interview with Luke

1 → Luke: When people come into the studio and whether it's my dealer, or whether
2 it's studio mates, whether it's, you know, family, whether it's people
3 outside, you're always aware of the language that people use and how
4 they talk about your work, and often if somebody says something and
5 I'm a little bit, you know, I go, what do you mean by that, I generally ask
6 them to expand upon it.

The theme of dialogue also appears in Luke's responses to questions regarding the influence his dealer has on the brief for his work (Extract 9.13; *a really good dialogue that opens up between us … we talk about*, lines 1–2; *it's a complete conversation*, line 8; *he will actually pose questions,* line 5). Luke emphasises the extent of his own agency (*he's always working to what my brief is,* line 4; *so it's not a dictatorial role that he takes*, line 6–7), although critically, it could be reasoned that the *respect* (line 4) Luke receives from the dealer for his creative work is based on the constraints originally set by Luke at the art institution in the United Kingdom.

Extract 9.13: Interview with Luke

1 → Luke: …there's a huge, there's actually um a really good *dialogue* that opens
2 → up between us, you know, we *talk about* which works he may prefer or
3 → not prefer, but it's never a decision about what fits a particular brief, he's
4 → always working to what my brief is, um, because he has respect for what
5 → I do, um but he will actually *pose questions* around, you know he thinks
6 → well that's interesting, have you thought about this, and so it's not a
7 → dictatorial role that he takes.

(…)

8 → it's a complete *conversation* and it's one I actually really relish, um
9 because in actual… in the end this person is actually going to represent
10 your work in a verbal manner to whomever might want to come and look
11 at it, whether it's a curator, or somebody willing to purchase, so for me
12 that's really important[1]

The strategy of dialogue is also employed by his dealer. In his public talk, he rejects the concept of the artist working in isolation while producing work. Instead, he states that he is 'nosey' and likes to engage in 'seamless conversations' and 'ongoing discussions' with his artists as they work towards their exhibitions. He makes the point that these ongoing conversations 'are not dictatorial', but instead due to the good relationship he builds with his artists, they are 'facilitating', 'sustained', and 'candid'. By interacting with Luke in the studio about his works in process, the dealer can better represent Luke to his potential buyers, but also so that he might perhaps facilitate the direction of the works produced for his gallery. This latter point is perhaps supported by Luke in the comment in Extract 9.13 above that, *we talk about which works he may prefer or not prefer* (lines 2 and 3). This emphasis on dialogue strongly reinforces the view underpinning this book that interaction is a central component of creative activity, and as such, creativity is primarily a collaborative and discursively accomplished activity. This view is again emphasised in Luke's comment that 'you can't create works on your own' and that it is 'discussion' and 'debate' which 'actually form the work'.

Motivation

The inner-directed desire to be identified as a professional artist or designer, which was identified as motivating the students' emerging creative practice in Chap. 5, is understandably absent from Luke's interview and ethnographic data. Instead, it would appear that this motivating desire has, for the most part, been replaced with the necessity to earn a living; that is, that the 'job' of being a professional artist must be carried out and that a professional 'profile' must be maintained. In a number of instances, however, Luke exhibits a degree of motivation beyond the activity of simply 'going through the motions'. This occurs firstly, when he discusses his increasing interest in developing his work beyond the existing expectations of his audience and when he discusses his desire to re-enter postgraduate study in order to do this. For Luke, the primary advantage of a return to study would be the increased dialogue around his creative processes, a dialogue which Luke conceptualises will provoke the desired shifts in his practice (Extract 9.14).

Extract 9.14: Interview with Luke

1 → Luke: … for me to actually head back into the place is really to go and get the

discourse to get the *discussion* around the work and work with people
who are like-minded, students and staff, and debate those kinds of
issues which actually form the work.

This motivating nature of dialogue for Luke is also captured in Extract 9.15 below, where Luke expresses a desire (*want*, line 1; *have to have*, line 2) that his audiences will engage on a personal and subjective level with his creative works, but adds that in order for this to occur it is necessary that he is cognisant of how they might *respond* (lines 1 and 2) to his works.

Extract 9.15: Interview with Luke

→ I *want* to know how those people will *respond* to what I do. I don't want
→ to dictate to them how to *respond*, but at the same time *I have to have*
some awareness of, of, the particular nature or particular environment
that will inform how they perceive what I do. It's not about controlling,
it's about understanding.

The repeated use of the word *respond* here and elsewhere throughout the interview is metaphorically connected to the concept of dialogue and reinforces the role of interaction as shaping Luke's creative practice.

Exploration

The most prominent of the systematic metaphors found in the situated context of the university art and design studio, *CREATIVE ACTIVITIES INVOLVE A JOURNEY OF EXPLORATION*, also occurs in the interview with Luke (Extracts 9.16–9.19).

Extracts 9.16–9.19: Interview with Luke (Relevant Metaphors Underlined)

Ex. 9.16: … or something I read um in some ways kind of articulates what I'm thinking, or where I'm thinking about heading.

Ex. 9.17: … and I think that a lot of artists began to realise that, we've left all that behind

Ex. 9.18: … and I think a lot of artists began to explore that, what does it mean for me to say that I have this understanding or this certain reaction to things before, without prior knowledge or concept …

Ex. 9.19: … the student has a really good ability to understand this area and to explore, innovate, expand, all those kind of things which actually says that the student has this ability to be aware of the whole practice …

Luke also characterises his creative practice through another related metaphor found in the university art and design studio, *CREATIVE ACTIVITIES ARE AN EXPERIMENT* (Extracts 9.20–9.21).

Extracts 9.20–9.21: Interview with Luke

Ex. 9.20: I think the practice of actually working through something is experimental …

Ex. 9.21: … it's very easy for them, just to get lost and for their practice to stop,
and where we could actually experiment …

Similarly, in a public lecture given by Luke about his creative work, he pointed out that his work is the result of 'experimenting in a number of fields'. This comment, along with Extract 9.21, reinforces the relationship between the *EXPERIMENT* and *JOURNEY OF EXPLORATION* metaphors discussed in Chap. 6. Additionally, in the ethnographic context of his studio, Luke described the pouring of numerous layers of paint onto the canvas as an 'experimental phase'.

However, and as indicated in Extract 9.13 above, further examination finds that the metaphor vehicle *respond* pervades Luke's interview (Extracts 9.22–9.25), suggesting that a systematic metaphor *CREATIVITY IS A DIALOGUE* interacts with the other systematic metaphors (e.g. *JOURNEY OF EXPLORATION* and *EXPERIMENT*) to facilitate Luke's creative practice.

Extracts 9.22–9.25: Interview with Luke (Relevant Metaphors Underlined)

Ex. 9.22: … so there's a whole point about how, about effect, how we respond to surfaces, colours, places.

Ex. 9.23: I do actually have to have some understanding of who they are and how they will respond …

Ex. 9.24: I have to think, okay how is my audience going to respond to this …

Ex. 9.25: I think it's very difficult to cut yourself off from an audience and presuppose how they are going to respond or relate to it

Luke's desired anticipation of his audience's *response*, which evokes Bakhtin's (1981) notion of dialogicality in speech, clearly broadens the extent of the *DIALOGUE* metaphor. This characterisation of his creative work as an utterance in a larger 'flow' of conversation is further emphasised in Extract 9.26, where he uses a literary metaphor to reject the conceptualisation of his creative practice as a linear, one-way process.

Extract 9.26: Interview with Luke

1 → Luke: I'm not giving somebody a narrative which has a beginning,
2 a middle and an end.

Ideas

Luke's description of his practice reproduces the ideas discourse discussed in Chap. 7. In Extract 9.27, for example, Luke describes his work as being motivated by an *idea* or *issues* (line 3), which have been extended (*extension,* line 2). In the student brief corpus, the verb process *extend* occurred twice as a collocate of *ideas* (Table 7.7), and in a tutorial with student 3 the tutor Anna suggested that the student might 'extend that idea a little bit more'.

Extract 9.27: Interview with Luke

1	→	Luke:	So it's a prior body of work and generally
2	→		everything that I think about is an extension
3	→		of an idea or based on issues in that work.

The centrality of idea extension as motivation for Luke's practice can be seen in his preceding comment that it is *generally everything that I think about* (lines 1–2). However, in Extract 9.28, Luke expands further on the development of his work.

Extract 9.28: Interview with Luke

1	→	Luke:	[It], is something which is conceptual and it's something I think
2	→		about through what I read or what I'm influenced by and I'll take notes
3	→		and I'll build up a scrap book. It may be visual and it may also have
4			visual elements. And then there's the other side of it which is actually the
5			making process, so through the actual process of layering on paint,
6			preparing the surfaces there are certain things that happen in that process,

7 the way in which the paint may move or may not move, the certain
8 nature of the grounds, the materials, a whole lot of factors which the
9 actually influence the next stage

In the first part of Extract 9.28, Luke reiterates the *conceptual* as facilitating his creative practice (line 1) and suggests that his ongoing readings provide sources for his concepts (lines 1–3). This comment is perhaps supported by a bookcase, which sits in the corner of his studio and contains numerous theoretical books by authors such as Deleuze and Guattari, Jamieson and Heidegger, among others. In fact, Luke mentions Deleuze and Guatarri's (1988) concepts of 'affect' (bodily experience) and the 'haptic' (the sensation of touch), as important impetuses for his work. His particular interest in the haptic, which he personally expresses as 'anything done by hand or made through the process of modelling which involves visiting something over and over again', might be seen as shaping Luke's comments in the second part of Extract 9.28 where he focuses on the material processes of making as central to his practice.

Interestingly, Luke's focus on these theoretical concepts has led him to reject the dominance of theory and the conceptual in shaping creative practice (Extract 9.29).

Extract 9.29: Interview with Luke

1 → Luke Yeah, well I think conceptual concerns have run their course, and I think
2 → for a lot of people they have kind of dried up as a discussion …

I asked Luke whether his rejection of conceptualism was not itself conceptually driven (Extract 9.30) given that it was supported by the theories of Deleuze and Guattari.

Extract 9.30: Interview with Luke

1 → Luke: Um, it is but then again to say that, you know, if I'm walking down the
2 street, and I, you know, am affected by some surface, whether it be the
3 edge of a building or an architectural space, that's not theoretically
4 → driven, that's coming down to pure affect, which actually is in some
5 → respect devoid of concept.

Luke supported his rejection of the conceptual by implying that the *pure affect* (line 4) that a materially driven artwork has on the viewer parallels the responses an individual might have to an architectural surface, in that it is *devoid of concept* (line 5). Hence, it is clear that while the ideas of affect and the haptic provide an impetus for Luke's creative practice, he is not interested in his works being read as a vehicle for communicating these specific theoretical ideas. This is in contrast to the situated context of the university art and design studio in Chap. 7, where the communication of the initial idea or concept was expressed as an important concern (Extract 9.31).

Extract 9.31: Studio Tutorial between the Tutor Anna and Student 3

1 → Anna: ... that actually might that might improve
2 the the well the communication
3 because we're sort of talking about communicating um
4 ideas, quite a bit.

Identity

The interview data suggests that Luke makes sense of his practice through an orientation to the following membership categories: viewers, dealers, curators, buyers, studio-mates, artists, and painters, which together could

Table 9.1 Concordances containing the node word *people* from Luke's interview

1	well, I want to know how those	people	will respond to what I do, I don't want to dictate
2	but also—and allowing people	people	to experience those different kinds of modis
3	it, because I don't like to direct	people	in terms of how they (...) read the painting, um
4	because often it's what actually	people	say in relation to your work, like I say I set up works
5	practice, context, concept, how	people	relate to it, how they do it. Um, I might say that
6	something I find that for a lot of	people	it's really difficult to expand on something that's
7	aware of the language that	people	use and how they talk about your work
8	narrative rules and so I listen to	people	and I actually encourage people to say well what
9	I'm very careful about what I ask	people	, when I'm doing that. I don't say to them, you
10	because descriptions channel	people	too easily, in terms of what they're supposed to see

be identified as belonging to a membership category device, 'the art world'. A further category that appears in the interview data and warrants further attention is the category 'people'. A list of concordances containing the node word *people* from Luke's interview can be seen in Table 9.1.

Luke partly uses 'people' as a synonym for the category viewers, and in a few places throughout the interview, the two words are used interchangeably. Perhaps his preference for the category 'people' may indicate a desire for a wider group of individuals to be interested in his work than might typically be reflected in the category 'viewers'. More importantly, the category 'viewers' connotes those who simply look, rather than speak, and in contrast, many of the concordance lines in Table 9.1 contain references to verbal communication, for example, *respond* (line 1), *say* (lines 4, 8, and 9), *language* (line 7), *talk about* (line 7), *listen* (line 8) and *ask* (line 9). The expression *expand on something* in line 6 is also making reference to verbal communication. Hence, Luke constructs, and employs as a resource throughout his interview, the category-based attributes of people as those who are interested in engaging verbally about the work and as being active participants in the production of his practice.

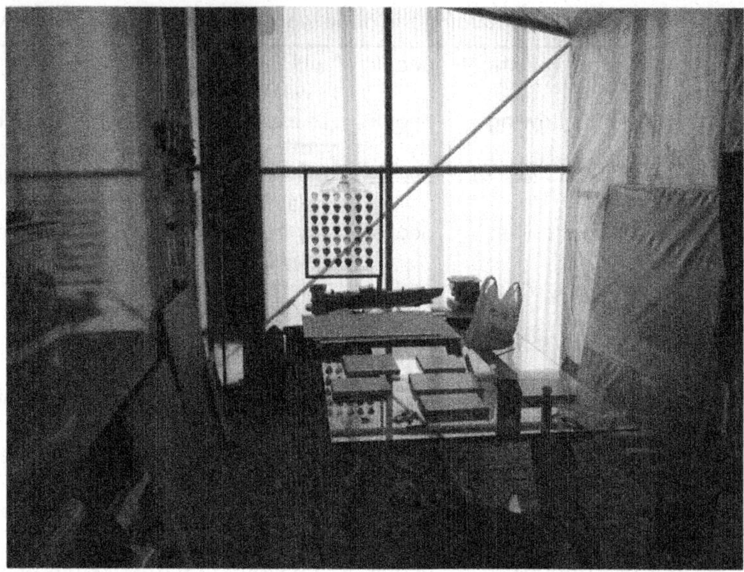

Fig. 9.1 Luke's studio

In Chap. 8, identity was also discussed semiotically, primarily focusing on the contrasting layout of the design students' and the visual arts students' studios. Luke's studio clearly resembles the layout of the visual arts students in Chap. 8, in that the table sits in the centre of the room, rather than against a wall (Fig. 9.1). However, unlike the untidy clutter of the visual arts students' table, evidence of Luke's creative practice is neatly organised across the table. Furthermore, completed large-scale paintings are covered for protection and lean tidily against the wall. The room is entirely sealed in a layer of cellophane, in order to avoid dust entering the room and settling on the drying canvases. Such a level of organisation and order is perhaps representative of Luke's professional status and the concern he has for the quality of his completed works.

The Case of the Professional Designer

The data for the second case study was collected from the following sources:

1. An interview with the designer
2. A visit to the designer's studio
3. The designer's website
4. The designer's 'Brief Document'
5. Documents from a design project in progress:
   (a) The Brand Strategy Document
   (b) The Brand Design Brief
   (c) The Phase One Document containing preliminary designs

Carl runs his own small successful design company located in an inner city neighbourhood. The company employs one other full-time designer, and hires other staff on an ad hoc basis when necessary. Like the visual artist Luke, Carl completed a Foundation Certificate in Art and Design. Carl described his foundation year as 'really, really cool' and stated that 'it encouraged me to think I did have a future doing design'. After completing the foundation programme, he attended a 3-year undergraduate degree in industrial design. Here, Carl found the interaction with fellow student designers and the access to the industrial workshops and facilities more 'rewarding' than the tutors, whom he described negatively as 'three or four guys who'd been working away in an institution for ten years'. He stated that like the other students, he was 'gasping to get more involved with industry and people who were at the cutting edge'. Some parts of the case study of Carl are specifically related to the design of a product label.

Perceptions of Creativity

Carl differentiates design creativity from technical skill. He states that creativity is about 'ideas', rather than 'sitting in front of a computer and being a master of Illustrator or Photoshop'. This distinction is further clarified in Extract 9.32, where Carl describes creativity as capturing the essence of the client's requirements in an uncomplicated way (lines 1–2), or encompassing a special characteristic in a design, for example, *quirky, appealing, or engaging* (line 5) that is also consistent with the constraints of the brief.

Extract 9.32: Interview with Carl

1 → Carl: I think it's just sort of distilling what the client wants in a very- don't
2 → over complicate things, I think that's what, you know, designers can do,
3 so there's creativity in that, you know, actually trying to, what, you
4 know, come up with something that fits the brief but is, you know, has
5 → got some layer of, that makes it quirky, or appealing, or engaging, or so.

What is evident in this extract is that Carl perceives creativity as fundamentally connected to the constraints of the design brief. However, he states that the occurrence of creativity is *very rare* (Extract 9.33, line 1). He implies that one reason for this is the difficulty of developing a design that meets the requirements of the brief and is accepted by the client, but simultaneously encompasses what Carl himself believes is a successful design.

Extract 9.33: Interview with Carl

1 → Carl: … but it's very rare to actually get that thing that, you know, you think
2 that it's really cool and they run with it, you know. It's cool and they
3 love it…

It would appear, then, that for Carl, creativity is a personally motivated, rather than an externally determined, phenomenon.

Work

Carl perceives his design practice as a commercially oriented business, which involves 'commercial realities'. However, what also emerges through the case study data is that Carl's work ethic is not one that is solely profit-driven, and he shows an empathy and rapport with those he designs for, even when a client's budget is limited (Extract 9.34).

Extract 9.34: Interview with Carl

1 → Carl: I never give anyone less care and attention than anyone else, so it's not a,
2 it's not a, umm, I'm not really very good at doing kind of budget jobs. If
3 there's two days required, you know, to do something, you just do it in
4 two days.

As a specific example, halfway during the process of designing a product label, Carl was informed by his clients that the name of their product title required changing due to a copyright infringement. Rather than begin the design process again, as would have been the convention (Extract 9.35, *it should've done*, line 2), Carl was particularly considerate of the clients' limited budget and time constraints.

Extract 9.35: Interview with Carl

1 → Int: Did the process have to begin again?
2 → Carl: No, I mean, it should've done, but, um, you know, because, I knew that
3 → they didn't have enormous amounts of money to throw at the project and I
4 → liked them, they were a really nice couple, we, um, kind of scratched our
5 → heads and thought about the new direction, whether there were any tie
6 → ups with where they were going already, (…)
7 → So, um, but anyway, we, so the next stage was, kind of, to try and think

8 → how we could possibly use some of the work we'd done before, and then
9 introduce some new, new, stuff and also to try and-because we were
10 ahh aware that they had, um, you know, (…) [a] date they wanted to
11 stick to, so there was a certain amount of, um, pressure, from a time
12 → point of view to try and help them with that …

Carl's professional consideration for his clients, who were not prior acquaintances, can be seen as being motivated by a sense of personal engagement (*I liked them*, lines 3 and 4; *they were a really nice couple*, line 4), which resulted in a desire to *help* (line 12). As indicated in the extract above, Carl was able to develop a new design and still meet existing budget and time constraints by identifying connections (*tie-ups*, lines 5–6) from the earlier designs (lines 7–8).

Carl's empathetic work ethic also extends to his creative processes. When questioned on whether he might attempt to meet budget constraints, or increase profit by quickly resolving a design project, he replied that he was *not that kind of designer* (Extract 9.36, line 1) or *person* (line 3).

Extract 9.36: Interview with Carl

1 → Carl: Um, I'm not that kind of designer. I've worked with people who do, you
2 can nail it instantly, you just think wow that was amazing, you know, but
3 → I'm not that kind of person. I'm a little bit more structured than that, um.
4 → Int: So if you have more time available before a deadline, you're likely to
5 keep contemplating the design?
6 → Carl: Oh yeah, well I am. I'm a perfectionist as well, so you know, if I could, I

7 → would keep on just tweeking and tweeking and tweaking. I mean, I'm
8 → not as bad as I used to be, but I think that yeah, you know, I'm never one
9 → hundred percent satisfied

Carl's rationale for working continually on a design (*keep on just tweaking and tweaking and tweaking*, line 7) until a deadline is reached is, firstly, because his design process is *structured* (line 3) and, secondly, because he is a *perfectionist* (line 6) who is never *one hundred percent satisfied* (lines 8–9). I would also argue that this incessant focus on a particular project is motivated by his desire to develop that *very rare* design (Extract 9.33 above).

In his interview, Carl uses the metaphor vehicle *played* (Extract 9.37), which metaphorically characterises his approach to the design process as involving fun and enjoyment. This characterisation is also consciously reproduced in his Phase One Document, where the preliminary designs for the product label are presented to the client as *playful* (Extracts 9.37–9.39).

Extract 9.37: Interview with Carl (Relevant Metaphors Underlined)

Carl: … we actually played about with a, a symbol …

Extracts 9.38–9.39: Phase One Document (Relevant Metaphors Underlined)

Ex. 9.38: … offers us some interesting textural opportunities as does a more playful look at …

Ex. 9.39: These are playful but provide a number of opportunities.

Carl's metaphorical characterisation of his design practice as play could be seen as contributing to what appears to be an 'anti-business' work ethic; one that foregrounds an empathy towards his client and a playful search for an often elusive perfect design. Coyne et al. (2002) discuss the PLAY metaphor in the context of design practice and suggest that it conveys the designer's avoidance of rules or constraints.

Agency

It would appear that an increased agency is attributed to Carl and his associates who, unlike the students in the university context, are largely in control of designing the briefs and directing the briefing and design process themselves, albeit in consideration of the client's budget and time constraints. This increased agency perhaps emerges from the designer's (and his brand design associates') conceptualisation of themselves as design experts (Extract 9.40).

Extract 9.40: Interview with Carl

1 → Carl: … you could just (…) allow them to interpret them themselves, but I
2 → think it's just, you know, (…) a lot of people aren't design savvy, you
3 know, and so, you know, you kind of almost need to just kind of support,
4 now that isn't true for everyone, of course, you know, I mean, a lot of the
5 → work we do for a corporate client, I mean, they are way more
6 → sophisticated …

With the possible exception of the corporate client (lines 5–6), Carl's general perception of the client as lacking *design savvy* (line 2) or sophistication is further reinforced in Extract 9.41 where, in a partly imagined interaction with a client, he presupposes that the client will have difficulty understanding the complexity of the design idea (*look, you know, this is a complicated thing*, line 1–2), or will lack the ability to conceptualise the finished design (*the finished thing, they can't picture it*, line 4).

Extract 9.41: Interview with Carl

1 → Carl: … so you present something, and say look, you know, this is a
2 → complicated thing, or, this is, you know, we gotta do this, this, this, you

3 know, I think that this is- and because you can't actually without doing
4 → the project and giving them the finished thing, they can't picture it, you
5 know, whereas I can think, you know, and I can sketch it and say look,
6 I think this is the way to resolve these aspects of this …

However, it would also appear that Carl's agency is reduced when decisions are made by the client whether to proceed with a preliminary design idea (Extract 9.42) or a completed design concept (Extract 9.43).

Extract 9.42: Interview with Carl

1 → Carl: … we actually played about with a, a symbol,
2 which they weren't very keen on, actually …

Extract 9.43: Interview with Carl

1 → Carl: I had a dust up with one client, who I don't think there was anything
2 → wrong with our work, actually, but he came into a meeting and
3 had already decided that what we were doing, he didn't like.

In the second Extract 9.43, Carl reproduces the perception of a client as lacking design knowledge through the way they are described as rejecting work that Carl himself considered successful (*I don't think there was anything wrong with our work, actually*, lines 1–2).

Motivation

Carl's post-secondary experience in his foundation programme, which encouraged him to consider a future in design, could be described as a critical motivating moment in Carl's career trajectory as a designer. Such comments reinforce the key points to emerge from Chap. 5, where the students' motivation was viewed as closely connected to their imagined future orientations as professional artists or designers. In a similar vein, Carl's interaction with fellow students during his undergraduate degree, whom he described as 'very talented designers', was also discussed as a career-motivating factor in the interview. The professional artist Luke also repeatedly identified the relationships formed with other 'like-minded' students as a motivating influence for his creative work, and as with the designer Carl, he also described his co-students as often more influential than his tutors.

It would also seem that profit creation, while important, is not a primary motivating factor for Carl. Instead he speaks of his desire to create the perfect design, one that he personally thinks is 'really cool' and that the client will also 'love'. His company's website reinforces this passion for his creative practice by explicitly stating that he cares about what he does. Moreover, as previously indicated, an important motivating factor for Carl is the relationship he forms with his clients. This was seen in the example where he was motivated to help clients who had a small budget and tight deadline because they were 'a really nice couple'. Similarly his website also explicitly states that strong relationships between the designer and the client result in 'great creative energy'.

Exploration

The *JOURNEY OF EXPLORATION* metaphor is evident in the interview with Carl and is most prominently realised in his account of the product label design as seen in Extracts 9.44–9.49. The extracts are all related to the design project where the client announced that the name originally selected for the product was infringing copyright.

Extracts 9.44–9.49: Interview with Carl (Relevant Metaphors Underlined)

Ex. 9.44: … he was actually quite upset that he'd allowed it to <u>go so far</u>

Ex. 9.45: … we'd really like to use the name can you free it up, but anyway, in the end they decided to <u>change direction</u> …

Ex. 9.46: … we, um, kind of scratched our heads and thought about the new direction …

Ex. 9.47: … we just (…) took them, you know, not right back to the start again.

Ex. 9.48: I don't support one route, you know, as being better than, you know, the other …

Ex. 9.49: … it was interesting to watch them debating the merits of where they were going …

While the journey entailments of movement and direction are manifest in the interview, those of exploration are relatively absent. They do explicitly occur, however, in the text of the Phase One Document of preliminary designs presented to the client (Extract 9.50, lines 2 and 4).

Extract 9.50: Phase One Document (Relevant Metaphors Underlined)

1 Creative Rationale
2 → The following couple of pages show some examples of our exploration
3 of texture. (…)
4 → These are explored in our look at background or pattern and texture.

An interesting elaboration on Carl's use of the *JOURNEY* metaphor to characterise his design practice can be seen in Extract 9.51. In this extract, he negatively characterises a bothersome deviation to a completed journey as a needless walk *around the houses* (lines 2–3).

Extract 9.51: Interview with Carl (Relevant Metaphors Underlined)

1 → Carl: … what you finish up doing is you've gone A to B and you've nailed it

2 → straight away, what you finish up doing is going all the way around the
3 → houses, until you finish up back where you were.

Carl's compassion for his clients is evident in his repeated deployment of *CLIENTS SHOULD BE COMFORTABLE* metaphors, which, as seen in Extracts 9.52 and 9.53, often intersect with the *JOURNEY* metaphor.

Extract 9.52: Interview with Carl (Relevant Metaphors Underlined)

1 → Carl: … to make sure they were comfortable with the way we were
2 going to approach it …

Extract 9.53: Phase One Document (Relevant Metaphors Underlined)

1 Naturally I have my own feelings about where we should be heading but
2 this is not about me it's all about finding a fit that you feel comfortable to
3 live with.

Ideas

The conceptualisation of design as ideas clearly emerges in the interview with Carl. It is evidenced through his summation of design creativity as *ideas* (Extract 9.54) and his description of his Phase One Document of preliminary designs as *ideas* (Extract 9.55).

Extracts 9.54–9.55: Interview with Carl (italics added)

Ex. 9.54: Carl: Because a lot of what I think design is about is creativity, you know, *ideas*.

Ex. 9.55: Int: What's this document called?
Carl: This was phase one of our *ideas*.

Furthermore, this description of his creative work as ideas is entextualised in the introductory page of the Phase One Document itself (Extract 9.56, lines 1 and 4).

Extract 9.56: Phase One Document (Italics Added)

1 → All or most *ideas* can easily be interchanged and certainly remain early…
2 'sketches'.
(…)
4 → Commencing page 11 we have included a few more developed *ideas* that
5 may provide work moving into phase 2 next week.

The data suggests that professional design practice is structured around a metaphorical conceptualisation of idea transference, one resembling the 'conduit metaphor' (Prior 1998; Reddy 1979) discussed in Chap. 7, where the idea as a word-container is transferred from one mind or medium to the next. In Extract 9.57, for example, Carl describes the design idea as one that is initiated (*you think about it*, line 1), developed (*it's going on and it's going on*, line 2), and then resolved, in the designer's *head* (line 3).

Extract 9.57: Interview with Carl

1 → Carl: So, it's more of a kind of a, you know, you go away you think about it,
2 → and then, you know, it's going on and it's going on and it's going on and
3 → then, you know, when it comes to actually putting it down on paper, it's
4 starting to resolve in your head.

This resolved idea is subsequently transferred from the designer's mind to *paper* (line 3), or as in Extract 9.56 above, to the pages of the Phase One Document (*we have included a few more developed ideas*, line 4). Furthermore, as evidenced in the text of the Brand Strategy Document (Extract 9.58), the design idea, semiotically representing a brand value, is viewed as being transferred to the *minds* of the clients' *audiences* (line 2–3) or *consumers* (line 6–7). Reinforcing the CONDUIT metaphor, The Brand Strategy Document concludes with a summative brand statement, which revealingly is referred to as 'The Single *Minded* Proposition' (italics added).

Extract 9.58: Brand Strategy Document

1 The Brand Essence
(…)
2 → It characterises what a brand stands for in the minds of your key
3 → audiences and embodies the brand's core competencies, advantages,
4 culture and values.
(…)
5 Brand Values
(…)
6 → These values are the triggers that create associations in your consumers'
7 → minds about your brand and its positioning

Extract 9.59 from Carl's website explicitly brings together the overlapping discourses of exploration, idea, and the related entailment of idea transference that have been discussed throughout this and the proceeding chapters.

Extract 9.59: Company Website[2]

> No matter how designers *make the trip from* the *brief to* the final design presentation, the procedure must commence *with an idea*. The challenge lies in *transferring* the *idea* to *paper*.

Identity

From the interview data it would appear that Carl structures his practice around the following membership categories: clients, brand development experts, consumer, and designers, all of which could be heard as belonging to the membership categorisation device of 'professional design practice'. Throughout the interview, Carl also describes two different membership categories of client: 'husband and wife team' and 'corporate client'. Some of the significant category-based properties of the husband and wife team are that they are busy with other jobs and often find it inconvenient to meet, they are not design savvy, they have limited economic resources, they generally require brand strategy expertise, and they are equal partners in their business relationship. In terms of category-bound activities, they put love and attention into their products, they have a tendency to change their minds, and they are unable to picture the final designs in their minds. The category-based property of the client's company is that it is very small and involves a handcrafted product. For Carl, the category-based property of the corporate client is that they are sophisticated and have a good reputation, while the category-bound activities are that they are used to dealing with the design discipline, and do not put love and attention into their product. It is also in relation to these different conceptualisations of the client that Carl constitutes the category-based properties and category-bound activities that describe his own identity. For example, in relation to the category of 'husband and wife team', Carl constructs himself as approachable, as used to dealing with clients who change their minds, as having design magic, as knowing where to start with the project, as needing to support and wanting to help the clients, as being able to sketch the design and resolve it in his head. In relation to the corporate client Carl constructs his identity as less 'worried' about their interpretation of his work.

The layout of Carl's design studio resembles the layout of the designers in the university art and design studio. The worktables are placed alongside the walls, rather than in the centre of the room. The designers sit at these worktables facing their computer screens and keyboards which are placed parallel to the walls (see Fig. 9.2).

Concluding Comments

A number of general comments can be made about the role of discourse in the respective professional practices of Luke and Carl. Luke's case clearly highlights the primacy of dialogue and interaction for his practice.

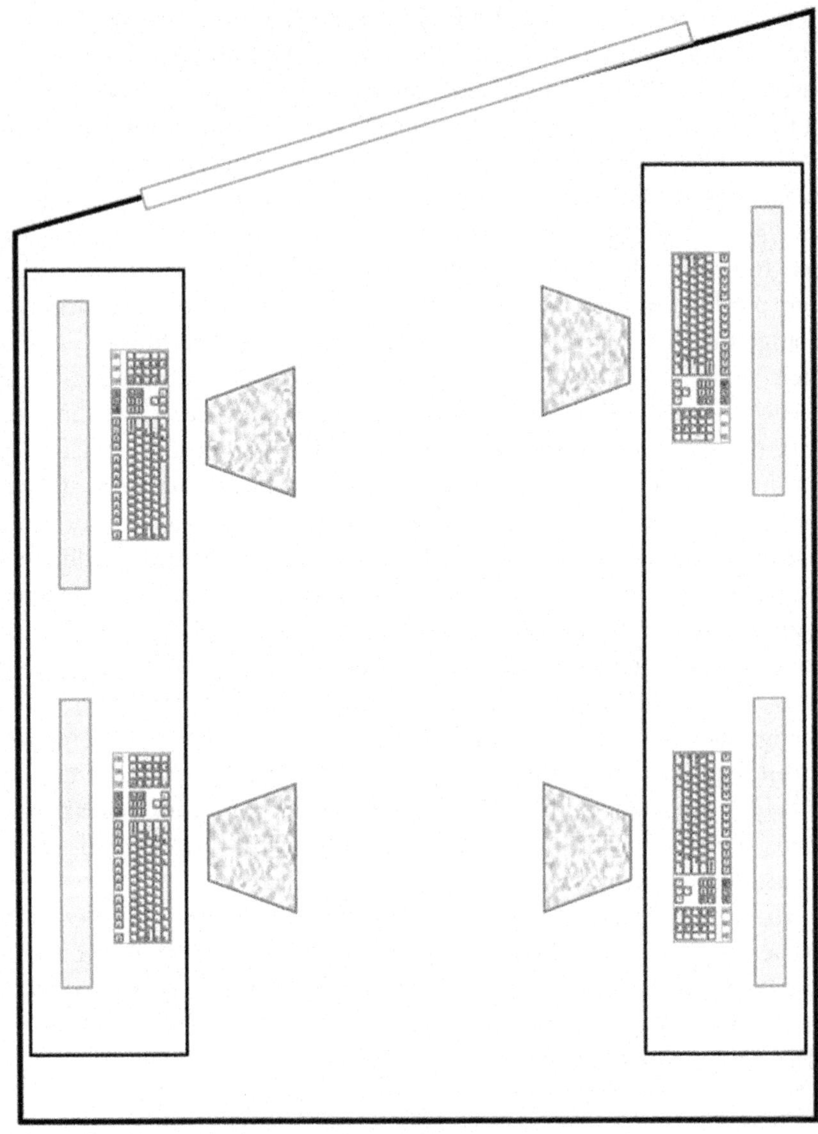

Fig. 9.2 The layout of Carl's design studio (not to scale)

This occurs at both a literal level (e.g. the way his practice is shaped through the interactions he has with his dealers, audience, studio-mates, family, dealers, co-students, tutors, and critics) and at a metaphorical level (e.g. the desire for his audience to *respond* to his creative works). Interestingly, a number of 'ideological dilemmas' (Billig et al. 1988), that is, opposing themes that frequently occur in the discourse of common-sense everyday practice, are evident in Luke's conceptualisation of his art practice. For example, he is critical of overly conceptual creative work, yet the conceptual guides his working processes. Luke also describes creativity as simply the act of making, but also refers to the importance of the creatively 'innovative'. Elsewhere in his interview he conceptualises art practice as dependent on shifts in fashion, but simultaneously describes his dealer as interested in work with a 'longevity' and 'integrity' that defies fashion. According to Billig et al., such dilemmas are '*not* the oppositions which might be associated with a careless lack of thought' (Billig et al. 1988, p. 143, italics added), but are philosophically demanding struggles which necessarily reflect the 'historical and ideological complexity of the social world' (p. 162). As a result, Billig et al. (1988) state that ideological dilemmas 'give rise to both problems and opportunities for reflection, doubt, thought, invention, argument, counter-argument' (p. 163), which in contexts such as Luke's professional practice can be viewed as both highly constructive and creative.

In contrast to what might be expected of a professional, Carl's work ethic does not come across in the data as primarily profit-driven. Instead, he foregrounds a compassion for his clients and a personal investment in his designs, a trait which Oak (2009) also finds in her study of the role relationships between an architect and his clients:

> As the architect talks about the early stages of the crematorium's design, it is apparent that he was personally highly invested in the project. For instance, he states that: 'of course it's every architect's dream' to work on such a building. Also, he notes that, for him, the project: 'was a dream come true' and: 'amazing'. (Oak 2009, p. 53)

Nevertheless, Carl's design practice is his primary source of income, and as such, it functions to financially support his family and pay the salary of his employees. Sarangi and Candlin (2011), citing the work of Parsons (1951), comment on this tension between altruistic behaviour and the need for profit creation in professional practice:

> ... on the one hand, professions manifest altruistic rather than self-interested behaviour; but, on the other hand, in terms of economic utilitarianism, all behaviour is self-interested. (Sarangi and Candlin 2011, p. 14)

They follow this observation with a relevant quotation from the social critic Ivan Illich (1977), which may provide a rationale for the absence of any reference to the profit-making element of Carl's practice.

> Neither income, long training, delicate tasks nor social standing is the mark of the professional. Rather, it is his authority to define a person as client, to determine that person's need and to find the person a prescription. (Illich 1977, pp. 17)

Illich's claim that the professional primarily defines their practice through the influence they construct over their clients, in particular the authority to define a client and their needs, is clearly reinforced in the case study data. Carl, for example, provides evidence of having defined his clients as a 'husband and wife team' needing 'brand strategy', while the Brand Strategy Document defines the clients through their conceptualisation of the product brand, using classifications such as 'tiny', 'family run', and 'eco-friendly'. The Brand Strategy Document even goes so far as to classify the consumer of the product, that is, the clients of the clients, through expressions such as 'connoisseurs' or 'image conscious'.

Finally, while Luke and Carl both foreground the dialogue or interactions they have with their professional peers and their audience/clients, and are cognisant of the particular role these interactions play in the facilitation of their creative practices, there are a couple of notable distinctions between the two practices. Luke, for example, is interested in his buyers' responses to the ongoing developments of his creative work, because their continuing patronage is dependent on his ability to meet their expectations. He believes that his wider audience should construct their own interpretation of his creative works, and he respects their ability to do so. In contrast, while Carl is aware that his clients ultimately make the choice whether to proceed with a particular creative project, he appears, in general, less confident of their views on design, or their ability to comprehend the design idea. Instead, he believes that his clients may need to be directed towards an understanding of the creative work. His does, however, foreground the important relationship between client and designer, and develops a strong rapport with his clients.

While, on occasion, Luke draws upon a traditionalist socio-cognitive discourse of creativity as novelty, he primarily views creativity as the habitual actions carried out by the artist as they produce work. Carl, in contrast, relates creativity to the construction of ideas that capture the essence of the client's initial requirements. He suggests this is a rare occurrence. They also both make repeated reference to the financial context of their practices. For Luke, earning a living from his creative practice is crucial for it to be sustained. As a result he suggests that it sometimes feels like a job where he is simply going through the motions. For Carl the focus is on the budgetary constraints of his client and how this affects his creative activity. Although he is cognisant of his own commercial interests, his creative practice appears to be motivated by the desire to create the unique design that appeals to both himself and his client.

Notes

1. Of relevance is Luke's comment in Extract 9.12 that he is always aware of the *language that people use* (line 3), and his comment in Extract 9.13 that the dealer represents his work in a *verbal manner* (line 10). Here again is evidence of the centrality of language to the production and reception of what is essentially a visual artifact.
2. To protect the anonymity of the case study participant, some of this extract is paraphrased to make any search for the website difficult.

References

Amabile, T. M. (1996). *Creativity in context*. New York, NY: Springer-Verlag.

Bakhtin, M. M. (1981). *The dialogic imagination: Four essays*. Austin, TX: University of Texas Press.

Billig, M., Condor, S., Edwards, D., Gane, M., Middleton, D., & Radley, A. (1988). *Ideological dilemmas: A social psychology of everyday thinking*. London, UK: Sage.

Candlin, C. N., Bhatia, V. K., & Jensen, C. H. (2002). Must the worlds collide? Professional and academic discourses in the study and practice of law. In P. Cortese & P. Riley (Eds.), *Domain-specific English textual issues: From communities to classrooms* (pp. 110–114). Tübingen, Germany: Peter Lang.

Coyne, R., Park, H., & Wiszniewski, D. (2002). Design devices: Digital drawing and the pursuit of difference. *Design Studies, 23*(3), 263–286.

Deleuze, G., & Guattari, F. (1988). *A thousand plateaus: Capitalism and schizophrenia*. London, UK: Athlone Press.

Flyvbjerg, B. (2006). Five misunderstandings about case-study research. *Qualitative Inquiry, 12*(2), 219–245.

Illich, I. (1977). Disabling professions. In I. Illich, I. K. Zola, J. McNight, J. Caplan, & H. Shaiken (Eds.), *Disabling professions* (pp. 11–39). London: Marion Boyars.

Molesworth, H. (2003). Work ethic. In H. Molesworth (Ed.), *Work ethic* (pp. 25–51). University Park, PA: Pennsylvania State University Press.

Oak, A. (2009). Performing architecture: Talking 'architect' and 'client' into being. *CoDesign: International Journal of CoCreation in Design and the Arts, 5*(1), 51–63.

Parsons, T. (1951). *The social system*. London, UK: Tavistock.

Prior, P. A. (1998). *Writing/disciplinarity: A sociohistoric account of literate activity in the academy*. Mahwah, NJ: Laurence Erlbaum Associates.

Reddy, M. (1979). The conduit metaphor: A case of frame conflict in our language about language. In A. Orotony (Ed.), *Metaphor and thought* (pp. 284–324). Cambridge, UK: Cambridge University Press.

Robinson, C. (2002). The national curriculum for Art: Translating it into practice. In R. Prentice (Ed.), *Teaching art and design: Addressing issues and identifying directions* (pp. 124–133). London, UK: Continuum.

Sarangi, S., & Candlin, C. N. (2006, June 23). *Aligning research and practice in professional discourse: The case for case studies*. Invited plenary presented at the meeting of the 3rd International IVACS Conference, University of Nottingham, England.

Sarangi, S., & Candlin, C. N. (2010). Applied linguistics and professional practice: Mapping a future agenda. *Journal of Applied Linguistics and Professional Practice, 7*(1), 1–9.

Sarangi, S., & Candlin, C. N. (2011). Professional and organisational practice: A discourse/communication perspective. In C. N. Candlin & S. Sarangi (Eds.), *Handbook of communication in organisations and professions*. Berlin, Germany: Mouton de Gruyter.

Scheff, T. J. (1997). *Emotions, the social bond and human reality*. Cambridge, UK: Cambridge University Press.

Schnell, C. (1992). *The value of the case study as a research strategy*. Manchester, UK (Available from the Manchester Business School).

Steinberg, L. (1972). *Other criteria: Confrontations with twentieth-century art*. Oxford, UK: Oxford University Press.

Sternberg, R. J. (1999). *Handbook of creativity*. Cambridge, UK: Cambridge University Press.

Yin, R. (1981). The case study crisis: Some answers. *Administrative Science Quarterly, 26*(1), 58–65.

10

Conclusion

Introduction

The six focal themes, *work*, *agency*, *motivation*, *exploration*, *ideas*, and *identity*, that frame the discussions in Chaps. 3–8 of this multi-perspectival study represent a network of historically formed, intersecting discourses, which facilitate creative practice and constitute the nature of creativity in the educational context. As indicated in Chap. 2, Fairclough (1992, 2003, 2010) and Chouliaraki and Fairclough (1999) refer to a collection or configuration of discourses, constitutive of a particular social practice (such as creative activity in the university context), as an *order of discourse*, a term which has been adapted from Foucault (1971). Using a multi-perspectival methodological approach, this book has identified the ways in which the order of discourse of art and design education shapes, and is shaped by, the communicative practices and genres (i.e. the student brief, the studio tutorial) of the university art and design studio. It has also shown how this order of discourse remains present in the practices of creative professionals long after they have completed their studies at the type of institutional context examined in the preceding chapters. To begin this conclusion, the discourses identified in Chaps. 3–8, which

D. Hocking, *Communicating Creativity*, Communicating in Professions and Organizations, https://doi.org/10.1057/978-1-137-55804-6_10

collectively (though not exclusively) give rise to, and are part of, the order of discourse of art and design education are briefly reviewed. Next the way in which these creativity-facilitating discourses intersect and are collectively articulated in and through the communicative practices of the art and design studio are examined. The chapter will then identify implications for creativity research and educational practice, followed by a brief summary discussion of the points raised in this chapter. As something of a coda, the chapter will close with an evaluation of the multi-perspectival approach to discourse analysis which identifies issues and concerns in its implementation, both as a research method and as a written report of research.

The Order of Discourse of Art and Design Education

Chapter 3 focused on the *discourse of work*. Defined by Weeks (2011) as 'a disciplinary mechanism that constructs subjects as productive individuals' (p. 54), the discourse of work is articulated in the texts, interactions, and accounts of tutors and students to constitute successful creative activity through an emphasis on production and a habitual work ethic. The discourse, at least in the context of visual arts practice, has its formations in the cultural and economic changes that took place in the mid-twentieth century, including a shift in the gravitational centre of the art world from Western Europe to the United States. A consequence of this shift was that artistic culture became increasingly associated with the practical and economic, and the act of being creative could be justified by the notion that work was being done.

Chapter 4 examined the creativity forming nature of *future-oriented* or *anticipatory discourses*. These were identified as closely connected to linguistic systems of agency, in particular modality and practices of tutor authority. The chapter argued that the conceptualisation of students' art activities as an act of self-expression, which emerged during the 1970s and is still valued by many educators as the primary purpose of art practice (Atkinson 2002), results in the strategic occlusion of tutor authority at the linguistic level. This is particularly noticeable in studio interactions, for example, the brief writing meeting or the studio tutorial, where the freedoms and constraints of the students' creative practices are established.

Chapter 5 was oriented around the *discourse of motivation*. According to Ahl (2008), the discourse of motivation has its contemporary origins in the theories of industrial psychology regarding the motivation of workers, and as evidenced in the chapter, produces an oversimplified dialectic of the student subject as either creatively motivated or unmotivated. In the context of the students' creative practice, motivation was discursively constituted as involving the exploration of ideas through experimentation, a view seemingly in conflict with the students' own motivations which were driven by their future desires as creative professionals.

Chapter 6 focused on the *discourse of exploration*. The chapter suggested that the discourse of exploration, which facilitates creative activity through metaphors of exploration and experimentation, emerged out of the widespread nineteenth-century culture of exploration and discovery. The chapter also argues that the discourse of exploration is now a taken-for-granted discourse within contemporary creative practice, after having been colonised and disseminated by art and design educationalists in the early twentieth century as a response to the political shifts and industrial advances taking place in Europe at the time.

Chapter 7 identified how the students' creative practice was articulated through a *discourse of ideas*. A number of studies discuss the contemporary significance of ideas in shaping contemporary arts practice, including Leuthold (1999), who states that:

> This emphasis on the 'idea' as the most important element in artistic development in some cases replaces or deemphasizes formal, representational, and expression-based aspects of art education, especially at advanced levels of artistic training. (Leuthold 1999, p. 37)

The chapter suggested that a discourse of ideas emerged in visual arts practice in the mid-twentieth century as a resistance against the early modernist focus on form. It was also discussed how the metaphorical conceptualisation of idea transference and a *discourse of ambiguity* are entrenched within the discourse of ideas in the context of art and design practice.

Finally, Chap. 8 provided evidence that a crucial function of the university art and design institution involves the separation of creative activity into distinct disciplinary-based categories, and the orientation of students towards one of these institutionally constrained, albeit often locally shaped, identities. This taken-for-granted belief that orientation to a specific art and design discipline is a fundamental objective of art and design education (even through art and design disciplines are constantly in a state of flux) might be referred to as a *discourse of disciplinarity* (Geisler 2006).

The discourses in the order of discourse of art and design education, as described above, are continually in a state of flux and change as they overlap and interconnect with other discourses, and it is this interdiscursivity and hybridity which produces their facilitative power. This means that a discourse of exploration is not, alone, strongly facilitative of creative practice. It intersects with a discourse of ideas (the exploration of ideas), as well as the category-based constraints and affordances of a particular disciplinary category. It may also require a discursive orientation to a hypothetical future to prepare the present for future creative action, and necessitate the discourse of work to accomplish this action. The way in which the discourses in the order of discourse of art and design education intersect to articulate creativity-facilitating communication in the university art and design studio can be demonstrated in an examination of the first two pages of a student brief from the student brief corpus (Extract 10.1).

Extract 10.1: Brief 12 (Original Caps)

1 What is important is how you explore various options for translating
2 your on site material so that it can be used to convey your ideas
3 and thoughts efficiently and effectively. (…)
4 Essential items required include:—an assortment of work books
5 and sketch pads with a hardback or cover to act as a drawing board. (…)
6 Throughout the duration of this project you will be working individually

7 on site gathering information and source material which will be used back
8 in your studio space at (name of institution) to complete a series of further
9 studies and finished works.
10 IMPORTANT—Be prepared !! When at the beach you will need:
11 – appropriate clothing for working at the beach.

The discourse of work (Chap. 3) is apparent in this extract through the circumstantial adjunct patterns *working individually* (line 6) and *working at the beach* (line 11). It is also emphasised by the binomial *on site* (lines 2), which evidence from the British National Corpus would suggest is 'primed' (Hoey 2005) for usage in work-related contexts (see Table 10.1). The use of future-oriented anticipatory discourse (Chap. 4), which I have argued facilitates creative action through an occluded discourse of obligation, can be seen in the repeated use of the modulated verb phrases involving *will* in lines 6, 7, and 10. Such obligation is also further marked through the use of the imperative *Be prepared* (line 10) and emphasised by

Table 10.1 Fifteen most frequent collocations within two places to the left of the node expression 'on site' using the British National Corpus (Davies 2004)

No.	Collocation	Freq.	M.I.
1	**work**	11	3.86
2	already	8	4.83
3	**facilities**	6	6.56
4	arrived	4	5.82
5	**staff**	4	4.39
6	commences	3	11.31
7	arrive	3	6.97
8	progress	3	5.46
9	**pay**	3	4.04
10	centre	3	3.96
11	start	3	3.94
12	available	3	3.72
13	**working**	3	3.63
14	skip	2	8.77
15	caravan	2	7.94

Those collocations which can be explicitly identified as being primed for the context of 'work' are in bold double exclamation marks. Discourses of exploration (Chap. 6) are manifest in the choice of the verb *explore* (line 1), the concept of *gathering information* to be taken *back* (line 7) and observed (lines 7–8), and the documentation of the (metaphorical) journey in *work books and sketch pads* (lines 4–5) in a scientific-like manner (*efficiently* and *effectively*, line 3). The discourse of ideas (Chap. 7) and the feature of idea transference are evident in the somewhat ambiguous requirement that the students *convey* (line 2, a synonym of carry, transport, send, and deliver) *ideas* (line 2) through the *translating* (line 1, signalling both transference and transformation) of on-site material. As indicated in Chap. 7, the brief constitutes the ideas as belonging to the student (*your ideas*, line 2), even though these are typically established by tutors in brief writing meetings. A discourse of (tutor-led) motivation (Chap. 5) is also represented through the emphatic use of the sentence adjunct *What is important* (line 1), and the single word IMPORTANT which is also repeated in bold in line 10. Furthermore (and not seen in Extract 10.1), the last two pages of the brief are organised as a set of milestones indicating what has to be completed by each successive day of the week. Finally, the brief is titled 'Landscape Painting' and necessitates students going to the particular setting of an isolated beach in order to generate resources for their studio work, which will involve developing two 'series' of paintings. The brief stipulates essential materials as including 'graphite pencils', 'charcoal', 'coloured pencils or pastels', and 'watercolour or acrylic paint'. Students are also required to work 'individually' (line 6). In these examples, we see the brief discursively constructing the discipline of painting, and as such, students' identities as painters (Chap. 8), including the typical subjects of painters (isolated landscapes), their methods (the development of a series of related works), their materials (graphite pencils, charcoal, etc.), and the nature of painting as an individual pursuit. Evidence of the early twentieth-century discourse of creative practice as a study (*studies*, line 8) is also apparent in this brief.

Implications for Research into Creativity

As discussed in Chap. 1, most research that investigates creativity overlooks the presence of discourses acting upon their participants' creative practices. By considering creativity and creative practice as a complex dynamic of historically formed discourses which are articulated in and through the texts, interactions, and beliefs of creative individuals, groups, and institutions, it could be argued that a more complex, insightful, and critical understanding of creativity and creative practice is possible. This is illustrated using two published studies of creativity.

In the first study, Griffin (2008) primarily uses participant interviews to evaluate the difference between the creative processes of beginner level (first semester) and advanced level (third semester) graduate students in an advertising course. He finds that beginner and advanced level students appear to have very different perceptions of the student brief. Advanced students, for example, believe that paying too much attention to the brief can stifle their creative thinking, while in contrast, beginner level students strictly adhere to the requirements of the brief. Griffin surmises that the rationale for this and other differences is due to the increasing cognitive sophistication of the advanced students, along with their ability to draw upon the strategies accumulated from previous successes. Such findings, however, could be further supported by a discourse-based analysis of the students' accounts, to see how this increasing sophistication has, in part, been shaped over time by the order of discourse of art and design education through the students' cumulative engagement with the written texts (including the brief itself) and verbal interactions of the studio context. For instance, the advanced students' dismissal of the brief may have been mobilised by their repeated exposure to discourses of idea ownership (e.g. *I wanted to come up with those ideas myself*, p. 97) and exploration (e.g. *I wanted to explore*, pp. 97–98) in the studio. Moreover, many of the discovery values associated with the exploration discourse, as identified earlier in Chap. 6, are also evident in Griffin's advanced students' accounts of their practice and engagement with the brief (e.g. *I didn't want someone telling me where to go with this*, p. 98; *you just go your own way*, p. 98). It is also of interest that the advanced students are positively identified as *idea* people, in contrast to the beginner students who are described as *ad* people.

In the second example, Cowdroy and Williams (2006) examine how creativity can be assessed in architectural education. While they view the concept of creativity as embracing many different notions involving a range of different models, it is nevertheless understood as an outcome of ability to which they ascribe the essentialist notion of higher-order intellectual ability. From this perspective, they develop a definition of creativity as a three-stage process beginning with the conceptualisation stage, which is 'exclusively intellectual' and 'involving the generation of imaginative original ideas' (p. 104). This proceeds to the schematisation stage, which involves 'thinking through the development of the original idea' (p. 104), and then moves to the actualisation stage, consisting of 'thinking out the final work' (p. 105). Based on this arrangement, the authors surmise that 'creative ability in our students could be entirely ideas (concepts)' (p. 105). Considering that in the architectural education context, their conceptualisation stage is most likely facilitated by some type of brief-based document (a point not discussed by the authors), what Cowdroy and Williams have arguably reproduced is the conduit model identified in Chap. 7, which I have argued recontextualises the discourses of twentieth-century conceptualism. Interestingly, the authors cite the way in which an 'originating idea (concept) is *translated*' (p. 104, italics added) first into sketches and then into a final form, as an important influence for their definition of higher-order creativity in contemporary visual arts practice. Furthermore, and through making comparisons to science, they go on to state that 'exploration and experimentation' (p. 110) are central to this three-stage higher-order process of creativity, thus unconsciously referencing discourses of exploration, which I have pointed out are commonplace in contemporary conceptualisations of art and design creative activity.

Research, such as the two examples discussed above, could be further enhanced if consideration was given to an understanding of creativity as a discursively constituted, and historically located social practice, rather than necessarily the result of an essentialist set of criteria or objective psychological state. As a discursive practice, and drawing upon the multi-perspectival approach, researchers would need to examine how the verbal and other interactional modes that occur in the site of engagement, along with the other textual and semiotic resources, are constitutive of creativity and creative action. As a historically located practice, the social and institutional histories relevant to the site of engagement would also need to be taken into account. In short, developing an awareness of the historically situated and emergent discourses which intersect to shape what is understood by participants—including the researchers themselves—as creativity or creative action should be at the forefront of creativity research.

Implications for Practice

This section provides suggestions for the practice that keys into the practical relevance (Roberts and Sarangi 1999) of the study. It is aimed at those who, after reading this book, are perhaps interested in its practical implications for art and design education and beyond. The implications are organised into five brief sections: increasing awareness of communicative practices, making the discourses transparent, the use of case studies, transforming the order of discourse, focus on the brief, and role for the discourse analysis in art and design education. Of course it is possible that the art and design educator has already considered some or all of these implications in their practice.

Increasing Awareness of Communicative Practices

Given that communication plays a crucial constitutive role in both the production and reception of contemporary creative practice, an increased analytical focus on the types of communicative practices that appear in the educative and professional worlds of art and design could be beneficial for art and design students. This could involve a focus on the writing of explanatory texts (e.g. gallery wall panels, labels, or online descriptions of creative works), gallery brochures, artists' statements, grant applications, and the various kinds of design briefs, among others. An important component of this focus could be establishing how each of these genres might be specifically designed for the expectations of different audiences, for example, how an artist statement written for a non-profit gallery might differ from that written for a commercial gallery. The types of verbal interactions central to art practice might also be examined, for example, how a designer most effectively interacts with a client, a professional associate, or an employee or how an artist successfully engages with a gallery dealer or an exhibition curator.

Making the Discourses Transparent

It is palpable that an awareness of the discourses, their historical origins and their effect on art and design practice, how they are realised in the studio (through metaphor, layout, etc.), how they interdiscursively interact with one another, and the nature of their underlying power effects, could be made transparent to art and design students. As an example, and following the discussion of the discourse of work in Chap. 3, this might involve a focus on the difference between Kantian universal aesthetics and Bourdieuian socio-economic notions of artistic production. It could also look at the twentieth-century post-structural reimagining of creativity as production. It might include a focus on how the cultural and economic shift of the art world from Europe to North America reconceptualised visual arts practice as concerned with the practical activities of work. Examples of contemporary and historical creative practices that have shaped, and been shaped by, a discourse of work could complement this discussion, for example, Marcel Duchamp's conceptualisation of the artist as craftsman, Frank Stella and Jackson Pollock's conscious construction of their identities as art workers, Tehching Hsieh's work symbolism, or Andy Warhol's frequently cited comment that 'making money is art and working is art and good business is the best art'. Within the context of these discussions, the discourse of work might form an explicit provocation for studio practice, for example, students could produce work that draws attention to technical and industrial processes, or references art practice as an economic commodity. The interdiscursive relationship between the discourse of work and other discourses, for example, exploration (i.e. working to explore an idea), might also be used as a provocation for the students' art practice, as could oppositional discourses, such as those of leisure and play.

The Use of Case Studies

The use of case studies discussing professional practice might also be included as a component of the studio curriculum. Again concentrating on the discourse of work, a focus on Luke's professional practice, for example, would provide students with real-world insights into the impact that shifting economic conditions and the necessity to earn a living has on creative practice. It could also provide insights regarding the role of the market, and the necessity to maintain the economic value of creative work. A focus on Luke's case would also provide information about the economic importance of the artist's relationship with the dealer and the effect this has on creative practice.

An increasing body of research is identifying the benefits of using case studies with students in a variety of fields (e.g. Krain 2010; Saleh et al. 2013). Sarangi and Candlin (2006) have also made a case for the increased use of case studies in interdisciplinary applied linguistics research. In the art and design educational context, case studies of professional practice could be developed by the students themselves as projects, or alternatively provided to the student as required reading from a pre-compiled bank of case studies, developed by the tutors, or reproduced from textbooks such as *Networks: Case studies in web art and design* (Burrough 2011). Perhaps with the exception of architectural design (see Francis 2001), the use of case studies of professional practice is traditionally an under-used pedagogical resource in the practice-based contexts of university art and design education.

Transforming the Order of Discourse

As well as making the discourses in the order of discourse of art and design transparent to students, a more critical approach might look at how more problematic aspects of these discourses could be transformed or resisted. Discourses of exploration, for example, are arguably saturated with colonial discourses of European dominance, shaped by a taken-for-granted and uncritical belief in the benefits of unrestrained discovery and scientific pursuit. According to a number of design scholars (e.g. Findeli 2001), the resulting modernist aesthetics of novelty (metaphorically captured in this book as the exploration of new forms and materials), and the accompanying focus on the making of an artifact as the normal outcome of design practice, are responsible for the production of an increasingly unsustainable number of design artifacts. As a result they call for a paradigm shift in art and design education towards a more sustainable practice, one which seeks to 'end the fetishism of the artifact' (Findeli 2001, p. 14). One way that this might be achieved by a shift towards the deployment of an ecological or sustainability discourse, involving the conscious use of metaphors, for example, *carbon footprint*, *cradle-to-cradle management*, *upcycling*, in the writing of student brief and in the studio interactions that follow. According to Goatly and Hiradhar (2016), as with the changes that took place as a result of the feminist critique of language, metaphors can be purposefully replaced or modified to challenge common-sense ways of thinking and facilitate social and ideological change. Indeed, some scholars, particularly in the area of architecture (e.g. Muller 2007), have already begun advocating for metaphorical change in both educational and professional contexts as a way of promoting a more sustainable, ethical, and ecological design discourse.

Focus on the Brief

In his guide to developing design briefs, Phillips (2004) makes the observation that the brief itself as an object of study is absent in the design educational context:

> Typically, the design brief is not covered in most school curriculums. Designers and design managers have had to fend for themselves to develop processes and formats for the design brief. (Phillips 2004, p. ix)

Due to the fundamental role played by the brief in the art and design educational context (and in the future vocations of many students), a curriculum that provides focused formal instruction on the brief and its use could be helpful for students. Such instruction might include an examination of how and why the discourses described in this book shape the text of the student brief, perhaps using a corpus of briefs collected from the institution concerned. One important pedagogical focus for brief-related study might involve examining the different modes of ambiguity in the brief (see Chap. 7), how these modes of ambiguity are produced through certain lexico-grammatical and visual choices in the brief texts, and how they work to facilitate creative action in different ways. A further implication involving the brief itself is directly related to the noticeable linguistic differences between the student and professional briefs. Taking into consideration the findings from this study, a central reason for these often distinctly different characteristics is that unlike the professional brief, the student brief plays the dual role of firstly identifying the parameters of the creative project (the primary function of professional briefs) and secondly facilitating the student into creative action; the latter typically accomplished through the creativity-facilitating discourses discussed here and in the preceding chapters.

Role for the Discourse Analyst in Art and Design Education

In a study that looked at the relationship between creative practice and student written and verbal interactions in university fine art study, Turner and Hocking (2004) concluded that a case existed for collaborative strategies between art tutors and language tutors in the wider development of students' communicative practice.

> Art staff can assist language staff in identifying what the targets are for the students, and language staff can therefore help those students (not only those from overseas) who need to develop their understanding of how language works or can work. Language staff can assist in making their art colleagues aware of the rhetorical complexity and subject specificity of the language and genres that frame their teaching and assessment processes, hopefully resulting in the integration of appropriate courses into the curriculum which seek to make such processes transparent. (Turner and Hocking 2004, p. 160)

Their view is based on evidence of a synergistic relationship between art and language, manifested in the way in which the studio tutorial and the theoretical written components of the dissertation mediate, and are mediated by, the development of the students' creative work. For Turner and Hocking (2004), the importance of this relationship is most evident when students are unable to meet the linguistic expectations of these genres, often resulting in a failure to further their creative practice. As evidenced throughout this book, the discursive nature of creative practice and the centrality of communication in the facilitation of creativity could suggest a role for the language specialist, particularly one with an in-depth knowledge of discourse analytical (and multimodal interactional) methodologies, in art and design education (see also Hocking and Fieldhouse 2011).

The final section of this book returns to a discussion of the multi-perspectival approach, to reflect on certain issues and concerns in its implementation. This section aims to provide advice to those who might draw upon the multi-perspectival approach for their future research

Reflections on Methodology

These reflections are divided into three stages: issues of planning and data collection, issues of data analysis, and issues of writing up multi-perspectival research. It should be pointed out that for many researchers these latter two stages are often completed in tandem, in that the process of writing up research is an integral part of the discovery process and often produces outcomes not initially observed in the data (Green 2009). In this study, the analysis of data (e.g. the examination of corpora, coding the ethnographic data, listing and coding metaphors) was routinely carried out well before the formal writing-up stage; however, inevitably, the writing process produced significant and novel outcomes that required an often lengthy return to the data. Nevertheless, for the purposes of clarity, the analytical and writing stages will be kept separate in this reflective discussion.

Planning and Data Collection

A defining principle of multi-perspectival research is that a diverse range of data will be collected that represent the different, albeit overlapping, central perspectives. This requires a detailed planning stage, which includes preparatory meetings with participants and an initial examination of the site of engagement in order to establish what data can be collected, and when and where this can occur. This planning stage is often made easier if the researcher is an 'insider' (Hammersley and Atkinson 2007, p. 86), with a broad knowledge of the participants' situated contexts, semiotic resources, written and interactional genres, and socio-histories. Sarangi and Candlin (2003) suggest that the benefits of being an insider can include increased trust between researcher and informants, greater access to data, and the provision of 'insights otherwise unavailable to the external researcher' (p. 279). If the researcher is an outsider, however, an initial period of ethnographic observation in the context of the site of engagement will facilitate a better understanding of the different types of data that might be collected. In both cases, the multi-perspectival model (Fig. 2.1 in Chap. 2) provides a useful planning tool.

As pointed out in Chap. 2, multi-perspectival research is an emergent process. As such, data sets that are not initially considered as vital may become relevant once the process of analysis commences. For example, in this particular study of creative practice, the benefits of collecting and analysing video-based multimodal data were only realised after initial data collection and ongoing preliminary analysis were already underway. As a result, and given the difficulty of anticipating at the outset which of the many potential data sets representing each of the perspectives might provide the most useful findings, it may be helpful to overcompensate and gather a wider range of data than might normally be the case. While this can increase the researcher's workload—for example, due to additional transcription work—it may avoid having to return to the site of engagement, or apply for additional ethical consent, once the project has begun.

The planning stage also requires the researcher to consider the potential relationship between data collected and the methods required to analyse the data.[1] Multi-perspectival researchers require a broad knowledge of different discourse analytical (and sociological) methods along with their respective analytical tools to realise the full potential of the broad range of data collected. In preparation for a multi-perspectival research project, it may also be necessary for the researcher to review less familiar methodological approaches.

Data Analysis

A key issue in multi-perspectival research involves identifying the most productive entry point into the mass of data collected for the study. This includes establishing which data set will be examined first, from which perspective (or interdiscursivity of perspectives), and using which analytical resources. In this particular study, it was found that the tools of corpus analysis—in particular, keyword analysis—could often provide useful preliminary insights into the data and consequently assist in identifying orienting focal themes which could structure the analysis (see Fig. 2.2 in Chap. 2). Importantly, the potential significance of any findings emerging from a preliminary analysis of the data should also take into account the researcher's broader ethnographic awareness of the site of engagement being investigated.

Multi-perspectival research can often be at its most productive when there is a fluid and dynamic interplay between methods and data sets in order to corroborate, augment, or extend emergent findings (Crichton 2010). In many instances, establishing the subsequent method or data set to be brought into play is instinctual; however, on other occasions, it may be necessary to carry out an explorative probe into the data, using a range of analytical resources to determine the next stage of the analysis. Dillon (2008) refers to such an explorative approach as a 'reconnaissance mission' into the data. Using Chap. 5 as an example, an explorative probe of the data using the analytical tools of multimodal (inter)action analysis (Norris 2004, 2011) found that these would clearly augment and extend the existing ethnographic focus on 'motivation', the orienting focal theme for the chapter. Consequently, the findings from the multimodal (inter) action analysis became a crucial component in this stage of the study.

Given that the expanse of data collected from the four inner perspectives can be examined in multiple ways to produce a rich array of findings, it can often be difficult to determine the limits of a multi-perspectival study. This may be exacerbated by the dynamic nature of multi-perspectival research, in that the findings emerging from one perspective can impact upon those from the others, thus constantly reshaping and redefining emergent results. In the analytical approach taken for this study of creative practice, each of the orienting focal themes in Chaps. 3–8 provided a set of guiding and hence limiting parameters for the ongoing analysis. The analysis was deemed to be more or less complete when: (i) a degree of stabilisation became evident in the findings, (ii) there was a significant degree of corroboration across the perspectives, and (iii) together, the findings began to emerge in the form of a 'coherent overarching story' (Corbin and Strauss 2008, p. 104). In most cases, this coincided with a sense that data saturation had occurred. It was also inevitable that as the findings stabilised and the 'story' for each chapter took shape, the nature of the orienting focal theme as initially conceptualised often required redefining and reframing.

The dynamic and continually emergent nature of multi-perspectival research requires an approach to research that is always cognisant of, and in preparation for, the subsequent stages of the analysis. However, at times, this can cause a degree of analytical distraction or tension. For example, as the ongoing analytical process was taking place for this study, important new concepts and issues would become apparent, some of which exhibited potential to serve as new orienting focal themes in their own right. As an illustration, the theme of 'motivation' emerged as the chapter on 'agency' was being developed, appearing particularly strongly within the context of the participants' use of modality to constrain and produce creativity activity. While still working on the agency chapter, it became increasingly difficult to refrain from observing patterns in the data related to the emergent focus on motivation, especially once its conceptual relevance to the overall study became apparent. However rather than putting emergent focal themes aside, it is important that they are kept in play, so that relevant preparatory groundwork, of both a theoretical and methodological nature, can take place before they are examined further.

Writing Up the Analysis

Writing up the dynamic, multifaceted, explorative process of multi-perspectival research following the linear conventions of research report writing can be somewhat challenging. The use of focal themes (realised in this study as discourses) to frame and delimit the analytical focus provides a useful approach at the macro-textual level, but at the micro-textual level, it can be difficult to develop a representation of the research process that suits the linear format of written text. One way to meet this challenge in a written report involves focusing on each perspective in turn; however, this approach does not necessarily convey the rich interdiscursivity of the multi-perspectival analysis. As this book was developed, it was established that the findings were best captured in written form through a coherent to-ing and fro-ing between the various perspectives, data sets, and methods. Due to the demanding nature of this process, however, significant redrafting and rewriting was required. Often this drafting work focused on identifying ways to link the various perspectival and methodological components of the analysis into a coherent account. Fortunately, as the data from the different perspectives were corroborated, the narrative of the research often logically developed into a coherent whole. Some of the chapters (e.g. Chaps. 3 and 5) developed relatively straightforwardly into their respective structures, while a number of others contained a more complex array of interrelating sub-concepts (e.g. Chap. 7), and as such required more, often time-consuming, structural management.

Due to the range of methodological resources used, another issue in writing up multi-perspectival research involves establishing the amount and depth of methodological description to include for readers. This is a particular issue for shorter publications where an overemphasis on a precursory discussion of all methods used in a multi-perspectival study can leave little space for the analysis itself. The solution potentially involves a consideration of the target readers' likely knowledge of the methods employed. Established and regularly used methods, for example, might require less explanation, while newer or less familiar methods might require a more complete description. In this book, for example, a reasonably comprehensive methodological background was included for the discourse dynamic approach to metaphor (Cameron 2010). Similarly, membership categorisation analysis required a more detailed introduction, as it is less known and has also undergone a number of conceptual transformations since its foundation by Sacks (1992).

As a final point, because multi-perspectival research involves multiple data sets, perspectives, and methods, an introductory table, outlining the methodological resources used in relation to the data collected from each of the different perspectives, may assist the reader to comprehend the way the different analytical components are integrated in preparation for reading the report. For clarity, it can also be helpful to accompany this table with a rationalisation of the unfolding structure of the study, relevant to the different perspectival and methodological foci used. The central Chaps. 3–8 provide an example of this procedure.

As hopefully demonstrated throughout this book, the multi-perspectival approach can help provide a comprehensive and in-depth understanding of dynamically complex site-specific practice, such as art and design creativity. The approach can also show how such practices are interdiscursively constituted and accomplished through the interactions, semiotic resources, and narratives of those who participate in them and how these interactional genres and communicative resources both shape and are shaped by interdiscursive networks of historically contingent macro-level discourses. Finally, the multi-perspectival approach takes into account that the analyst's values, choices, and understanding of the research context are subject to their own historically, socially, and discursively informed interests, backgrounds, and motivations.

Notes

1. Crichton (2004, 2010) and Candlin and Crichton (2012, 2013) provide a valuable discussion on the relationship between methodologies and perspectives in multi-perspectival research.

References

Ahl, H. (2008). Motivation theory as power in disguise. In A. Fejes & K. Nicoll (Eds.), *Foucault and lifelong learning: Governing the subject* (pp. 151–163). Abingdon, UK: Routledge.

Atkinson, D. (2002). *Art in education: Identity and practice.* Dordrecht, Netherlands: Kluwer Academic Publishers.

Burrough, X. (2011). *Net works: Case studies in web art and design.* Abingdon, UK: Routledge.

Cameron, L. (2010). The discourse dynamics framework for metaphor. In L. Cameron & R. Maslen (Eds.), *Metaphor analysis: Research practice in applied linguistics, social sciences and the humanities* (pp. 77–94). London, UK: Equinox.

Candlin, C. N., & Crichton, J. (2012). Emergent themes and research challenges: Reconceptionalising LSP. In P. Margrethe & J. Engberg (Eds.), *Current trends in LSP research: Aims and methods* (pp. 277–316). Bern, Switzerland: Peter Lang.

Candlin, C. N., & Crichton, J. (2013). From ontology to methodology: Exploring the discursive landscape of trust. In C. N. Candlin & J. Crichton (Eds.), *Discourses of trust* (pp. 1–18). Basingstoke, UK: Palgrave Macmillan.

Chouliaraki, L., & Fairclough, N. (1999). *Discourse in late modernity: Rethinking critical discourse analysis.* Edinburgh, Scotland: Edinburgh University Press.

Corbin, J. M., & Strauss, A. L. (2008). *Basics of qualitative research: Techniques and procedures for developing grounded theory* (3rd ed.). Thousand Oaks, CA: Sage Publications.

Cowdroy, R., & Williams, A. (2006). Assessing creativity in the creative arts. *Art, Design & Communication in Higher Education, 5*(2), 97–117.

Crichton, J. (2004). *Issues of interdiscursivity in the commercialisation of professional practice: The case of English language teaching* (PhD thesis). Macquarie University, Sydney.

Crichton, J. (2010). *The discourse of commercialisation.* Basingstoke, UK: Palgrave Macmillan.

Davies, M. (2004). *BYU-BNC. (Based on the British National Corpus from Oxford University Press).* Retrieved from http://corpus.byu.edu/bnc/

Dillon, P. (2008). Reconnaissance as an unconsidered component of action research. *Action Learning Action Research Journal, 13*(1), 4–7.

Fairclough, N. (1992). *Discourse and social change.* Cambridge, UK: Polity Press.

Fairclough, N. (2003). *Analysing discourse: Textual analysis for social research.* Abingdon, Oxon: Routledge.

Fairclough, N. (2010). *Critical discourse analysis: The critical study of language* (2nd ed.). Harlow, UK: Pearson.

Findeli, A. (2001). Rethinking design education for the 21st century: Theoretical, methodological, and ethical discussion. *Design Issues, 17*(1), 5–17.

Foucault, M. (1971). The order of discourse. In R. J. C. Young (Ed.), *Untying the text: A post-structuralist reader* (pp. 48–78). London, UK: Routledge.

Francis, M. (2001). A case study method for landscape architecture. *Landscape Journal, 19*(2), 15–29.

Geisler, P. R. (2006). *Higher education at a crossroads.* New York, NY: Peter Lang.

Goatly, A., & Hiradhar, P. (2016). *Critical reading and writing in the digital age.* London, UK: Routledge.

Green, B. (2009). Introduction: Understanding and researching professional practice. In B. Green (Ed.), *Understanding and researching professional practice* (pp. 1–18). Rotterdam, Netherlands: Sense.

Griffin, G. W. (2008). From performance to mastery: Developmental models of the creative process. *Journal of Advertising, 37*(4), 95–108.

Hammersley, M., & Atkinson, P. (2007). *Ethnography: Principles in practice* (3rd ed.). London, UK: Routledge.

Hocking, D., & Fieldhouse, W. (2011). Implementing academic literacies in practice. *New Zealand Journal of Education Studies, 46*(1), 35–47.

Hoey, M. (2005). *Lexical priming: A new theory of words and language.* London, UK: Routledge.

Krain, M. (2010). The effects of different types of case learning on student engagement. *International Studies Perspectives, 11*(3), 291–308.

Leuthold, S. (1999). Conceptual art, conceptualism, and aesthetic education. *Journal of Aesthetic Education, 33*(1), 37–47.

Muller, B. (2007). Metaphor, architectural design, and environmental response. *Enquiry: The ARCC Journal, 4*(1), 69–78.

Norris, S. (2004). *Analyzing multimodal interaction: A methodological framework.* New York, NY: Routledge.

Norris, S. (2011). *Identity in (inter)action: Introducing multimodal (inter)action analysis.* New York, NY: De Gruyter Mouton.

Phillips, P. L. (2004). *Creating the perfect design brief.* New York, NY: Allworth Press.

Roberts, C., & Sarangi, S. (1999). Hybridity in gatekeeping discourse: Issues of practical relevance for the researcher. In S. Sarangi & C. Roberts (Eds.), *Talk, work and institutional order: Discourse in medical, mediation and management settings* (pp. 473–504). Berlin, Germany: Mouton de Gruyter.

Sacks, H. (1992). *Lectures on conversation: Volumes I and II.* Oxford and London: Blackwell.

Saleh, S. M., Asi, Y. M., & Hamed, K. H. (2013). Effectiveness of integrating case studies in online and face-to-face instruction of pathophysiology: A comparative study. *Advances in Physiology Education, 37*(2), 201–206.

Sarangi, S., & Candlin, C. N. (2003). Introduction. Trading between reflexivity and relevance: New challenges for applied linguistics. *Applied Linguistics, 24*(3), 271–285.

Sarangi, S., & Candlin, C. N. (2006, June 23). *Aligning research and practice in professional discourse: The case for case studies.* Invited plenary presented at the meeting of the 3rd International IVACS Conference, University of Nottingham, England.

Turner, J., & Hocking, D. (2004). Synergy in art and language: Positioning the language specialist in contemporary fine arts study. *Art, Design and Communication in Higher Education, 3*(3), 149–162.

Weeks, K. (2011). *The problem with work: Feminism, marxism, antiwork politics, and postwork imaginaries.* London, UK: Duke University Press.

Appendix: Transcription Symbols for Extracts

((*unintelligible*))	Double parentheses with italics enclose transcriber's comments.
raises hand	Italics without parenthesis describe non-verbal actions. These descriptions commence approximately where they occur in relation to the verbal data.
→	An arrow preceding a line indicates the analyst's signal of a significant line.
–	An en dash indicates a truncated intonation unit.
wor-	A hyphen indicates a truncated word.
↑	A rising arrow indicates a relatively strong rising intonation.
.	A period indicates a falling, final intonation.
word . word	Dots between words indicate silence.
:	A colon indicates an elongated vowel.
<u>word</u>	Underlined words are spoken louder than usual.
words [words [words	Square brackets indicate the commencement of simultaneous talk.
wo(h)rd	(h) indicates the word contains laughter.

D. Hocking, *Communicating Creativity*, Communicating in Professions and Organizations, https://doi.org/10.1057/978-1-137-55804-6

Index[1]

[1]Note: Page numbers followed by "n" refers to note.

D. Hocking, *Communicating Creativity*, Communicating in Professions and Organizations, https://doi.org/10.1057/978-1-137-55804-6

CPSIA information can be obtained
at www.ICGtesting.com
Printed in the USA
BVOW09*1932281017
6057BVAU00001B/3/P